PEER GYNT

THE NORDIC SERIES

Volume 2

Advisors to the Series

HENRIK IBSEN
PEER GYNT

Translated and Introduced by

ROLF FJELDE

SECOND EDITION

UNIVERSITY OF MINNESOTA PRESS
MINNEAPOLIS

Copyright © 1980 by Rolf Fjelde
All rights reserved.
Published by the University of Minnesota Press
111 Third Avenue South, Suite 290, Minneapolis, MN 55401-2520
Printed in the United States of America
Sixth printing, revised, 1997

Library of Congress Cataloging in Publication Data

Ibsen, Henrik, 1828-1906.
  Peer Gynt: a dramatic poem.
  Bibliography: p.
  I. Fjelde, Rolf. II. Title.
PT8876.A3293 1980   839.8'226   80-10315
ISBN 0-8166-0912-8
ISBN 0-8166-0915-2 pbk.

The University of Minnesota
is an equal-opportunity
educator and employer.

FOR MY FATHER AND THE MEMORY OF MY MOTHER

Udenom, sa'e Bøjgen!
            (hører sang i stuen)
                        Nej; denne gang
tvers igjennem, var vejen aldrig så trang!

CONTENTS

Foreword   ix

Acknowledgments   xxvii

Peer Gynt   1

Notes   213

Appendix I: *Peer Gynt:* Text/Translation/Script   231

Appendix II: *Peer Gynt* in the American Theater:
An Abbreviated Stage History   271

Selected Bibliography   293

FOREWORD

To have a self, to be a self, is the greatest concession made to man, but at the same time it is eternity's demand upon him.
Kierkegaard

In the spring of 1864, like countless other artists seeking a thaw of feeling and a renewal of hope, Henrik Ibsen passed for the first time through that towering continental rock barrier that separates two climates, two outlooks and two antiquities. What this transition meant to him, he could still remember clearly in a speech given thirty-four years later: "Upon the vast mountains hung clouds like great dark curtains, and underneath them we drove through tunnels, finding ourselves suddenly at Miramare, where the beauty of the South, a wonderful soft brightness, shining like white marble, was suddenly revealed to me and was destined to set its stamp on all my later production, even if that production was not all beauty."

For Ibsen the Alps were to separate more than the Gothic North from the Mediterranean South, though he could hardly have known it at the time. He had just turned thirty-six. Behind him were ten plays, most of which had failed in performance, some several dozen poems, a scattering of newspaper pieces and speculative papers on literary subjects. Behind him, also, lay Norway, which meant a proud, dead viking past and some of the most spectacular and legend-haunted scenery in Europe, but more importantly and immediately, humiliating childhood memories of his father's failure in business, social ostracism, grinding poverty in cheerless, wintry towns, a hard apprenticeship at the Bergen Theater, debts, unproductive overwork as a theater director in the capital city of Christiania (Oslo),

financial failure again, more debts, the recognition and prefer-
ment of less gifted contemporaries, contrasted with his own
customary reception in the press ("Herr Ibsen as a dramatic
author is a complete nonentity"). There were a few bright
spots—most recently, a modest government travel grant—but
the view to the north was largely dark. Ahead to the south lay
Italy and, unforseeably within three years, two of his greatest
plays, hinged like a diptych on one event, the dramatic poems
Brand and *Peer Gynt.*

That event was the brief Prusso-Danish War, then at its
height. The duchies of Schleswig and Holstein, strategically situated at the neck of the Jutland peninsula between Denmark
and Prussia, had for years been a focus of tension between
those countries. Schleswig traditionally and, with less justification, ethnically had long been considered a fief of the Danish
crown, and this status had lately been confirmed by treaty. In
1862, however, Bismarck became chancellor of Prussia; and
along with his vision of German unification and his maxim that
"the great questions of our time will be settled by blood and
iron," he held other views on the Schleswig-Holstein controversy. "From the beginning," he wrote, "I kept annexation
steadily before my eyes." When, in March 1863, King Frederick
III issued a royal proclamation unequivocally making Schleswig
Danish soil, the incipient crisis came to a head.

The policy that advocated closer ties between Denmark,
Sweden, and Norway and common action in the face of an external threat went by the name of Scandinavianism. It was fer-
vently championed among the students and young professionals; in December 1863, as the Prussian invasion was being
mounted, the Christiania students' club passed a resolution
vowing to take up arms for their "brothers" on the Danish
frontier. Joint action, on the other hand, was opposed by the
peasants, particularly in the rural areas of Sweden and Norway,
who feared Russian expansion more than Prussia and hoped,
by standing pat, to give offense to no one. For the history of
world drama, Scandinavianism has its major importance as the

one article of political faith that Ibsen consistently upheld throughout his lifetime.

Thus, when the newly reorganized and expanded Prussian army, dieted on Clausewitz and led by Moltke, invaded Schleswig in February 1864 and swept victoriously northward into Denmark, Scandinavianism and Ibsen's ideals were simultaneously put to the test. As Bismarck had so shrewdly foreseen and prepared through his manipulations, none of the great powers came to Denmark's aid. Charles XV of the dual kingdom of Sweden-Norway prudently opted for nonintervention. As Ibsen, traveling southward toward Italy, reached Berlin, he could see the cannon from the Danish forts at Dybbøl, those cannon that had fired without relief until they burst, hauled into the capital amid shouts of triumph, and he watched the crowds spit into the muzzles of the guns. "To me," he wrote, "it was a sign of how history someday will spit into the eyes of Norway and Sweden for the sake of this affair."

The outraged sense of personal betrayal that Ibsen felt was twofold. First through the isolation and defeat of Denmark, Scandinavianism had been vitiated; and this cause Ibsen had made particularly and powerfully his own. It was the contemporary implication of his most recent play, *The Pretenders,* in which the conflict between King Haakon and Earl Skule revolves around the analogous national consolidation of thirteenth-century Norway. Second, his ideals, based on inwardly evolving and as yet largely unarticulated insights into the laws of human nature, had been betrayed, so to speak, in the impotence of their childhood, much like the threadball thoughts that roll accusingly after Peer Gynt. Norway, since the Napoleonic Wars, had been joined to the Swedish crown as the inferior, backward partner; Ibsen's ideals therefore decreed that his country be "absolutely and in every respect independent." As with individuals, so with nations, there could be no true union except between equals. What credible reason was there for building up a national theater and a new dramaturgy, other than to strengthen the people by reminding them of their past best selves and teaching them to "think greatly." The Danish crisis had been an opportunity for Norway now to *act* greatly and with strength. Instead, noninvolvement was nothing more than self-defeat, something Ibsen could readily identify with his own sense of helpless rage.

And yet, in this coming together of roles and feelings, by that mysterious law in art and life which he had already affirmed in himself, that law whereby much must be suffered before much can be given, one can see that Ibsen had gained inestimably. Following the precedent of his first consequential modern play, *Love's Comedy,* two years before, he renounced once and for all his systematic excavations of a usable past in the Norse heroic ballads, the Eddas and the sagas. His work decisively entered the history of his time, and he began to speak, not for an aesthetic program or an archaic dream, but for an entire civilization and an age bewilderingly caught up in technological, economic, political, social, and intellectual change. Without this deepening and transforming connection to a larger life, Brand and Peer Gynt could never have emerged the archetypal figures that they are.

But the transformation did not occur instantaneously; it came about, as was characteristic with Ibsen, gradually, over many months, after false starts and hard struggle. First he merely subsided into the liberating experience of Italy. After two initial weeks in Rome, he moved out to Genzano in the Alban Hills for the summer. A stocky, genial figure with a short black beard and a broad-brimmed hat that gave him the name "Cappellone" among the townspeople, he spent his afternoons reading or exploring the countryside. In the evenings there were tours with friends around the Lake of Nemi. In the mornings he worked. His original intention had been to write a historical drama in five acts on the life of the Faroese pirate Magnus Heinesen; this, however, would only have been another of those costumed glorifications of the past that camouflaged the poverty of the present. He abandoned this idea and talked of writing a play about Julian the Apostate, reaching further back in history to the divided roots of Western civilization, the divergent ideals of paganism and Christianity. But in actuality he had already begun a long narrative poem about a fanatical country pastor locked in conflict with himself, his congregation, his mission, and his God. The protagonist's name was Koll, meaning "mountain peak," but presently he changed it to Brand, with its dual meaning of "fire" and "sword."

When he returned in the fall to Rome, joined there by his wife and small son, he felt he had found a second home in Italy. It was a year, however, before the new environment completed its work of liberation. The following July, living now largely on the dole of friends in Christiania, Ibsen threw away a whole year's effort and began again, casting his lot—for the rest of his life, as it proved—with the dramatic form. Writing long hours at an inspired pace, he had, in three months' time, the finished draft of a play whose power and scope were unprecedented in his former production or, for that matter, in the entire theater of the northern countries; when it appeared in March 1866, it won immediate acceptance throughout Scandinavia and ran through three large editions by the year's end. The ebb tide of defeat at last had turned.

"After *Brand*," Ibsen wrote, "*Peer Gynt* followed almost as of itself." In the earlier play, the God-intoxicated protagonist descends from the mountains, bringing the ruthless claims of the absolute down to the hearts of the villagers, forcing sacrifices first on his family, then on his congregation, inspiring them, goading them beyond themselves into building a new church to mark a new life, then repudiating this temple of idolatry to lead them out in the open, back up the mountain to worship freely in spirit and truth, until they lose faith, turn on him, stone him, and leave him to press on, like incarnate will itself, up to the ice-church to die in an avalanche alone. In shaping the tragedy of this Savonarola of the fjords, Ibsen's mind must have played with the possibility of creating his counterpart, the man with no ruling passion, no calling, no commitment, the eternal opportunist, the mirror of surfaces, the charming, gifted, self-centered child who turns out finally to have neither center nor self. After *Brand* was published and its success assured, he had both the buoyancy and the means to attempt it, and he proceeded rapidly to the composition of what, for many, remains the richest and greatest of his works.

Following a summer at Frascati, largely spent wrestling in vain with material for the play about the Emperor Julian, he returned to Rome. During the dark days of the writing of *Brand,* he had read nothing but the Bible; now he immersed himself in the broad humor and sparkling phrases of the eighteenth-century Danish playwright Ludvig Holberg, the "Molière of the North," born in Bergen, where his own initiation in theater had occurred. At the beginning of November, a letter to his publisher indicates that new subjects were stirring in him. By New Year's of 1867, he was hard at work on notes and a scenario for a dramatic poem about "one of the half mythical, romantic characters out of Norwegian folklore of recent times." Ibsen's confidence in his new conception is clearly apparent in the fact that, by early August, he could send the first three acts direct to press from his summer quarters on the island of Ischia. A few days later a slight earthquake disturbed his productive stay on the island; he promptly moved to Sorrento, where the last two acts were written and mailed off within two months. On November 14, 1867, *Peer Gynt* was published by Gyldendal in Copenhagen, and the diptych was complete.

The actual historical prototype for the legendary character of Peer Gynt is still open to debate. Some authorities derive the name from one Peder Laurisen Günter, of a seventeenth-century German aristocratic family settled in Norway. A more appealing and suggestive derivation, in view of the trollish propensity for distorted vision, would identify the name with a Peder Olsen Hage, nicknamed Gynt, conjecturally from the root *gjyne,* "to see." We know that Ibsen, in any case, believed in his hero's authenticity. In 1862, aided by a university grant, he had taken a two-month walking tour from Christiania northward to

Romsdal and Sunnmøre for the purpose of gathering folklore. From his findings at that time, he could report to his publisher that "Peer Gynt is a real person who lived in the Gudbrandsdal, probably at the end of the last, or the beginning of this century. His name is still well known among the people up there, but nothing particular is remembered of his doings, beyond what is to be found in Asbjørnsen's *Norwegian Fairy Tales.*"

The collections of popular tales by Asbjørnsen and Moe provide the single most important source of material for the play. In these, one finds not merely the original germ of the character Peer Gynt, but also Gudbrand Glesne's ride, the three farm girls, the Boyg, the Woman in Green, the eye operation of the trolls, the tale of the devil in the nut, the castles called Soria-Moria and East of the Sun and West of the Moon, and the talking threadballs. To these shards of folklore, Ibsen added his own observations of his more Gyntian contemporaries. Among others, the flamboyant virtuoso Ole Bull made his unwitting contribution, as did the poet and linguistic nationalist A. O. Vinje, who was to be still more devastatingly satirized as the language reformer Huhu. Not least among these were traits of the peasant class at large, sentimentally portrayed in most of the fiction of the time, but to Ibsen's mind the chief betrayers of Scandinavian unity and therefore, like Peer, windy exponents of the promise for the deed.

What really matters, however, in all these circumstances of composition is how the imagination of the poet succeeds in penetrating through historical material to myth, to the form of the irreducible event. In the characters and actions of his major plays, Ibsen always gives us three things: the sometimes obscure, sometimes documentable inflections of his subjective development at a given moment in historic time; the progressive psychological revelations of roles, characterizations, human destinies that live objectively on the page and in the actor's art; and behind these individual figures, insights into gigantic and mysterious principles that move, interact, and evolve out of the hidden depths of life. We can learn by studying the first and by perceptively appreciating the second, but we can never afford to lose sight of the last, for these are what give Ibsen's theater, which often seems on the surface so confined, its peculiar resonance and strength. In *Peer Gynt,* as nowhere else, we have the sense of ulterior forces brought up from a usually buried awareness, as if the whole action of the play took place with the top layers of the mind peeled off.

To show, in anything like their full complexity of pattern and meaning, the archetypes at work behind the personae of the actual in an Ibsen play would involve a commentary far too lengthy for this introduction. Once can perhaps suggest some part of their over-all structuring power, however, by focusing briefly on several aspects of the total design of *Peer Gynt,* namely, the opposing figures of Solveig and the trolls, the fate of the draft-evading farm boy, and the significant repetitions-with-variation in Act Four of motifs from Peer's youth.

It is no accident that Peer Gynt encounters both Solveig and the trolls within two or three days of each other. Peer, as we meet him at the opening of the play, is a powerfully built youth of twenty. His experience of religion, we learn much later, has come to him in easy doses in his middle years. Thus, though he has lived to himself in his fantasies to a great extent, he has had no cause, either physical or spiritual, to examine his life. When he acts, he does so unreflectively and irresponsibly, going off during his mother's busiest time on the farm to hunt reindeer. He may be said, at this stage, to represent existence without self-awareness, a state of harmonious union with nature. The emblem of this state is the ride on the reindeer's back, animal and man blended into one purposeless, blindly charging force. The course of the ride is down the dizzying razor's edge of unconditioned freedom, and the ride becomes, as it must, a leap and a fall. But it is the utter, intoxicating freedom, even of the fall, that stays with Peer ("Imagine—a reindeer, falling free—/ With never the hard earth under me!") Imagine—yes; because no man can live that unconditioned freedom except in dreams or in the imaginative play of childhood.

What makes Peer obscurely but decisively aware of his own existence, his own finite, yet marvelously potent—and potential—self is the encounter with Solveig. Their meeting, for him, is a true *ekstasis;* for the first time in his life, he comes poignantly and exaltedly outside himself. But to discover one's potentiality as a self-transcending being, no longer lapped in the mindless flow of nature and one's dreaming childhood, is also to discover the opposite, the potentiality of becoming less than oneself, of becoming, in other words, a troll.

What is it to be a troll? The genus is well described by M. C. Bradbrook when she speaks of a troll as being humanity minus the specifically human qualities. "The troll is the animal version of man, the alternative to man; he is also what man fears he may become." To reconstruct his origins in the Northern imagination, you need only take the train from Oslo through the Gudbrandsdal to Andalsnes. There, at the valley's upper end, in the pale green twilight of the brief summer night, the fjelds loom starkly black, abrupt, and menacing overhead, and to a sensitive eye, they may move slightly as you turn away. The genus troll comes out of these mountains and others like them. He is primeval and remorseless, permanent as rock in the nature of things. From another viewpoint, he may appear unreflective, irresponsible, purposeless—in other words, the animal that man remains if he fails to act upon his self-discovery. He exists, in fact, in the widest array of forms. In recent history he ran the death camps; and today as in Ibsen's time, he maneuvers spitefully and secretly against recognition of the best, or mouths the tribal chant of a complacent nationalism. Instinctively he dislikes the open and gravitates toward caves, back rooms, closed thoughts and feelings. Yet with all his affinity for dark places, he shies away from the darkest place of all, himself. There he lives indolently on the surface, cutting corners, following fashions, getting by on compromise, accepting himself through custom and habit, rather than making the painful struggle to realize himself in truth and freedom. His mind, shapeless and indulgent at the core, is like a distorting prism; and with his passion for conformity, he must coerce all others to see things on his own bias. Above all, behind whatever disguise he wears, he finds his own ideas, his own prejudices, his own way of life, his clan, his class, his nation-state—enough. In the Ronde Mountains, we have him pure, but he exists, to greater or lesser extent, in everyone.

The most impressive and formidable of all the trolls is that enveloping presence, that voice from the darkness, the Great Boyg. A rich symbol, suggestive of several interpretations, the Boyg receives one unmistakable definition within the play itself. In Act Four, Peer comes once again on what seems to be its likeness, in the shape of the Sphinx. We then recall that other self-made man who, centuries before, confronted and surmounted the crisis of the Sphinx. Significantly, now the roles are reversed. Oedipus was asked a riddle, and successfully responded. But here, Peer Gynt does the asking—and gets no response; the Sphinx is mute. If Peer were less the child of his age of unreason, he might see that the Sphinx is not there to be asked. It exists solely to be answered—with the risk and the commitment of one's whole being. And the answer, we remember, is "Man." To become man, to take on the total challenge of becoming human, is the only adequate reply to the riddle of the Sphinx.

The inducement for Peer to accept this challenge is, or ought to he, Solveig. Solveig is clearly no ordinary woman, a fact which considerably disturbs some critics. This patient Griselda who wastes herself in waiting is, they assert, hardly to be believed; how could she live out her years for so little? Such a judgment is founded on a too literal-minded realism. It is certainly true of most people that the bulk of their lives is a matter of bank statements and furniture bills, what to have for dinner and whether it rained all during vacation. But in *Peer Gynt*, Ibsen is not particularly interested in these surface levels of experience. Solveig is merely tangent to the everyday world; her real life is elsewhere. And that real life has to do with what she, as a woman, has most centrally or, one might say, religiously to give. Approach Solveig as a naturalistic character, and, even making allowance for the extremes of Lutheran pietism, she seems so far from ordinary as to be almost incredible; approach her as woman archetypally conceived, and she is not nearly so difficult to comprehend or portray.

In the over-all pattern of the play, Solveig is everything that the trolls are not. The trolls are the dark interior at the base of the mountain; she climbs to her proper home on the heights. The trolls drift and temporize; she stakes her life on one irrevocable choice. They go it alone, or at best join in an uneasy collective; she wants to share to the full. They are vindictive; she forgives. One of the things about her that troubles these same literalist critics is that, apart from some superficial signs of aging, she changes so little in the course of the play as to appear virtually static. But here I would trace Ibsen's meaning along the lines suggested by R. Ellis Roberts: that in Solveig's faith, her hope and her love is eternity's claim, from which she never departs. The real center of her life is in a timeless realm where love emanates and returns; and she participates in that timelessness. History, which fascinates Peer Gynt, we can be sure means nothing to her. World epochs rise and sweep to doom, thinkers perish and martyrs bleed, emperors wear their crowns of straw, while out of the waste spaces of the Sahara, the vast Egyptian night, where the stone idols wait, half-sunken like the wreck of Ozymandias in the sand, comes nothing but the endless blowing of the desert wind. Finding the truth in, and of, one human soul—for Ibsen, as for Shakespeare—outweighs all the pomps and casualties of time. Finding that truth is finally everything for Peer; making the discovery possible for one who, in her eyes, is a sufficient cause is finally everything for Solveig. How can she live for less?

With these two meetings then, the alternatives of the action are established, and Peer Gynt's life unrolls between them—the way of Solveig and the way of the troll. To be faced with alternatives implies the necessity of choice—and to choose so fundamentally, for Peer, is too difficult. The entire phantasmagoria of the play is the odyssey of an unmade choice, the choice of being what you can become, namely, that nature-transcending, contradiction-torn, purpose-evolving, suffering, striving and achieving self which is truly man, and that spiritually anesthetized, fantasy-swathed, self-sufficing unborn thing which is a troll.

To become man is the underlying objective, the Stanislavskian infinitive of the drama; but "man," like the genus troll, is an abstraction, a universal, whereas truth for Ibsen never lies in the abstract, but in the specific, the individual confronted with the problematic concreteness of reality. What is it to become, not Man, but simply—or not so simply—a man. The question is raised and particularized in what deserves to be called the subplot of *Peer Gynt,* although unlike standard Shakespearean dramatic construction and that of other Ibsen plays such as *A Doll House,* it is stated within the strictest limits, being confined to no more than two scenes: the dumb show in Act Three, in which the farm boy amputates his finger, and the moving eulogy in Act Five, in which his life is summed up by the country pastor. Condensed as the presentation is, this other life must be thought of as moving invisibly parallel to Peer Gynt's own through the fifty-year span of the play, a silent and ironic commentary on its inauthentic character.

The parallelism is asserted by a number of points of correspondence. Both young men, of about the same age, stand separate from their communities. Both undergo a bitter initiation, the farm boy by running a gauntlet of scorn, Peer Gynt by drinking the bowl of mead with the trolls. Each begets, in his own way, an illegitimate child. Each enters the world through a flight from responsibility and becomes as a result a cripple, the farm boy outwardly through his mutilated hand, Peer inwardly, as the Woman in Green observes, through being lame in his mind.

The similarities are clearly apparent, but so also are the contrasts. The farm boy's thoughts are restrained and tame; Peer's are impetuous and fantastic. The farm boy's voice lacks force;

Peer's strength, Aase declares, is all in his mouth. The bearing of the anonymous youth lacks manliness; Peer makes a flagrant display of his virility with the three mountain girls. As much as these two are paralleled, they are contrasted; and it is the contrasts, ultimately, that dominate.

In a sense, then, the paired lives constitute two faces of the same coin, opposing profiles of the same persona. What differentiates them finally is less native endowment than choice, the choice of self made by the one and not by the other. And yet what delays and obviates the choice for Peer is nothing other than his most salient character trait, that tendency toward excessive fantasizing that Ibsen knew too well in his own life, that tendency that arises as a double-edged compensation out of a childhood such as Aase reveals during the search following the bride-rape. It is in this scene that Solveig suddenly understands, that she discerns, under the riot of Peer's ambitions, the boasting, the rage and self-centeredness, a human being seeking to be born. She understands birth and children (Ibsen aptly gives her a little sister over whom she watches protectively at the wedding feast), and now she sees her work. At the end of the drama, Peer, to her, is still the groping, vulnerable child within the old, played-out, world-weary traveler.

What wearies Peer Gynt most is, in all his wandering, having missed so completely the springs of life; but his failure certainly stems in part from his mode of quest. Anyone who reads the text with some care is struck by the number of modulated repetitions of motifs from Peer's youth in the later action. His harsh treatment at Hegstad and at the hands of the troll-imps, for example, is duplicated in his encounter with the Moroccan monkeys and again in the final chaos of the asylum scene. His invocation of the inviolable Anitra snoring in her tent repeats, in satiric reduction, his original refusal to approach Solveig in the hut. The enormous pig becomes the miraculous horse. He begins to quote the Bible, the classics, proverbs, acquaintances, himself, incessantly — and never quite accurately. The Memnon statue seems like the Dovre King; the Sphinx is like the Boyg.

In this mosaic of repeating patterns, Ibsen suggests that experience takes its shape primarily from the set of the personality, and that the world we never made is, often to a surprising extent, an outgrowth of our own human powers or a denial thereof, and not, as Peer passively claims, of Fate. But the repetitions, we also see, are veiled, disguised, off key, inaccurate; and in this fact are further implications. The Gyntian mode of procedure in all things, large or small, is roundabout. To go by roundabouts—or by the Rotation Method, to use the comparable term from *Either/Or,* one of the works of Kierkegaard read by Ibsen in his Grimstad days—is to compromise between two extremes. One extreme would be to break the cycle of repetitions, to strike out, through struggle and suffering, for genuine novelty, for a new contribution to the life of man. But this would be to enter the refining creative matrix of the universe and have one's ego shrunk to scale and eventually lost, becoming only a moment in the evolution of intelligence. The other direct route would be to face repetition undisguised, head on. To confront one's life as repetition is to confront oneself; to confront oneself in such terms is to experience the paralysis of despair; but to accept despair would be to affirm at least the potentiality of self-transcendence in other dimensions of existence. In either case, there would be a risk, a leap, but this time the real would be grounded in the real and the Button-moulder sent packing. Peer's flirtation with pure research, however, is no more than another transitory bit of role-playing; and the first time he fully acknowledges despair is when the shooting star flashes down and out, and the mists shattered by his imaginary leap in the opening scene threaten to close in again. So, for the Gyntian personality, the cycle must hold; and the effective function of fantasy, in proceeding by roundabouts, we see, is to throw just enough of a veil over repetition to persuade the self that no really fundamental change or effort is necessary.

The great arc of the play's action, then—from Gudbrandsdal throughout the world and back again—though framed in the archetypal pattern of the hero's life, his adventure and return, is far from the fulfillment of a heroic destiny. In the three aspects of the play discussed above, comprising the hero's choice, his initiation, and his quest, each is presented in terms of its inverse, its antithesis, the negative — or, as the Lean One makes clear, not even that, since, photographically speaking, Peer Gynt is an undeveloped plate on which nothing has really registered. In this antiromantic work that employs the full resources of the romantic theater, the nonheroic hero is the pilot model of the hollow man of our own time, rendered perplexed and anxious by problems of identity and direction.

"If the modern age has been rightly called the age of anxiety," Erich Fromm has written, "it is primarily because of . . . anxiety engendered by the lack of self." To the extent that we *are* all brothers in old Peer Gynt, Ibsen's image of the human condition takes its place as one of the invaluable reference points in mapping the present world and one of the major landmarks indicating the course of the past. Again, as Georg Groddeck has remarked, there is so much to learn from this play, it is quite impossible to refer to everything.

Deficient as he is in a strong sense of self, Peer has a personality that picks up and reveals the pressures and conflicts of an age of transition the way iron filings strewn on a sheet of paper bring out the lines of force of a magnet underneath. In his young manhood, Peer's life is outwardly restricted; he is the son of a *bondemand,* a peasant farmer, tied to his limited milieu of parish, village, and farm. The bent of his mind is feudal and romantically medieval; women are princesses, mountains are castles, trees are warriors cloaked in chain mail. He sees himself as a knight-at-arms, needing only an unapproachable lady to serve in the manner of the *fin aman.*

Then, with a masterfully bold stroke, Ibsen opens Act Four on his middle-aged protagonist suavely presiding over the banquet years of the latter nineteenth century as an exemplar of the international, cosmopolitan world of finance capitalism.

Peer has made his fortune, after the manner of the empire builders, in slaves and idols, the two logical products of reductive Gyntian opportunism, which turns even the essence of the human and the divine into commodities. (Appropriately, it is as an Americanized European that Peer engages in the slave trade, the shame of Europe and the guilt of America.)

The transition from an organic community based on land and blood ties, from which Peer Gynt is outlawed, to a collective based on abstract contractual relationships—the uneasy company of self-made men among whom he finds an insecure perch—is paralleled by the loosening, the blurring of traditional sanctions and prohibitions. The result is a state of inner disorientation and drift, the background of which can be traced through a number of literary antecedents. For, quite as much as the community defines for Oedipus what he has to do ("Now, Oedipus, Greatest in all men's eyes/here falling at your feet we all entreat you,/find us some strength for rescue"), so the Ghost in *Hamlet* lays his charge upon the prince ("If thou hast nature in thee, bear it not"). But, by the time of *Faust,* the bonds are clearly in dissolution; the hero has saved the community a long while back, and his present ties are rather with Mephistopheles, the destructive principle, conceived still in its traditional form. *Peer Gynt,* however, brings us up to date, as the hero wanders the whole world over, trying to discover what it is he ought to be or do. The community, the ancestors, even self-knowledge, are no longer sufficient guides. Life becomes a feat, or a series of feats, or subjective choice.

In this awareness, Kierkegaard had already modified the original Greek imperative accordingly. "'Know thyself' cannot be the real goal of life," he wrote, "if it is not also the beginning. The ethical individual knows himself; but this knowledge is no mere contemplation. . . . It is a reflection about oneself, which is itself an action, and therefore I have purposely used the expression 'choose yourself' instead of 'know yourself.'" The transformation of the classic hero of reason and virtue, or the tragic departure therefrom, into the modern hero of existential will, or the lack thereof, implies a new conception of tragedy, which Ibsen then strives to articulate. In the later plays, he is ceaselessly preoccupied with the question: To what extent *is* one free to choose oneself, and to what extent is self-knowledge, the uncovering of the obstinate past, a determinant in making that choice?

What is made clear in this earlier work is the fact that the hero is not free *not* to choose himself, not free to expand his personality in the romantic or Faustian pattern to include all knowledge, all experience, all phases of consciousness. It is part of its significance that *Peer Gynt* stands as a cenotaph for the Renaissance man. At some time in the progressive nineteenth century with its immense and varied innovations in fact and theory, the Goethes, the Ben Franklins, the leisured men of parts, cease to be possible; and, with that abruptness that struck Henry Adams, the eighteenth-century man who was, at his best, still the Renaissance man, the microcosm of all learning, becomes the specialized twentieth-century man, locked in the pressure chamber of his career, seeking fulfillment in the utilitarian ethic. Peer experiments with that ethic briefly, after his manner, by envisioning himself as a canal builder, but the solution for the aged Faust is not for him. It is after this that he sees that, if he cannot be one thing, he must be all things; that he is, in reality, the sum of man, the whole of the past, the Emperor of all Human Life—but this last and greatest of his visions, which is essentially the Renaissance belief in the plenitude and perfectibility of the individual, is, by itself and in this advanced age, only one more waystage on the road to the Cairo asylum. Like his brother under the skin, Don Quixote, two and a half centuries before, Peer Gynt is a dreamer patching together the tatters of an outworn ideal, no longer of medievalism and *courtesie*—he has graduated from that—but of an aspiration that has its origins in Castiglione and Petrarch.

And what is Peer left with in the last analysis, under the tatters, under the patchwork coat of many colors? Only his life, his having lived, the fountain of his vitality. Every peeling of the onion—if one is looking for more in life—is a detour, a delusion; and yet at the same time, every peeling was himself, some part of himself that he could not deny. To give him due credit, we have to say of Peer that, in this one sense, he holds nothing back. There is no staid bourgeois façade, as in the later plays, in which chink after chink of the truth will open. And for this reason Groddeck is right when he speaks of him as sincere. For this is exactly what Peer Gynt is. This chronic liar whose life blows away like the desert wind, this clump of nothing who creeps back to the beginning and end of everything in Solveig's lap, is amazingly sincere, extraordinarily significant. He was hardly far wrong about what he should do—what Ibsen did do with him—when, in the passage projecting the Renaissance ideal, he first thought of writing his life story down as a guide to others. But we, more fortunate, scarcely need his book when we can have him alive on the stage. And with his flamboyance, his roguish variability, his innumerable masks and emotions, the theater is where he belongs, along with all the chiaroscuro of his motley world. Aase scolding on the hill, Peer spellbinding his mother into death, the near-blind Solveig speaking forgiveness at the end—the theater is only beginning to discover the potentialities of portrayal in their roles. The shifting illusions and realities of the stage are the counterpart and fit medium of the selfsame shifts within Peer's life, by which we are eventually brought up to that last and most impressive change of scene when, for him as perhaps for us, before the ultimate hour, a light breaks; and out of the strange mercy of the universe, the sun rises still one more time.

ACKNOWLEDGMENTS

Information for inclusion in the appendixes to this second edition of my translation of *Peer Gynt* has been compiled through the cooperation of a number of libraries and institutions, among them the Theater Collection of the Performing Arts Research Center at Lincoln Center, the New York Public Library, the Museum of the City of New York, the Information and Research Program of the Theater Communications Group, the library of Goethe House, the Malmö Stadsteater, the Arkiv and Bibliotek of the Kungliga Dramatiska Teatern, and the American Conservatory Theater. I am greatly indebted to helpful members of their respective staffs. A number of individuals have also been generous with usable suggestions and material, including Harry Carlson, Fru Rachel Due, Bernard Dukore, Einar Haugen, Gerald Kahan, Brian Johnston, Steve Lawson, Edward Mabley, Rollo May, George New, Tom J. A. Olsson, Karl Skare, and Carla Waal.

Toward a revision that would further enhance the theatricality of the original translation, I have accumulated ideas and insights from a decade and a half of observing, discussing, and corresponding about individual scenes staged by groups as diverse as the Actor's Studio in New York and the English Theater Company of Norway in Oslo, not to mention full-scale productions in England and America; but I am particularly grateful to Robert Corrigan, Sanford Robbins, and Jewel Walker at the University of Wisconsin in Milwaukee for their invitation to participate with them and their actors in a series of in-depth, pre-producton workshop sessions at exactly the time that my thoughts on the specifics of a new edition were sharpening into resolution.

It is likewise both a pleasure and the repayment of a debt of gratitude to make acknowledgment to the American-Scandinavian Foundation for assistance through grants that both prompted the original conception and aided the consultative phase of the first edition of this translation; and to the Pratt Mellon Foundation Programs in the Humanities, and its director Carl Craycraft, for many supportive considerations that have eased the sometimes frustratingly detailed labor of revision and amplification for this second edition. The main part of this latter work was carried out on a semester's sabbatical leave from teaching, for which relief my appreciation goes to the administration of Pratt Institute.

Again, I would like to thank Professor Gunnar Høst and his wife Else Høst, as well as Professor Daniel Haakonsen, for their past help in resolving certain references familiar only to native-born Norwegians. Professor Einar Haugen of Harvard University contributed invaluable expertise on moot points of the Norwegian original through his close reading of the translation. Finally, this long-term project has benefited in innumerable ways by the active interest of my parents, Paul and Amy Fjelde, and more recently from that of my wife Christel, whose acuity of critical judgment has been right more times than I could hope to remember.

Rolf Fjelde

New York City
January, 1980

PEER GYNT

THE CHARACTERS

AASE, *a farmer's widow*
PEER GYNT, *her son*
TWO OLD WOMEN *with sacks of grain*
ASLAK, *a blacksmith*
WEDDING GUESTS. MASTER OF CEREMONIES. FIDDLER, *etc.*
A NEWCOMER
HiS WIFE
SOLVEIG
LITTLE HELGA   } *their daughters*
THE FARMER AT HEGSTAD
INGRID, *his daughter*
MADS MOEN, *the bridegroom*
HIS PARENTS
THREE HERD GIRLS *from a mountain hut*
A WOMAN IN GREEN
THE TROLL KING
A TROLL COURTIER. OTHERS LIKE HIM, TROLL GIRLS *and*
    TROLL CHILDREN. A PAIR OF WITCHES. GNOMES, GOBLINS,
    ELVES, *etc.*
A VOICE IN THE DARKNESS. BIRD CRIES
KARI, *a cottar's wife*
AN UGLY BRAT
MR. COTTON
M. BALLON   } *traveling*
HERR VON EBERKOPF   } *gentlemen*
HERR TRUMPETERSTRAALE
A THIEF *and a* FENCE
ANITRA, *daughter of a Bedouin chief*
ARABS. FEMALE SLAVES. DANCING GIRLS, *etc.*
THE STATUE OF MEMNON (*singing*). THE SPHINX AT
    GIZEH (*mute*)

1

PROF. BEGRIFFENFELDT, *Ph. D., director of the insane
     asylum at Cairo*
HUHU, *a language reformer from the Malabar coast*
A FELLAH *with a royal mummy*
HUSSEIN, *a Near Eastern cabinet minister*
OTHER INMATES, *along with their* KEEPERS
A NORWEGIAN SEA CAPTAIN *and his* CREW
A STRANGE PASSENGER
A PASTOR. MOURNERS
A SHERIFF
A BUTTON-MOLDER
A LEAN PERSON

*The action opens in the early years of the nineteenth century
and ends in the late 1860s. It takes place partly in Gudbrandsdal and the surrounding mountains, partly on the coast of
Morocco, in the Sahara Desert, in a Cairo insane asylum, at
sea, etc.*

ACT ONE

SCENE ONE

A wooded hillside near AASE's *farm. A stream runs brawling through, past an old mill set on its farther side. It is a hot summer day.* PEER GYNT, *a powerfully built youth of twenty, comes down the path.* AASE, *his mother, small and frail, trails after him, angrily scolding.*

AASE
  Peer, you're lying!

PEER GYNT *(without stopping)*
                No, I'm not!

AASE
  Well, go on then—swear it's true!

PEER GYNT
  Swear? Why should I?

AASE
                Hah! Know what?
  You don't dare; they're lies right through!

PEER GYNT *(stops)*
  It's truth I've told you, altogether!

AASE *(confronts him)*
  And no shame before your mother?
  First you run off to the mountains
  In my hardest months, to go
  Tracking reindeer through the snow;
  Come back with your clothes in ribbons,
  Lose your quarry—*and* your gun—
  Then, to boot, with big wide eyes,
  You scheme to see me taken in

3

By the worst of hunters' lies.
Well — where did you meet this buck?

PEER GYNT

West of Gjendin.

AASE *(laughs derisively)*

Oh, of course!

PEER GYNT

I'm stalking down a wind that roars
About me; hid up behind a grove
Of alders, he's pawing in a pack
Of snow for moss —

AASE *(as before)*

Oh yes, of course!

PEER GYNT

My breath stops short; I freeze and listen,
Hear the scraping of his hoof,
See a glint of antler horns.
With that I'm flat between the stones,
Worming up so's not to miss him.
Then, screened by rocks, I feast my eyes on —
Such a buck, so sleek and fat,
You've never seen his equal yet!

AASE

I'm sure of that!

PEER GYNT

So bang! I shoot.
He hits the dirt, whump, like a mallet.
But in that instant as the brute
Lies still, I'm there astride his back,
Seize him by the left ear tight,
And poise to drive my knife in right
Below the jawbone for his gullet —
When hi! the scum lets out a shriek,
Scrambles bolt up on his feet
And, with this one head-backward flip,
Knocks knife and scabbard out of reach

Clamps me neatly at the hip,
Rams his horns down on my legs
To pin me like a pair of tongs —
And then with dizzy leaps he springs
Along the brink of Gjendin ridge![1]*

AASE *(involuntarily)*

Oh, my Jesus — !

PEER GYNT

Have you seen
The way the cliffs of Gjendin hang?
They run out nearly four miles long,
Lean as a scythe edge at the top.
Past glaciers, ledges, rockslides,
Herbs clinging to the gray-green slope,
You can look down either side
Straight into water, where in a slow
Black heavy sleep it lies one
Thousand yards, almost, below.

He and I, on that blade of ground,
Cut a channel through the wind.

I've never had me such a run!
Sometimes in the headlong pace
The air seemed full of flashing suns.
In the reeling gulfs of space
Eagles with brown backs would float
Midway between us and the water —
Then fall away behind, like motes.

I could see ice floes crack and shatter
On the shore, without a sound to hear.
Only the imps of swimming senses
Came singing, swirling, weaving dances
In rings around my eyes and ears.

AASE *(giddy)*

Oh, God help me!

---

* Notes will be found on pp. 213-28.

PEER GYNT

> Suddenly,
At a spot where the cliff drops violently,
This great cock ptarmigan explodes
Into wings, squawking terrified
From some nook where he'd thought to hide
Till the hoofs came on too loud.

> The buck goes spinning half around
And takes off with a tremendous bound,
Plunging both of us straight for the deep.

> (AASE *sways and steadies herself against a tree.*
> PEER GYNT *continues.*)

Behind us, rock walls sheering up,
Beneath us, gaping nothingness —
And we two dropping, first through veils
Of mist, then through a flock of gulls
That wheel off, scattering their cries
To all the corners of the sky.

> Downward, endlessly, we go.
But in the depths something shows
Dim white, like reindeer's belly fleece.
Mother, it was *our* reflection
Shooting upward in the lake from
Silent darkness to the glassy calm
On top with the same breakneck
Speed as we were hurtling down.

AASE *(gasping for breath)*

> Peer! Dear Lord, what happened? Quick!

PEER GYNT

My buck from above, the other
From below lock horns together
In one huge shower burst of foam.

> Well, there we lay and thrashed awhile —
Then at last, somehow, we struck
Out for the northern shore, the buck

He swam, and I hung on his tail —
So, here I am ——

AASE

                    But the reindeer?

PEER GYNT

Oh, I guess he's out there somewhere —
          (*Snaps his fingers, turns on his heel, adding:*)
Finders keepers — you can have him!

AASE

And you didn't break your neck?
Or both your legs? What an escape!
You really didn't crack your spine?
Oh, great God — all thanks and praise
To Thee for delivering my son!
Your trousers got a little torn,
It's true; but that's of no concern
When you realize just how black
Things might have been after such a leap — !

(*Stops abruptly, stares at him wide-eyed and open-
          mouthed, struggles for words until, at length,
                              she bursts out.*)

Oh, you tricky little devil —
God in heaven, you can lie!
I remember all this drivel
Now; it happened to Gudbrand
Glesne, back when I was twenty.
This is his ride secondhand,
Not your own, you — !

PEER GYNT

                    His *and* mine.
Things like that can happen twice.

AASE (*angrily*)

Yes, give a lie a new disguise,
Twist it , turn it out so fine
The bony carcass can't be seen

7

Spruced up in the fancy dress.
That's the only thing you've done—
Run wild in your imagination,
Trotted out those eagles' backs
And all your other rotten tricks,
Lied the sun and moon away,
And stirred up such a misery
Of fright that one forgets old
Things one heard once as a child.

PEER GYNT

If anyone else talked like that
To me, I'd cripple him for life!

AASE *(weeping)*

Oh, God, please let me die; oh, let
Me sleep in the earth and rest!
Prayers and weeping leave him deaf—
Now and forever, Peer—you're lost!

PEER GYNT

You pretty little mother, you,
Every word you say is true;
So give us a happy smile—

AASE

                            Be still!
How can I be happy while
I have such a pig for a son?
Don't you think it's hard for me,
A helpless, struggling widow, to be
Always put to shame again?

                    (Once more weeping.)
What have we got now from the days
When your grandfather's fortunes rose?
Those sacks of coin that Rasmus Gynt
Willed us—you know where they went?
Your father! Him, with his open hand,
And the money running through like sand,
Buying property right and left,

Driving his gilded carriages —
Where's it gone now, all the waste
Poured out for that winter feast
When the guests flung every glass
And bottle to the wall to smash?

PEER GYNT

Where are the snows of yesteryear?[2]

AASE

Don't talk back to your mother, Peer!
Look at the farm there! Nearly half
The windows plugged with rags and stuff.
Railings, fences, hedges down;
Cattle shifting to the wind and rain;
Fields and pastures gone to weeds;
And every month the sheriff takes——

PEER GYNT

That's enought of this old maid's
Talk! One's luck has losing streaks
Only to spring up good as new!

AASE

The ground is barren where it grew.
Lord, aren't you the country squire —
Just as haughty and cocksure
And impudent as when the preacher,
Newly come from Copenhagen,
Hearing you blab your name, at once
Swore the brain in your little noggin
Outclassed the mind of many a prince,
So that your father, true to nature,
Went and gave him a horse and sleigh
For talking in such a generous way.
Ah, but things looked rosy then!
Bishops, captains — how they all came
Flocking daily to drink and eat,
Stuffing themselves till they nearly split!
Who knows his friends in an easy time?

No one, not a soul, stopped in
The day "Jon Moneybags" took
To the road with a peddler's pack.
                    (Drying her eyes with her apron.)
Ah, Peer, you're big and strong;
You should be the mainstay now
That your mother's getting on —
Keep the farm in trim, and show
Some fight to save your nest egg.
                    (With a new burst of tears.)
Oh, God help me if I owe
Any thanks to you, you lazy slug!
Loafing in the chimney-corner
Home,[3] and poking up the fire,
Or out at dances where you scare
The local girls with your crazy manner —
You make me a common laughingstock;
And now, brawling with the lowest pack ——

PEER GYNT *(moves away from her)*
Leave me alone.

AASE *(following him)*
                    Go on, make
Believe you didn't lead that row
The other day at Lunde[4] when you
Boys all wound up swapping blows,
Mad as dogs. Oh, I suppose
It wasn't you that laid Aslak
The smith's arm up in a splint?
Or at least didn't you crack
One of his fingers out of joint?

PEER GYNT
Who fed you all that foolishness?

AASE *(hotly)*
Kari, downhill, heard the yelling!

PEER GYNT *(rubbing his elbow)*
Yes, but I made all the noise.

AASE
    You?

PEER GYNT
        That's right — *I* got the mauling.

AASE
    What —?

PEER GYNT
        He can raise a bruise.

AASE
    Who can?

PEER GYNT
        He, Aslak, can. Who else?

AASE
    You — pah, you! I could spit!
    You mean a blubber-bellied sot,
    A walking sponge, a piece of tripe
    Like that could ever beat you up?
                        (Weeping again.)
    Shame and scandal, how it fills
    My life — and now, worst of all, this
    Has to happen, this disgrace.
    Let him be brawny as an ox —
    Why should you be the one he licks?

PEER GYNT
    Win or lose, it doesn't matter —
    You boil me in the same hot water.
                    (Laughing.)
    Ah, cheer up ——

AASE
            What! Were you lying
    Once again?

PEER GYNT
        Just this once.
    Dry your tears now; stop crying.
            (Clenches his left hand.)

    Look—in these tongs, what chance
    Did he have, bent double, glowing
    Under the hammer of my right—

AASE

    Oh, you fire-eater! You'll put
    Me in the grave, the way you act.

PEER GYNT

    Oh no, what you can expect
    Is twenty thousand times finer
    Than that! Dearest, ugly, little
    Mother, be patient with it all:
    This whole parish'll do you honor;
    You just wait till I come out
    With something—something really great!

AASE *(snorting)*

    You!

PEER GYNT

        Who knows what's in the cards?

AASE

    If only someday you'd have sense
    Enough to make an effort towards
    Sewing the holes up in your pants.

PEER GYNT *(hotly)*

    I'll be a king, an emperor!

AASE

    An emperor? God help me, there
    He's losing the little mind he had!

PEER GYNT

    But I will! Just give me time!

AASE

    Yes, time brings all things to him
    Who waits, or so I've heard it said.

PEER GYNT

    You'll see, Mother!

AASE
                              Hold your tongue!
          The madhouse, that's where you belong —
              Still, you're not completely off —
          Something is what you might have been
          If you hadn't sunk yourself in
          Lies and windy dreams and bluff.
          The Hegstad girl was fond of you.
          That plum was ripening to fall,
          And would have, if you'd had the will —

PEER GYNT
    Think so?

AASE
                    The old man hasn't got
          The strength to tell his daughter "no."
          He's strict with her, or tries to be,
          But Ingrid always gets her way;
          And where she goes, Old Stumble-shoe
          Clumps after, angry as a beet.
                            (Starts crying again.)
          Ah, my Peer, a girl with land,
          Clear property, an heiress! Think —
          If you'd only had the will,
          You could have married into rank —
          You, in your tatters, black as coal.

PEER GYNT *(briskly)*
    Well, let's go courting someone's hand.

AASE
    Where?

PEER GYNT
            At Hegstad!

AASE
                      You poor child,
          Your hopes are locked out in the cold.

PEER GYNT

  What do you mean?

AASE

                Oh, it's too much!
  The moment's flown, and so's the luck —

PEER GYNT

  Why?

AASE *(sobbing)*

      While you went riding your buck
    Through the air over the western ridge,
    Mads Moen proved the plum was ripe.

PEER GYNT

  What —? You mean that scarecrow! Him!

AASE

  Yes, he's going to be the groom.

PEER GYNT

  Wait here till I harness up
  The horse and cart —

             (Starts off.)

AASE

              No use leaving.
  The wedding's set now for tomorrow.

PEER GYNT

  Ffft! I'll be there this evening!

AASE

  For shame! Don't you think my sorrow's
  Enough, without their ridicule?

PEER GYNT

  Don't worry; it'll all go well.
  Cheer up, Mother! Let the cart stay here;
        (Shouting and laughing at once.)
  There isn't time to get the mare.
          (Lifts her in his arms.)

AASE

  Put me down!

PEER GYNT
                    No, like this you'll
Arrive in style at the wedding farm.
                    (Wades out in the stream.)

AASE
  Help! Oh, God, be merciful!
  Peer! We'll drown —

PEER GYNT
                              I was born
  To die a nobler death —

AASE
                              That's true,
  Hanging's more in line for you!
                    (Pulls his hair.)
  Oh, you monster!

PEER GYNT
                    Now be calm;
  The footing here is slippery-smooth.

AASE
  Jackass!

PEER GYNT
          Sure, just use your mouth;
  Words do no one any harm.
  There, you see, it's shelving up —

AASE
  Don't let me drop!

PEER GYNT
                    Hi, giddap!
  Time to play at Peer and the buck —
                    (Cavorting about.)
  I'm the reindeer, you be Peer!

AASE
  I don't know who I am, I swear!

PEER GYNT
  We're almost in the shallows, look —

(Wading ashore.)
    So be nice, give the buck a kiss
    And thank him for the ride across——
AASE *(clouts him on the ear)*
    There's my thanks for the ride!
PEER GYNT
                                    Ow!
    Your sense of gratitude is low.
AASE
    Let me go!
PEER GYNT
                To the wedding first.
    Be my spokesman. You're clever;
    Have a talk with the old crust;
    Tell him Mads is a real loafer——
AASE
    Let go!
PEER GYNT
            Then give him a chance to hear
    Something about *my* character.
AASE
    Oh yes, you can bet I will!
    You'll have a testimonial
    And your portrait painted front and back;
    I'll spill out every devil's trick
    I've seen you do, till his ears are limp——
PEER GYNT
    Oh?
AASE *(kicking furiously)*
        This tongue of mine will wag
    Until the old man sics his dogs
    On you, as if you were a tramp!
PEER GYNT
    Hm, then I'll have to go alone.
AASE
    Yes, but I'll be right behind you!

PEER GYNT
    Mother, you're not strong enough to —
AASE
    Strong enough? I feel so violent
    Inside that I could crumple stone!
    Hoo, I could make a meal of flint!
    Let go!
PEER GYNT
                All right, if you'll promise —
AASE
    Nothing! We're going, both of us.
    They have to find out who you are!
PEER GYNT
    No, you'd better stay right here.
AASE
    Never! To the feast! Let's be off.
PEER GYNT
    I can't allow it.
AASE
                What will you do?
PEER GYNT
    I'll set you up on the millhouse roof.
                (Lifts her up there. AASE *screams.)*
AASE
    Lift me down!
PEER GYNT
                Will you listen now —?
AASE
    Rubbish!
PEER GYNT
                I'm asking you, Mother dear —
AASE *(throws sod from the roof at him)*
    Get me down this instant, Peer!
PEER GYNT
    If I dared, you know I would.

(Comes closer.)

Now, see if you can't stay quiet, glued
To one spot. Try not to kick and flop
About, and don't pull the shingles up—
Or you might find out you've gone from bad
To worse with a nasty fall.

AASE

You beast!

PEER GYNT

Stop wiggling!

AASE

Oh, for a wind to blast
You like a changeling[5] off this earth!

PEER GYNT

Mother, shame!

AASE

Pah!

PEER GYNT

Aren't I worth
Your blessing in taking on this struggle?
Can't you give it?

AASE

I'll give a whipping
To you for all your size, that's what!

PEER GYNT

Then fare thee well, Mother, my sweet.
Just be patient; I won't be long.

(Starts off, then turns and shakes his finger at her.)

Remember now: you mustn't wiggle!

AASE

Peer! God help me, there he goes!
Reindeer rider! Liar! Hi!
Will you listen—? No; now he's
Running—! *(Shouts.)*

Help, I'm dizzy! Hurry!

(TWO OLD WOMEN, *with sacks on their backs, come down the path toward the mill.*)

FIRST OLD WOMAN
    Mercy, who's that screaming?

AASE

                            Me!

SECOND OLD WOMAN
    Aase! You've come up in life.

AASE
    This won't give me much relief —
    But soon I'll rise to eternity!

FIRST OLD WOMAN
    Enjoy the trip!

AASE

                            Go fetch a ladder;
    Get me down! That devil Peer ——

SECOND OLD WOMAN
    Your son again?

AASE

                Only consider
    This a sample of what I have to bear.

FIRST OLD WOMAN
    We're witnesses.

AASE

                    If you'd just
    Help me, I could be at Hegstad fast ——

SECOND OLD WOMAN
    Is he there?

FIRST OLD WOMAN

                You'll have your vengeance
    The smith's left, too, for the celebration.

AASE *(wringing her hands)*
    Oh, God save me! The poor boy,
    They'll kill him, if they have their way!

FIRST OLD WOMAN
   It's time and again we've heard that talk;
   Take heart: if it's going to be, it will!
SECOND OLD WOMAN
   Her wits are scattering everywhere.
                              (Calling up the hill.)
   Eivind! Anders! Hey, come here!
A MAN'S VOICE
   What's the matter?
SECOND OLD WOMAN
                              Peer Gynt's stuck
   His mother up on top of the mill!

SCENE TWO

A small rise of ground covered with shrubs and heather. Up-slope and behind a fence runs the high road. PEER GYNT *comes along a footpath, hurries up to the fence and stands gazing out over the landscape.*

PEER GYNT
   There it lies, Hegstad. I'll be there soon.
          (Climbs half over the fence, then hesitates.)
   Wonder if Ingrid's at home alone?
              (Shades his eyes and looks off.)
   No, the guests are swarming in like flies —
   It might be better just to return.
                  (Climbs down again.)
   They whisper behind your back, always
   Sneering, and it sears you like a burn.
   *(Goes a few steps from the fence and begins aimlessly
                  plucking leaves.)*
   If I only had something strong to drink —
   Or I could slip in without being seen —

Or just be unknown —— For numbing the pain
Of their laughter, nothing beats getting drunk.
(*Looks about him in a sudden fright, then hides among
some bushes. Several* WEDDING GUESTS, *with presents,
go by on the road toward the farm.*)

A MAN (*in conversation*)
With his father a drunkard — and that mother's a case.

A WOMAN
Yes, it's not hard to see why the boy's such a mess.
(*The* GUESTS *pass on. A moment later* PEER GYNT *emerges,
blushing with shame, and stares after them.*)

PEER GYNT (*softly*)
Were they speaking of me?
(*With a forced shrug.*)
Well, let them speak.
They can't kill the life in my veins with talk!
(*Throws himself down in the heather and lies on his back
awhile, hands under his head, gazing up into the sky.*)

What an odd-shaped cloud! Like a horse almost.
Someone's riding him — he's saddled and reined —
And there's an old witch on a broom behind.
(*With a quiet little laugh.*)
It's Mother. She's scolding and yelling: "You beast!
Hi, wait for me, Peer!"
(*Slowly closing his eyes.*)
She's frightened now —
Peer Gynt rides ahead, with an army in tow —
His harness is silver, his mount is gold-shod.
He wears gauntlets, a scabbard, a fine saber blade,
And a cape flowing long and silken-lined.
They're the salt of the earth, the men of his band;
Yet not one sits so bold in his saddle as Peer,
Or glitters like him in the sunlit air.
Below by the road people gather in groups,

Tipping their hats, and everyone gapes.
    The women curtsy. They're all impressed
By the Emperor Peer Gynt and his thousand-man host.
    Pieces of silver and new copper coins
He scatters like sand till his pathway shines,
    And every citizen's rich as a lord.
Then Peer makes the ocean his boulevard.
    On a far-off shore stands Engelland's[6] prince,
And all Engelland's maidens wait in suspense.
    And Engelland's nobles and Engelland's king,
As Peer canters up, rise from parleying.
    Their emperor takes off his crown and speaks —

ASLAK THE SMITH *(to some others, passing on the road)*
    Well, look; it's Peer Gynt, the drunken swine — !

PEER GYNT *(half rising with a start)*
    My sovereign — ?

ASLAK *(leaning over the fence and grinning)*
                Get off your haunches, son!

PEER GYNT
    What the devil! Aslak! What do you want?

ASLAK *(to the others)*
    He's still hung up from his Lunde jaunt.

PEER GYNT *(springing up)*
    Get out of here!

ASLAK
            Yes, I can do that.
    But where have you been, lad? Out of sight
    For six whole weeks. Trolls get you, what?

PEER GYNT
    Aslak, I've done fantastic things!

ASLAK *(winks at the others)*
    Give us the word, Peer!

PEER GYNT
            Can't waste my lungs.

ASLAK *(after a pause)*
  You going to Hegstad?
PEER GYNT
                              No.
ASLAK
                              They say
  That girl there used to give you the eye.
PEER GYNT
  You filthy crow—!
ASLAK *(drawing back a little)*
                              Easy now, Peer!
  If Ingrid's dropped you, there's plenty more—
  Think—Jon Gynt's son! Join the carouse;
  There'll be tender lambs and bouncy widows——
PEER GYNT
  Go to hell!
ASLAK
                    You'll find someone who'll have you.
  Good day! I'll be giving the bride your love now.
  (They move on, laughing and whispering. PEER *stares after
  them briefly, then tosses his head and turns half around.)*
PEER GYNT
  Anyone Ingrid wants to marry
  She's welcome to. Who gives a damn!
                    (Inspecting himself.)
  Trousers torn. Ragged and grim—
  I could use some new clothes in a hurry.
                    (Stamps on the ground.)
  If I could just take a butcher's knife
  And cut the mockery out of their chests!
                    (Staring suddenly around.)
  What—! Who's that? Did somebody laugh?
  Hm, I was sure——Nothing but ghosts—
  I'll go home to Mother.

(Turns up the hill, stops again and stands, ears cocked toward the farm.)

The dancing's begun!

(Gazing and listening, then moving downslope step by step, his eyes kindling, his palms rubbing his thighs)

What a swarm of girls! Seven, eight to a man!

Hell and blazes! To the wedding I'm off!

But Mother, perched on top of the roof —

(His eyes are drawn back to Hegstad; he kicks up his heels and laughs.)

Ah, the halling![7] How it floats and swirls

For Guttorm; how sweetly his fiddle's stroked — !

It sparkles and dips like a cataract.

And that flock, that shimmering flock of girls!

Oh, hell and blazes, To the wedding, I'm off!

(Leaps the fence and heads down the road.)

SCENE THREE

The grounds at Hegstad. Farthest to the rear, the farmhouse. A THRONG OF GUESTS. *Lively dancing on the grass. The* FIDDLER *is seated on a table. The* MASTER OF CEREMONIES[8] *stands in the doorway.* KITCHEN MAIDS *go back and forth between the buildings.* ELDERLY PEOPLE *sit here and there, conversing.*

A WOMAN *(joining a group seated on some logs)*

The bride? Oh yes, she's crying some,

For the usual reasons, mostly vague —

MASTER OF CEREMONIES *(in another group)*

Now, folks, let's see you drain the keg.

A MAN

How — when you're filling it all the time?

A YOUTH *(to the* FIDDLER, *as he flies past with a girl by the hand)*
  Hi, Guttorm, don't spare the bow!

THE GIRL
  Stroke till it rings through every meadow!

OTHER GIRLS *(around a young man dancing)*
  That's kicking!

A GIRL
                    He's got legs like steel!

THE YOUNG MAN *(as he dances)*
  It's high to this ceiling[9] and wide to the wall!
  (The BRIDEGROOM, *whimpering, comes up to his* FATHER,
      who is talking to several others, and tugs at his sleeve.)

BRIDEGROOM
  Father, she won't; she's just too proud!

FATHER
  Won't what?

BRIDEGROOM
                    She's locked herself away.

FATHER
  Well, it's up to you, then, to find the key.

BRIDEGROOM
  I don't know how.

FATHER
                    You're a knucklehead!
  (Turns back to the others. The BRIDEGROOM *wanders off.)*

A BOY *(rounding the house)*
  Hey, girls! The party's coming alive!
  Peer Gynt—!

ASLAK *(newly arrived on the scene)*
                    Was he asked?

MASTER OF CEREMONIES
                    Not by my leave.
  (Goes toward the house.)

ASLAK *(to the girls)*

    If he talks to you, don't listen to him!

A GIRL *(to the others)*

    No. Pretend that we look right through him.

PEER GYNT *(hot and ardent, enters, stops in front of the*
        group and claps his hands)

    Which one of you girls can really move?

A GIRL *(as he approaches)*

    Not me.

ANOTHER

        Not me.

A THIRD

             Nor me either.

PEER GYNT *(to a fourth)*

    All right, *you* — before I'm lured by another.

THE GIRL *(turning aside)*

    Too busy.

PEER GYNT *(to a fifth)*

        Then you!

THE GIRL *(as she leaves)*

            I was just going home.

PEER GYNT

    So early? You must be out of your mind!

ASLAK *(after a moment, in a low voice)*

    See, Peer, she'll dance with the first man around.

PEER GYNT *(turns quickly to an elderly man)*

    Where are the unattached girls?

THE MAN

        Find them.

(He walks away. PEER, *suddenly subdued, glances shyly and*
furtively at the group. They all look at him, but nobody
speaks. He approaches other groups. Wherever he goes, there
is silence; as he moves on, looks follow him and smiles.)

PEER GYNT *(in an undertone)*

    Glances, hard thoughts and mocking smiles —

They grate, like a saw blade under a file!
(He slinks along the fence. SOLVEIG, *leading* LITTLE HELGA
by the hand, comes into the yard with her parents.)

A MAN *(to another, close by* PEER GYNT)
Look, the new neighbors.

THE OTHER
                                        From the west country, right?

FIRST MAN
I think, from Hedal.[10]

THE OTHER
                                Yes, that was it.

PEER GYNT *(steps in the newcomers' path and, pointing at*
        SOLVEIG, *asks her father)*
Can I dance with your daughter?

THE FATHER *(quietly)*
                                        You may; but first
We'll go in and pay our respects to the host.
                        (They enter the house.)

MASTER OF CEREMONIES *(to* PEER GYNT, *offering him a drink)*
Since you're here, you'll want the bottle passed.

PEER GYNT *(staring fixedly after the newcomers)*
I'll be dancing, thanks. I have no thirst.
(The MASTER OF CEREMONIES *moves away.* PEER GYNT
        looks toward the house and laughs.)

How fair! Who's ever seen one like this!
Eyes on her shoes and snow-white apron—!
And how she held onto her mother's dress,
And the kerchief she carried her prayer book in—![11]
I must see her again.
        *(Starts into the house, but is met by several young
                        men coming out.)*

A YOUTH
                        Hey, Peer, you leaving
The dance?

PEER GYNT
              No.

THE YOUTH
              Then you're headed wrong.
        (Takes his shoulder to turn him about.)

PEER GYNT
  Let me pass!

THE YOUTH
              Are you scared of the smith?

PEER GYNT
  Me scared?

THE YOUTH
              So, the memory of Lunde has teeth!
        (The group laughs and goes on to the dancing.)

SOLVEIG *(appears at the door)*
  Aren't you the boy that wanted to dance?

PEER GYNT
  Why, yes; didn't you know me at once?
                (Taking her hand.)
  Come on!

SOLVEIG
             Mother says, not too far.

PEER GYNT
  Mother says? Mother says! Were you born last year?

SOLVEIG
  You're making fun —!

PEER GYNT
                 But you're nearly a child.
  Are you grown?

SOLVEIG
             I'm just confirmed[12] — that old.

PEER GYNT
  Tell me your name, girl, and things'll go lighter.

SOLVEIG
  My name is Solveig. And who are you?

PEER GYNT
  Peer Gynt.
SOLVEIG *(draws back her hand)*
              Oh, my goodness!
PEER GYNT
                              What's wrong now?
SOLVEIG
  My garter's come loose; let me tie it tighter.
                    (Leaves him.)
BRIDEGROOM *(pulling his mother's sleeve)*
  Mother, she won't — !
MOTHER
                    She won't? Won't what?
BRIDEGROOM
  Just won't, Mother!
MOTHER
                What?
BRIDEGROOM
                      Unlock the door.
FATHER *(in quiet fury)*
  Uf! A stall — that's all you're good for.
MOTHER
  Now don't scold. Poor boy, he'll be all right.
                    (They go off.)
A YOUTH *(coming up with a crowd from the dancing)*
  Little brandy, Peer?
PEER GYNT
                No.
THE YOUTH
                    Ah, come on.
PEER GYNT *(looking somberly at him)*
  You have some?
THE YOUTH
                  Oh, it just might be.

(*Pulls out a pocket flask and drinks.*)

Ai, that burns—! Well?

PEER GYNT

Let me see.

(*Drinks.*)

ANOTHER YOUTH

Now you can have a taste of mine.

PEER GYNT

No.

THE OTHER

Ah, rubbish! Don't be a mope.

Drink up, Peer!

PEER GYNT

Well, maybe a drop.

(*Drinks again.*)

A GIRL (*in an undertone*)

Come on, let's go.

PEER GYNT

You afraid of me, puss?

A THIRD YOUTH

Who isn't afraid of *you*?

A FOURTH

We saw

You in action at Lunde, you know.

PEER GYNT

You should see me when I really cut loose!

FIRST YOUTH (*whispering*)

Now he's started.

OTHERS (*thronging around in a circle*)

Tell us! Say what

You can do!

PEER GYNT

Tomorrow—!

MORE VOICES

No, now; tonight!

A GIRL

    Can you conjure, Peer?

PEER GYNT

                  I can call up the devil.

A MAN

    My grandmother, before I was born, did that!

PEER GYNT

    Liar! What *I* do, no one can equal.

    Once I conjured him inside a nut.

    Through a wormhole, that is.

SEVERAL *(laughing)*

                Obviously!

PEER GYNT

    He wept and swore and tried bribing me

    With all kinds of things——

ONE OF THE CROWD

              But he had to remain?

PEER GYNT

    Oh yes. I'd closed up the hole with a pin.

    You should've heard him buzzing and booming——

A GIRL

    Imagine!

PEER GYNT

          It was like a bumblebee humming.

THE GIRL

    You still have him trapped in the nut?

PEER GYNT

                  Oh, no,

    The devil's made off on his own by now.

    It's *his* fault the smith has it in for me.

A YOUTH

    How come?

PEER GYNT

          I went to the smith and, "Say,"

    I asked him, "could you crack this shell?"

"Sure"—and he laid it down on his anvil;
But that man's got fists like a couple of hams
When he swings his sledge, so he just let fall——

VOICE FROM THE CROWD

Did he kill the devil?

PEER GYNT

He came down, wham!
But the devil was quicker and shot like a flame
Straight through the roof and split the walls.

SEVERAL VOICES

And the smith?

PEER GYNT

Just stood there with charred hands.
From that day on, we've never been friends.

(General laughter.)

MORE VOICES

That's a good one!

OTHER VOICES

It's nearly his best!

PEER GYNT

You think I'm inventing it?

A MAN

No, I agree
With you there; my grandfather told me most
Of this——

PEER GYNT

Liar! It happened to me!

THE MAN

Yes, everything has.

PEER GYNT *(tossing his head)*

Why, I can ride
Through the air like the wind going past!
The things I can do, the things—oh, God!

(Another roar of laughter.)

ONE OF THE CROWD
    Peer, ride in the air a bit!
MANY VOICES
                                      Yes, Peer, do —
PEER GYNT
    Don't be so anxious begging me to.
    I can ride like a hurricane over your lot,
    And you'll fall, all of you, fall at my feet!
AN OLDER MAN
    Now he's raving mad.
ANOTHER
                                      What audacity!
A THIIRD
    Loudmouth!
A FOURTH
                    Liar!
PEER GYNT *(threatening them)*
                              You wait and see!
A MAN *(half drunk)*
    You wait, and you'll get your coat dusted, hey!
OTHERS
    Your back gone over! A fat black eye!
    *(The crowd disperses, the older ones angry, the younger
                ones laughing and jeering.)*
THE BRIDEGROOM *(close by PEER)*
    Say, Peer, is it true you can ride in the air?
PEER GYNT *(brusquely)*
    Anything, Mads! I'm a rare kind of man.
BRIDEGROOM
    Then you have the invisible cloak, I'm sure.
PEER GYNT
    The hat, you mean? Yes, I have one.
        *(Turns from him. SOLVEIG comes across the yard,
                leading HELGA by the hand.)*

PEER GYNT *(goes toward them, his face lighting up)*
    Solveig! Oh, it's good to see you again!
                    (Seizing her by the wrist.)
    Now you're going to be swung and held!

SOLVEIG
    Let go of me!

PEER GYNT
             Why?

SOLVEIG
                 You're much too wild.

PEER GYNT
    Wild like the reindeer when summer dawns.
    Come on, lass; don't be contrary!

SOLVEIG *(pulls her arm free)*
    I don't dare.

PEER GYNT
          Why?

SOLVEIG
               Because — you've been drinking.
         (Moves away with HELGA.*)*

PEER GYNT
    Oh, to feel my knife blade sinking
    Into the hearts of each and every
    One of them!

BRIDEGROOM *(nudging his elbow)*
            Help me get in to the bride?

PEER GYNT
    The bride? Where is she?

BRIDEGROOM
             The storehouse.

PEER GYNT
                    So.

BRIDEGROOM
    Oh, please, Peer Gynt, give it a try!

PEER GYNT

No, you can do it without my aid.

(*A thought strikes him. In a low, hard voice:*)

Ingrid! The storehouse! (*Goes over to* SOLVEIG.)

Now what do you say?

(SOLVEIG *turns to leave; he bars the path.*)

You're ashamed; I look like a tramp to you.

SOLVEIG (*hastily*)

No, you don't! That just isn't true!

PEER GYNT

Yes! And now I've gone a little askew.

But that was for spite, when you slighted me.

Come on!

SOLVEIG

If I wished to, I still wouldn't dare.

PEER GYNT

Who are you scared of?

SOLVEIG

Mostly my father.

PEER GYNT

Your father? I know; he's a living prayer!

The soul of piety,[13] eh? Well—answer!

SOLVEIG

What should I answer?

PEER GYNT

Is he one of the saints?

And you and your mother sing the same tune?

Well, will you answer?

SOLVEIG

Leave me alone.

PEER GYNT

No. (*In a low, bitter, intimidating voice.*)

I can turn myself into a troll.

I'll come to your bed at midnight, I will.

If you hear something that hisses and grunts,
Don't try to pretend it's only the cat.
It's me, child! I'll drain off your blood in a cup;
And your little sister—I'll eat her up;
Because, you know—I'm a werewolf at night—
I'll bite you all over the loins and back—

   (Suddenly changes his tone and begs, as if in anguish.)

Dance with me, Solveig!

SOLVEIG *(looking darkly at him)*

                                   That was ugly talk!

                    (Goes into the house.)

BRIDEGROOM *(wanders up again)*

   I'll give you an ox if you'll help me.

PEER GYNT

                                   Come!

(They go behind the house. At the same time a crowd comes up from the dancing, most of them drunk. Noise and confusion. SOLVEIG and HELGA, their parents, and a number of older people come out the door.)

MASTER OF CEREMONIES *(to the SMITH, leading the crowd)*

   Calm down!

ASLAK *(pulling off his jacket)*

                   No, this is the reckoning time.

   Peer Gynt or I will get laid out flat.

SEVERAL VOICES

   Yes, let them fight!

OTHERS

                                   No, argue it out!

ASLAK

   We'll settle with fists; no more blather.

SOLVEIG'S FATHER

   Control yourself, man!

HELGA

                         Will they hit him, Mother?

A YOUTH

    Let's tease him instead with all his lies!

ANOTHER

    Boot him out of here!

A THIRD

                     Spit in his eyes!

A FOURTH *(to* ASLAK*)*

    You backing down?

ASLAK *(throwing his jacket away)*

                   I'll murder the swill!

SOLVEIG'S MOTHER *(to* SOLVEIG*)*

    Now you see what they think of that fool.

AASE *(coming up with a stick in her hand)*

    Where's my son? He'll be getting it, fore and aft!

    Ah, the pleasure I'll have in walloping him!

ASLAK *(rolling up his shirt sleeves)*

    For his kind of carcass, a stick is too soft.

SEVERAL VOICES

    The smith's going to wring him!

OTHERS

                    Bung him!

ASLAK *(spitting on his hands and nodding at* AASE*)*

                     Hang him!

AASE

    What! Hang my boy! Yes, try, if you dare—!

    Me and myself, we've got claws that tear—!

    Where is he? *(Calls across the yard.)*

            Peer!

BRIDEGROOM *(running up)*

              Hell and damnation!

    Come, Father and Mother—!

HIS FATHER

                What, on my soul—?

BRIDEGROOM

    It's Peer Gynt——

AASE *(screams)*
>   Have they killed my son?

BRIDEGROOM
    No, he's—! Look, up there on the hill——

THE CROWD
    With the bride!

AASE *(lets her staff sink)*
>   The beast!

ASLAK
>   It's a sheer drop;
    But he climbs, God, like a goat on a crag!

BRIDEGROOM *(sobbing)*
    Mother, how he carries her—just like a pig!

AASE *(shakes her fist at him)*
    I hope you fall down and—!

>   *(Shrieks in fright.)*
>   Hi, watch your step!

INGRID'S FATHER *(comes up, bareheaded, white with rage)*
    For stealing the bride, I'll have his head!

AASE
    If I ever let you, God strike me dead!

ACT TWO

A narrow path, high in the mountains. It is early morning.
PEER GYNT *comes hurrying sullenly along the path.* INGRID,
partly dressed in bridal costume, tries to hold him back.

PEER GYNT
  Just go away!
INGRID *(weeping)*
                After this!
  Where?
PEER GYNT
             Anywhere away from me.
INGRID *(wringing her hands)*
  Oh, you cheat!
PEER GYNT
                Don't make a fuss.
  We'd each better go off separately.
INGRID
  We're bound by sin—and sin again!
PEER GYNT
  The devil take all memories!
  The devil take all women; that is—
  All but one—!
INGRID
             Who is that one?
PEER GYNT
  It isn't you.
INGRID
           But what's her name?

PEER GYNT

   Go away! Back where you came from!
   To your father, quick!

INGRID

                      My dearest own—!

PEER GYNT

   Don't!

INGRID

       You can't possibly mean
   What you're saying.

PEER GYNT

               I can and do.

INGRID

   Ruin me first—then cast me off!

PEER GYNT

   And what kind of future can you give?

INGRID

   Hegstad farm, and a lot more too.

PEER GYNT

   What do you wrap your prayer book in?
   Does your hair fall golden at your throat?
   Do you gaze down into your apron?
   Your mother's skirt, do you hold it tight?
   Answer!

INGRID

      No; but—?

PEER GYNT

            And were you just
   Now confirmed?

INGRID

      No, but Peer——

PEER GYNT

   Do I feel your shyness like a wound?
   Can you refuse what I'm craving for?

INGRID
    Oh, God, I think he's lost his mind—!
PEER GYNT
    Does the very sight of you bless the air?
    Well!
INGRID
        No, but—
PEER GYNT
                Then what's all the rest?
                (Starts off.)
INGRID *(blocking his way)*
    Don't you know it's a hanging crime
    If you run off now?
PEER GYNT
                I don't care.
INGRID
    You could have property and honor
    If you'd take me—
PEER GYNT
                Can't afford them.
INGRID *(bursting into tears)*
    How you lured me!
PEER GYNT
                You were willing!
INGRID
    I was desperate!
PEER GYNT
            And I was mad.
INGRID *(threatening)*
    You won't escape till the price is paid!
PEER GYNT
    The highest price would seem like nothing.
INGRID
    You're really set on that?

PEER GYNT

Like stone.

INGRID

Good! We'll see who's going to win!

(*Starts down the slope.*)

PEER GYNT (*silent a moment, then cries out:*)

The devil take all memories!

The devil take all women —

INGRID (*turns her head and calls up mockingly*)

That is —

All but *one*!

PEER GYNT

Yes, all but *one*.

(*They go off separately.*)

SCENE TWO

Soft marsh country near a mountain lake. A storm is gathering.
AASE, *in despair, is peering in every direction and calling out.*
SOLVEIG *finds it hard to keep up with her.* SOLVEIG'S *parents*
and HELGA *follow close behind.*

AASE (*flailing her arms and tearing her hair*)

Everything spites me with a vengeance —

Sky and water and these wicked mountains!

Fog pouring out of the sky to confound him,

The water luring him in to drown him,

The mountains poising their rocks to fall —

And those people! All of them out for the kill!

Oh Lord, not that! I musn't lose him.

The lout! Why the devil has to tease him —?

(*Turning to* SOLVEIG)

It's hard enough to believe, God knows —

He who was nothing but dreams and lies,

He whose strength was all in his mouth,
Who'd never done work of any worth,
That he—! You want to both laugh and cry!
   Oh, we've had to stick close in misery.
Because, you know, my man—he drank,
Roamed the parish with a line of bluff,
Scattered and trampled our goods to dust—
While back at home my Peer and I sat.
All we could do was try and forget;
I'm no good when something has to be faced.
It's so painful staring fate in the eyes;
You'd much rather shake your troubles off
And just do anything not to think.
Some turn to brandy, others to lies,
And we—well, we took to fairy tales
Of princes and trolls and strange animals.
Stolen brides too. But who'd have thought
Those infernal stories would be in him yet.
          (Terrified again.)
Hoo, what a scream! It's a draug[14] or a troll!
Peer! Peer! Up there on the hill—!
*(Runs to the top of a small rise and looks out over the
    lake.* SOLVEIG'S *parents come up.)*

  Not a trace!
THE FATHER *(quietly)*
        The worse for him.
AASE *(in tears)*
  Oh, my Peer, my poor lost lamb!
THE FATHER *(nodding gently)*
  Yes, he *is* lost.
AASE
          Oh, forget his faults!
He's so fine. He's like no one else.
THE FATHER
  You foolish woman!

AASE
                              Yes, that's it,
    I'm a fool; but the boy's all right!

THE FATHER *(continues quietly, looking gently at her)*
    His heart is hardened; his soul is lost.

AASE *(anguished)*
    Not true! The Lord isn't so unjust!

THE FATHER
    You think he can feel his weight of sin?

AASE *(hotly)*
    No; but he and a buck have flown!

THE MOTHER
    My stars, are you crazy?

THE FATHER
                              What was that?

AASE
    There's nothing he can take on too great.
    You'll find out, if he lives that long —

THE FATHER
    You'd be better off to see him hang.

AASE *(shrieks)*
    Oh my Jesus!

THE FATHER
                      A length of rope
    Might turn him toward our eternal hope.

AASE *(dazed)*
    Don't talk like that, you'll make me ill!
    Let's find him!

THE FATHER
                      To save his soul!

AASE
                                  And skin!
    If he's stuck in the marsh, let's bring him in;
    And ring the church bells to ward off trolls.

THE FATHER
Hm — ! Here's a cow path —

AASE
                                          God repay
You for helping me!

THE FATHER
                              It's Christian duty.

AASE
Then they're heathens, all the other
Ones! Not *any* of them would bother —

THE FATHER
They knew him too well.

AASE
                          He's above their like!
                    (Wringing her hands.)
And to think — to think his life's at stake!

THE FATHER
Here's a man's footprints.

AASE
                              Better make sure!

THE FATHER
We'll scatter downhill across the pasture.
                    (He and his wife go ahead.)

SOLVEIG *(to* AASE*)*
Tell me some more.

AASE *(drying her eyes)*
                    Of my son?

SOLVEIG
                                          Yes —
Everything!

AASE *(smiles and throws back her head)*
                    Everything — ? You'll weary of this.

SOLVEIG
You'll grow tired of talking long
Before I'm done listening.

SCENE THREE

*Low treeless knolls under a towering waste of mountain;
high peaks farther off. The shadows are lengthening; it is
late in the day.* PEER GYNT *comes running full tilt and stops
on the hillside.*

PEER GYNT

The whole parish is hot on my tracks
Armed to the teeth with rifles and sticks!
Old Hegstad's in front, you can hear him howl —
The news is out, Peer Gynt's on the prowl!
This is no row with a blacksmith here!
This is life! I feel strong as a bear.

> *(Leaping in the air and lashing out.)*

To crush, overthrow! Swim cataracts!
Smash! Rip fir trees up by the roots!
This is life! How it toughens and frees
The soul! To hell with those sickly lies!

(THREE HERD GIRLS[15] *from a mountain hut come running over the hill, shouting and singing.)*

HERD GIRLS

Trond of the Valfjeld! Kaare and Baard!
Trolls, come sleep with us, hold us hard!

PEER GYNT

Who're you shouting for?

HERD GIRLS

Trolls! For trolls!

FIRST GIRL

Trond, go easy!

SECOND GIRL

Baard, be rough!

THIRD GIRL

The beds are all lying empty at home!

46

FIRST GIRL
    Rough is easy.

SECOND GIRL
                            And easy is rough!

THIRD GIRL
    When there aren't any boys, a troll's good enough.

PEER GYNT
    And where are your boys then?

ALL THREE *(roaring with laughter)*
                                    They can't come!

FIRST GIRL
    Mine called me near and dear as his shadow.
    Now he's hitched to a middle-aged widow.

SECOND GIRL
    Mine met a gypsy bitch up north.
    Now they roll on the country earth.

THIRD GIRL
    Mine put our bastard out of his pains.
    Now his head sticks on a stake and grins.

ALL THREE
    Trond of the Valfjeld! Kaare and Baard!
    Trolls, come sleep with us, hold us hard!

PEER GYNT *(leaps in among them)*
    I'm a three-headed troll[16] and a three-woman man!

THE GIRLS
    Do you ride so well?

PEER GYNT
                            Find out if I can!

FIRST GIRL
    Up to the cabin!

SECOND GIRL
                        We've mead!

PEER GYNT
                            Let it flow!

47

THIRD GIRL
> We won't have a bed lying empty now![17]

SECOND GIRL *(kissing him)*
> He sputters and glows like white-hot steel.

THIRD GIRL *(kissing him)*
> With his baby eyes from a bottomless pool.

PEER GYNT *(dancing among them)*
> Heart like a stone, blood like a goat,
> Eyes full of laughter, tears in the throat!

THE GIRLS *(thumbing their noses at the mountaintops, shouting and singing)*
> Trond of the Valfjeld! Kaare and Baard!
> Did you sleep with us once? Did you hold us hard?
> *(They dance away over the heights with* PEER GYNT
> *in their midst.)*

SCENE FOUR

In the Ronde Mountains.[18] *Sunset. Snow-capped mountains gleaming on all sides.*

PEER GYNT *(enters, wild and distraught)*
> Castle on castle soaring!
> See, what a glittering gate!
> Stay! Will you stay! It's veering
> Farther and farther about!
> The cock on the weathervane's lifting
> His golden wings into flight.
> He fades in a blue mist, drifting;
> The mountains freeze in for the night.
>   What are those trees there, rooted
> In crevasses of the rock?
> They're warriors, heron-footed!
> Now they're passing into the dark.
>   The air, like a rainbow streaming,

Cuts into my eyes and soul.
What far-off bells are chiming?
What's pressing down on my skull?
My head swells bigger and bigger;
It's clamped in an iron band—!
I can't for the life of me figure
How that got wrapped around!

> (*Sinks down.*)

A race along Gjendin's ridges.
Dreams and damnable lies!
Up over the sheerest ledges
With the bride—then a drunken daze;
Hunted by hawks and falcons,
Menaced by trolls and gnomes,
Wenching with crazy women—
Lies and damnable dreams!

> (*Gazing up for a long time.*)

Way up there, two brown eagles.
Southward, a flight of geese.
And here I wallow and straggle
Through mud and filth to the knees!

> (*Springing up.*)

I'll join them! Wash myself clean in
A bath of the flurrying wind
Fly to the heights, then dip down in
The waters and rise up christened!
I'll skim the mountain cabins,
Glide till my spirits dance,
Soar out over rolling oceans,
And high over Engelland's prince!
Yes, you can look, young maidens;
My flight won't touch you at all;
Your waiting is quite unbidden—!
Well, I might drop down for a while.
    That's funny. Those two eagles—?
They've vanished, devil knows where—

Wait! There's the peak of a gable,
And now the eaves coming clear,
Sprung up from the ruins—yes,
And look, the gate's open wide!
Why, I remember that house:
Grandfather's farm in its pride!
The rags are gone from the windows;
The fences are straight and tall.
Light blazes from every pane now;
They're feasting in the great hall.
I can hear a chinking of metal;
It's the bishop's knife on his glass—
Now the captain's flinging his bottle,
And the mirror shivers to smash.
Let's squander! This is tremendous!
Hush, Mother; who says we can't!
The rich Jon Gynt's behind us—
Three cheers for the house of Gynt!
What's that? Pandemonium
Breaking out at the feast—?
The captain calls me to join him;
The bishop makes me a toast.
Go in, Peer, in where your fate is
Sung out in prophecy:
Peer Gynt, thou art born of greatness,
And greatness is coming to thee!

*(Leaps forward, but bangs his nose against a rock
and falls senseless.)*

SCENE FIVE

*A hillside with great sighing shade trees. Stars twinkle through
the leaves; birds sing in the treetops. A* WOMAN IN GREEN[19]
walks on the slope. PEER GYNT *follows her, making all sorts of
amorous gestures.*

WOMAN IN GREEN *(stops and turns)*
   Is that true?
PEER GYNT *(drawing his finger across his throat* [20] *)*
                  True as my name is Peer,
   And true as you're a beautiful woman!
   Will you have me? You'll see the way I care;
   You won't ever have to weave or spin—
   Just eat; and the meals will be immense.
   I'll never pull your hair, not once—
WOMAN IN GREEN
   Nor beat me, either?
PEER GYNT
                        Am I the type?
   We kings' sons don't beat our women up.
WOMAN IN GREEN
   You're a king's son?
PEER GYNT
                  Yes.
WOMAN IN GREEN
                        I'm the Dovre King's daughter.
PEER GYNT
   You are? Well, that's a coincidence.
WOMAN IN GREEN
   Deep in the Ronde his castle stands.
PEER GYNT
   My mother's is bigger, if it's any matter.
WOMAN IN GREEN
   You know my father? His name's King Brose.
PEER GYNT
   You know my mother? Her name's Queen Aase.
WOMAN IN GREEN
   When my father's mad, the mountains blanch.
PEER GYNT
   When my mother scolds, there's an avalanche.

WOMAN IN GREEN

  My father can kick to the highest beams.

PEER GYNT

  My mother rides through the swiftest streams.

WOMAN IN GREEN

  Have you no other clothes than those tatters there?

PEER GYNT

  Ah, you should see my Sunday gear!

WOMAN IN GREEN

  Weekdays, I'm always in silks and gold.

PEER GYNT

  It looks more to me like straw and mold.

WOMAN IN GREEN

  Yes, but there's one thing to understand
  About Ronde customs: here you'll find
  Everything has to be seen two ways.
  You could easily think, if you went on
  To my father's court, that his royal house
  Was nothing more than a bleak moraine.

PEER GYNT

  Well, isn't it just the same with us?
  Our gold would look to you like dross,
  And every glittering pane might seem
  Like clouts of stockings, rags and grime.

WOMAN IN GREEN

  Black looks white, and vile looks fair.

PEER GYNT

  Great looks small, and foul looks pure.

WOMAN IN GREEN *(embracing him)*

  Oh Peer, I can see, we're like one and the same!

PEER GYNT

  Like a leg for a trouser; like hair for a comb.

WOMAN IN GREEN *(calls off across the hill)*

  My steed, my steed! Come, bridal steed!

(An enormous pig comes running in, with a rope end for a bridle and an old sack for a saddle. PEER *swings up onto its back and sets the* WOMAN IN GREEN *in front of him.)*

PEER GYNT

Giddap! Straight for the Ronde gate, ride!
Gee-up! Gee-up there, my prancer! Up, boy!

WOMAN IN GREEN *(caressingly)*

And just now my mood was so sad and grey —
How life provides, if you give it a chance!

PEER GYNT *(whips the pig to a trot)*

You can tell great men by the style of their mounts.

SCENE SIX

The Royal Hall of the King of the Dovre Mountains.[21] *A great assembly of* TROLL COURTIERS, GOBLINS, *and* GNOMES. *The* TROLL KING *sits on his throne, sceptered and crowned. His* CHILDREN *and* CLOSE RELATIVES *are grouped around him.* PEER GYNT *stands before him. Wild uproar in the hall.*

TROLL COURTIERS

Kill him! A Christian's tried to lure
The Dovre King's most beautiful girl!

A TROLL CHILD

May I slash his finger?

ANOTHER

                                    May I tear his hair?

A TROLL GIRL

Hei! Hoo, let me bite his rear!

TROLL WITCH *(with a ladle)*

Shouldn't we boil him down for gruel?

ANOTHER WITCH *(with a carving knife)*

Turn him on a spit, or brown him for stew?

THE TROLL KING

    Cool your blood!

               (Beckons his counselors to him.)

                 It's no time to crow.

We've been slipping downhill these latter years —

Who knows if things'll go better or worse,

So let's not discourage a new recruit.

Besides, the boy looks perfectly fit,

And he's well set up, if I see him clear.

It's true, he hasn't a head to spare,

But my daughter's only a one-headed troll.

Three-headed trolls have gone out of style;

You scarcely see two-headers any more,

And the ones you do see are pretty poor.

                 (To PEER GYNT.*)*

So — it's my daughter you want to have?

PEER GYNT

    Yes, and your realm for the dowry too.

TROLL KING

    You can have half while I still live,

    And the other half right after I go.

PEER GYNT

    That's fair enough.

TROLL KING

             Just a minute, boy —

There are some promises you have to give.

Break only one, and the contract's clay,

And you'll never get out of here alive.

First, you must promise never to care

For the world beyond our own frontier;

Renounce day, deeds, the things of light.

PEER GYNT

    If I can be king, there's nothing to that.

TROLL KING

    Next — I'll put your wits to the test —

(Draws himself up on his throne.)

THE OLDEST COURTIER TROLL *(to* PEER GYNT*)*
Let's see if your wisdom tooth can
Crack the shell of our king's request!

TROLL KING
What difference is there between troll and man?

PEER GYNT
No difference at all, from what I can see.
Big trolls roast you, and little trolls claw—
Same as with us,[22] if our nerves are raw.

TROLL KING
Yes, there and in other points, we agree.
But morning is morning and night is night,
And there *is* a difference down at the root.
I'll tell you what it is. Outside,
Among men, under the shining sky,
They say: "Man, to yourself be true!"
While here, under our mountain roof,
We say: "Troll, to yourself be—enough!"[23]

THE COURTIER TROLL *(to* PEER GYNT*)*
Can you fathom that?

PEER GYNT
                              Through a dark cloud.

TROLL KING
"Enough," my son—that severing term—
Must boldly stand on your coat of arms.

PEER GYNT *(scratching behind his ear)*
Well, but —

TROLL KING
                  It *must,* if you want to rule here!

PEER GYNT
Well, all right, I guess that's fair—

TROLL KING
Next, you must learn the value of
Our simple, domestic way of life.[24]

(He gestures; two trolls with pigs' heads and white
nightcaps bring food and drink. [25])
Our cows give cake and our bulls give mead;
Don't ask if the flavor is sour or sweet;
The main thing that you must never forget
Is—that it's home-brewed.

PEER GYNT (pushing the things away)
To hell with all your homemade brews!
I'll never get used to this country's ways.

TROLL KING
The bowl belongs with the drink; it's gold.
Who owns this bowl, my daughter will hold.

PEER GYNT (musing)
It's written: Thy nature must be subdued—
In time the drink may seem less crude.
So, here goes! (Drinks.)

TROLL KING
                        Ah, wisely put.
Did you spit?

PEER GYNT
                        One obeys the force of habit.

TROLL KING
Now, throw off your Christian dress.
Everything's mountain-made with us;
From the valleys we get nothing else
But the silk bows that adorn our tails.[26]

PEER GYNT (angrily)
I have no tail!

TROLL KING
                        We'll get you one.
Steward, my Sunday best! Tie it on.

PEER GYNT
Lay off! You think I've lost my mind?

TROLL KING
You can't court my daughter with a smooth behind.

PEER GYNT
Turn man to a beast!

TROLL KING
                              You're wrong, my son;
I want you decked out like a proper swain.
You'll get a flame-yellow bow to wear,
And that rates the highest honors here.

PEER GYNT *(thoughtfully)*
Well, they say that man is only a mote,
So custom and fashion have to guide us a bit.
Tie away!

TROLL KING
              What a responsive guest.

COURTIER TROLL
Show us how well you can wag your tail!

PEER GYNT
Ha, there's more you want of me still?
Would you also like my Christian faith?

TROLL KING
No, you can keep that under your breath.
Faith is free; we impose no tax;
A troll is known by the way he looks.
Once we're the same in manner and clothes,
You're free to believe in what a troll loathes.

PEER GYNT
You know, despite the conditions you make,
You're more sensible than I thought you'd be.

TROLL KING
Trolls aren't as bad, son, as people say;
It's one other point where we're unalike—
Well, that ends the party's serious side;
Now we'll enjoy what our senses bring—
Musician! Strike the Dovre harp-strings!
Dancer! Let the floor echo your tread!
                    (Music and dance.)

COURTIER TROLL
How do you like it?

PEER GYNT
Hm —

TROLL KING
Speak out.
What do you see?

PEER GYNT
A horrible sight.
A bell cow strumming a catgut lyre,
And a sow in stockings dancing to her.

COURTIERS
Eat him!

TROLL KING
He sees us with human senses,
Remember!

TROLL GIRLS
Tear out his eyes and ears!

WOMAN IN GREEN *(sobbing)*
Boo-hoo! The things we have to endure
When my sister and I put on our dances!

PEER GYNT
Oh no, was it you? Well, a little guying
At a banquet is hardly a sign of spite.

WOMAN IN GREEN
Do you swear to that?

PEER GYNT
Both dancing and playing —
May the cat claw my tongue — were pure delight.

TROLL KING
It's strange about this human nature,
Just how remarkably deep it goes.
If it gets gashed in some battle with us,
It heals right up and wears its scar.
Now my son-in-law's lenient as any man;

He willingly dropped the garb of a Christian,
Willingly drank the bowl of mead,
Willingly let his tail be tied —
In fact, was so willing in all we made him
Do that I really thought the old Adam
Had at last been safely kicked out of doors;
But, look, in a wink he's back in force.
Ah yes, my son, you need a cure
To reform your accursed human nature.

PEER GYNT
What do you mean?

TROLL KING
                                          I'll make a slit
In your left eye, till you see the world slant —
But all that you see will make you content.
Then I'll cut out the right windowpane —

PEER GYNT
Are you drunk?

TROLL KING *(puts some sharp implements on the table)*
                                 Here you see a glazier's kit.
You'll be blinkered like an unruly bull.
Then you'll realize your bride is beautiful,
And your eyesight will never again confuse
Her charms with pigs or musical cows.

PEER GYNT
You're raving mad!

THE OLDEST COURTIER
                                          You heard what he said;
It's he who's wise, and you that's mad.

TROLL KING
Think of the torments, the miseries
You'll save yourself in afterdays.
Vision, don't forget, is the source
Of tears, and the body's bitter light.

PEER GYNT

>That's true; and there's the Bible verse:
>"If thine eye offend thee, pluck it out."
>Wait! But tell me, when would it mend
>Back to human sight?

TROLL KING

>   Never, my friend.

PEER GYNT

>Hm! Well, then I'll say thanks, but no.

TROLL KING

>Where are you heading?

PEER GYNT

>   It's time to go.

TROLL KING

>Hold on! Here it's easy to enter in,
>But the gate isn't made to swing out again.

PEER GYNT

>You're not going to keep me here forcibly?

TROLL KING

>Now listen, be reasonable, Prince Peer!
>You're gifted for trollhood. Doesn't he bear
>Himself already quite trollishly?
>And you want the job—?

PEER GYNT

>   Of course I do.
>For a bride, and a well-run empire to boot,
>There are losses I can accommodate.
>Everything has its limits, though.
>I've taken a tail, that I'll admit;
>But what's been tied, my hands can unknot.
>I've shed my trousers; they were old and thin,
>But I surely can button them on again.
>And I'm sure as well that I can slough off
>All signs of your Dovre way of life.
>I'll gladly swear that a cow is a woman;

An oath one can always whistle away —
But *this* — to know you can never be free,
Never die decently as a human,
To run as a hill troll till kingdom come —
It's this — the fact that you can't go home
The way the book says, *this* you're intent on;
But it's what I'll never put my consent in.

TROLL KING

Now, bless my sins, I'm getting cross;
And I'll have no more of this foolishness.
You know who I am, you whey-faced rotter?
First, you're fast and loose with my daughter —

PEER GYNT

You lie in your teeth!

TROLL KING

You must marry her.

PEER GYNT

You dare to accuse me — ?

TROLL KING

What? Can you swear
She hasn't gone flickering through your desire?

PEER GYNT (*snorting*)

Is that all? Who's going to make *that* stick?

TROLL KING

You human beings are all alike.
You serve the spirit with your lips
And settle for what your hands can keep.
So you think desire doesn't matter, either?
You'll soon have visible proof, just wait —

PEER GYNT

You won't catch me with your liar's bait!

WOMAN IN GREEN

Peer, by the year's end, you'll be a father.

PEER GYNT

Open up; let me out.

TROLL KING

> You'll get the brat
Wrapped in a goatskin.

PEER GYNT *(mopping sweat from his brow)*

> Oh, to wake up!

TROLL KING

Should he go to your palace?

PEER GYNT

> To the poorhouse doorstep!

TROLL KING

Splendid, Prince Peer; you can manage that.
But *one* thing is certain: what's done is done,
And your offspring will sprout up like a weed;
These mongrels ripen remarkably soon.

PEER GYNT

Now don't be so stubborn-minded, dad.
Be sensible, girl. Let's compromise.
I'm neither a prince nor rich, God knows—
And no matter how you measure or weigh me
You're not going to gain much profit by me.

> *(The* WOMAN IN GREEN *faints and is carried out by
the* TROLL GIRLS.*)*

TROLL KING *(gives him a look of utter contempt)*

Dash him to bits on the rocks, children!

TROLL CHILDREN

Can we play owls and eagles then?
The wolf game! Gray mouse and glow-eyed cat!

TROLL KING

Yes, quickly. I'm vexed and sleepy. Good night!

> *(He leaves.)*

PEER GYNT *(hunted by* TROLL CHILDREN*)*

Let go, you devils!

> *(Starts to squirm up the chimney.)*

TROLL CHILDREN

> Come, goblins! Gnomes!

Bite his back!

PEER GYNT

               Ow!

               (Tries the cellar trapdoor.)

TROLL CHILDREN

                  Plug up the seams!

COURTIER TROLL

What fun for the young!

PEER GYNT *(struggling witha a tiny troll, who has bitten deep in his ear)*

                    Let go, you crud!

COURTIER TROLL *(raps his knuckles)*

Careful, you lowlife; that's royal blood.

PEER GYNT

A rathole —! *(Runs toward it.)*

TROLL CHILDREN

               Goblins! Head him off course!

PEER GYNT

The old man was foul, but the children are worse!

TROLL CHILDREN

Flay him!

PEER GYNT

            Oh, to be small as a mouse!

            (Runs aimlessly.)

TROLL CHILDREN *(swarming about him)*

Close in! Pen him!

PEER GYNT *(in tears)*

                The size of a louse!

               (He falls.)

TROLL CHILDREN

Now, get his eyes!

PEER GYNT *(buried in a heap of trolls)*

              Help, Mother, I'll die!

             (Church bells ring far off.)

TROLL CHILDREN

Bells in the mountains! Blackfrock's cows![27]
>   (*The trolls flee in a turmoil of howls and shrieks.
>   The hall collapses; everything vanishes.*)

SCENE SEVEN

Pitch blackness. PEER GYNT *can be heard striking and flailing
about with the branch of a tree.*

PEER GYNT

Speak out! Who are you?

A VOICE IN THE DARKNESS

>   Myself.

PEER GYNT

>   Move aside!

THE VOICE

Go roundabout, Peer! The heath is wide.

PEER GYNT (*starts to go through at another point, but is
     stopped by something*)

Who are *you*?

THE VOICE

>   Myself. Can you say the same?

PEER GYNT

I can say what I please; and my sword hits home!
Look out! Ahh! Now he feels his wounds!
King Saul killed hundreds;[28] Peer Gynt, thousands!
>   (*Hewing and slashing.*)

Who are you?

THE VOICE

>   Myself.

PEER GYNT

>   That stupid answer

You can keep; it makes nothing clear.
What are you?

THE VOICE
>   The great Boyg.[29]

PEER GYNT
>   I see!
> The riddle was black, and now it's gray.
> Out of my way, Boyg!

THE VOICE
>   Go roundabout, Peer!

PEER GYNT
> Straight through! *(Striking out.)* He's down!
>   *(Tries to go on, but again is stopped.)*
>   What? Still more?

THE VOICE
> The Boyg, Peer Gynt! The one only one.
> The Boyg that's unhurt, and the Boyg that's in pain.
> The Boyg that's dead, and the Boyg that's alive.

PEER GYNT *(flinging the branch away)*
> The sword's bewitched, but fists are enough.
>   *(Hammers his way ahead.)*

THE VOICE
> Yes, trust to your fists, your body's hope.
> Ho-ho, Peer Gynt, you'll reach the top.

PEER GYNT *(returning)*
> Forward and back, it's just as far.
> Out or in, it's a narrow door.
> He's *there*! And *there*! And beyond the bend!
> As soon as I'm out, he rings me around—
> Your name; Let me see you! Say what you are!

THE VOICE
> The Boyg.

PEER GYNT *(groping about)*
>   Not dead, nor alive. Slime; gray air,
> Not even a form. It's like trading jabs
> With a den of snarling, half-awake bear cubs.
>   *(Shrieks.)*

Stand up to me!

THE VOICE

               The Boyg's not insane.

PEER GYNT

  Strike!

THE VOICE

        The Boyg doesn't strike.

PEER GYNT

                  Fight! Come on!

THE VOICE

  The great Boyg wins, though no fighting rages.

PEER GYNT

  For a goblin raking my back with a knife!
  Or only so much as a year-old troll!
  Something to scrap with. But there's nothing at all —
  Now he's snoring! Boyg!

THE VOICE

             What?

PEER GYNT

               Get rough!

THE VOICE

  The great Boyg wins all by easy stages.

PEER GYNT (*bites his own hands and arms*)

  Gashing teeth and claws in the flesh!
  I've got to feel my own blood drop.

    (*A sound like the wingbeats of great birds*[30] *is heard.*)

BIRD CRIES

  Boyg, is he coming?

THE VOICE

           Yes, step by step.

BIRD CRIES

  Sisters far off, fly here in a rush!

PEER GYNT

  If you want to save me, girl, do it quick!

Don't lower your gaze, tender and shy —
The prayer book! Fling it straight in his eye!

BIRD CRIES

He wavers!

THE VOICE

We've got him.

BIRD CRIES

Sisters, attack!

PEER GYNT

If the price of life is this agony,
Even one hour's too much to pay.

(*Sinks down.*)

THE BIRDS

Boyg, he's fallen! Take him! End him!

(*Church bells and hymns in the distance.*)

THE BOYG (*dwindles to nothing, his voice a gasp*)

He was too strong. There were women behind him.

SCENE EIGHT

Sunrise. On the slope by AASE'S *mountain hut. The door is
bolted; everything is deserted and still.* PEER GYNT *lies asleep
alongside one wall. He wakes, looks about with a dull, heavy
stare, then spits.*

PEER GYNT

Oh, what I'd give for a pickled herring!

(*Spits again, and at the same moment notices* HELGA
approaching with a food basket.)

Well, what brings you up here, child? Exploring?

HELGA

It's Solveig —

PEER GYNT (*leaps up*)

Where is she?

67

HELGA
                              Back of your hut.
SOLVEIG *(hidden)*
   Come any closer, and I'm going to run!
PEER GYNT *(stops)*
   Afraid you'll wind up in the arms of a man?
SOLVEIG
   Shame on you!
PEER GYNT
                        Know where I was last night?
   The Troll Princess went after me like a bat.
SOLVEIG
   It's a good thing, then, that we rang the bells.
PEER GYNT
   Peer Gynt isn't one that her sort beguiles —
   What'd you say?
HELGA *(bursting into tears)*
                        Oh, she's running! Wait!
   Wait! *(Hurries after.)*
PEER GYNT *(seizing her arm)*
         Look here, in my pocket, I had
   This silver button. Take it! It's for you —
   If you just speak well of me!
HELGA
                              Please, let me go!
PEER GYNT
   It's yours.
HELGA
               Please — in the basket, there's food!
PEER GYNT
   If you don't, God help you —
HELGA
                              Oh, you upset me!
PEER GYNT *(gently, releasing her)*
   No, I mean — ask her not to forget me!
                  (HELGA runs off.)

ACT THREE

Deep in a pine forest. Gray autumn weather, with snow falling.
PEER GYNT *stands in his shirt sleeves, felling timber. He is hew-*
ing away at a great fir with crooked branches.

PEER GYNT
    Ah, you're tough, you old mountain man —
    But it's no use; you're coming down.
                 (Hewing away again.)
    I see you're wearing a coat of mail;
    It's strong, but I'll stave it in for the kill —
    Go on; shake your crooked arm;
    Of course you're angry and out of form;
    But still you're going to bow to me — !
                 (Breaks off abruptly.)
    Lies! It's just a battered tree.
    Lies! It's no armor maker's work;
    Only a fir with peeling bark.
    It's weary labor, chopping wood,
    But to chop *and* dream is crazy mad.
    I'm through with it — this life of mist
    That weaves the living moment past.
    You're an outlaw, Peer! A hunted beast.
             (Chopping hard for a time.)
    An outlaw, yes. No mother glad
    To set your table and bring you food.
    If you're hungry, boy, you're on your own;
    Fetch it raw from woods or stream;
    Split your kindling, build your fire,

Putter and mend and make secure.
If you want to dress warmly, kill a buck;
If your house needs shoring, break the rock;
If you're short of timber, fell the logs
And haul them in on aching legs.

    (The ax sinks; he gazes off.)

Build it with splendor. A tower and vane
On the ridgepole, soaring high and clean.
And then I'll carve, for the end of the gable,
A mermaid, fish-shaped down from the navel.
The vane and the locks will be of brass —
And panes of glass, I can try for that.
Passing strangers will wonder what
It is that shines on this distant rise.

    (Laughs angrily.)

Infernal lies! I went off again.
You're an outlaw, Peer!

    (Chopping fiercely.)

    A plain bark roof
For the rain and frost is good enough.

    (Looks up at the tree.)

Now he's swaying. A kick, just one —
And there he falls to cut a swath
Across the shuddering undergrowth!

  *(Starts to trim off branches; suddenly
  he listens, motionless, ax in midair.)*

Someone's after me — ! Are you that kind,
Old Hegstad — to come here, sneaking around?

    (Crouches behind the tree and peeps out.)

A boy! And alone. He looks afraid.
He's staring about. What is that, hid
By his jacket? A sickle. His eyes keep scanning —
Now he's spread his hand on the fence rail.
What now? Why does he stand there, leaning — ?
Ugh, his finger, it's off! He's cut

The whole finger off! He bleeds like a bull—
He's running away with his fist in a clout.
(Rises)
The devil! An irreplaceable finger—
Lost! And through his, not another's anger.
Ah, now I know—! That's the price
For escaping his military service.
That's it. They want to send him to war;
And the boy, of course, doesn't want to go—
But to cut off—? For all time, never to—
Yes, think it; wish it; *will* it so—
But to *do* it! No, I can't follow him there.
(Shakes his head quietly, then returns to work.)

SCENE TWO

A room in AASE'S *house. Everything in disorder, boxes stand-*
ing open, clothing strewn about, a cat lying on the bed. AASE
and KARI *are hard at work, packing and straightening up.*

AASE *(running to one side of the room)*
    Kari, listen!
KARI
                Now what?
AASE *(back to the other side)*
                        Tell me—!
    Where's—? Where did I—? You know, where's the—?
    What do I want? My mind's in a whirl!
    Where's the key to the chest?
KARI
                            In the keyhole.
AASE
    What's that's rumbling?

KARI

>   The last cartload
>   Going over to Hegstad.

AASE *(weeping)*

>   I'd be glad
>   To be going myself in a long black box.
>   Ah, what a person suffers in heartbreaks!
>   Merciful God! The house stripped clean!
>   What old Hegstad left, the sheriff held —
>   Even the clothes on my back were sold.
>   Shame on a justice that can be so mean!

>   *(Sitting on the edge of the bed.)*

>   The farm and the land, lost to our name.
>   The old man was hard; but the law was a crime —
>   No one to help; no mercy given;
>   Peer far away; no counsel even —

KARI

>   But the house is yours till the day you die.

AASE

>   Yes, I and the cat can take charity!

KARI

>   God help you, Aase; you've paid for your son.

AASE

>   Peer? Now that's an odd opinion!
>   Ingrid got home safe, finally.
>   They ought to lay the blame on the devil —
>   He's the power in all that's evil;
>   The prince of hell possessed my boy!

KARI

>   Maybe I'd better send for the pastor?
>   You might have worsened without your knowing.

AASE

>   The pastor? I guess it would be best for —

>   *(Starting up.)*

>   God no, I can't! What am I saying?

His mother must help him; it's the least I owe—
To be there when the others all turn away.
They left him this coat. I'll patch it up.
Ah, the fur rug's something I'd like to keep!
Where are the stockings?

KARI

There, in that muddle.

AASE *(rummaging around)*

What's this—? Look, it's the casting ladle
From the old days! With this he used to play
Button-molder—melt and pour and ply
The metal. At a party once, he came in
And asked his father for a lump of tin.
"Not tin," says Jon, "but coin of the mint—
Silver, because you're the son of Jon Gynt."
God save him, he was a little wild
From drink, and couldn't tell tin from gold.
There, the stockings. And full of holes!
They ought to be darned.

KARI

They really should.

AASE

When that's been done, I'll go to bed.
I feel so weak, so sick and depressed—

(Joyfully.)

Two wool shirts, Kari—these they missed!

KARI

So they did.

AASE

It's something at least.
One of them's yours; we can settle with
That—or—no, we can take them both.
The ones he's got are wearing thin.

KARI

But, Mother Aase, stealing is sin!

AASE

Oh well, but you know the pastor brings
Forgiveness for that, and all our wrongs.

SCENE THREE

*Outside a newly built hut in the forest. Reindeer antlers over
the door. The snow lies deep. It is dusk.* PEER GYNT *stands in
front of the door, fixing a large wooden bar in place.*

PEER GYNT

There must be a bolt, one that can fasten
This door against trolls, and women and men.
There must be a bolt, one that can lock
The goblins out, all the merciless pack.
      They come with the dark; they hammer and hit:
   "Open up, Peer Gynt, we're as quick as thought!
      We're under the bed, in the ash of the fire;
   We stream down the chimney like dragons. Ah, Peer—
      What made you think that nails and slats
   Could shut out the merciless goblin thoughts?"
      (SOLVEIG *comes across the snowfield on skis; she has a
          kerchief on her head and a bundle in her hand.*)

SOLVEIG

God bless your work. Don't turn me away.
I've come to your call; now let me stay.

PEER GYNT

Solveig! It can't be—! Oh, but it is!
And you're not afraid to come so close!

SOLVEIG

Your call reached out in my sister's voice;
It came on the wind and in silences.
In your mother's words I felt it flame;
And it echoed out of my waking dreams.
The heavy nights, the empty days

Kept calling me, telling me, "Go where he goes."
My joy was gone, my life cut short;
I couldn't laugh or cry from my heart.
I couldn't be sure what your feelings were;
I only knew I had to come here.

PEER GYNT
But your father?

SOLVEIG
                          On this whole wide earth
I've no one for father or mother both.
I've left them forever.

PEER GYNT
                          Solveig, my own —
You did this for me?

SOLVEIG
                          Yes, for you alone;
You must be all to me — lover and friend.
                  (In tears.)
The worst was leaving my sister behind —
No, leaving my father, *that* was the worst;
But still worse, to leave her whose breast
Had nourished me; oh, God, no, the real
Pain and sorrow was leaving them all!

PEER GYNT
You know the judgment read last spring?
I'm stripped of my farm, of everything.

SOLVEIG
You think I cast off the ones I love
Just for some property you might have?

PEER GYNT
You've heard the sentence? Outside this wood
I'm fair game for all, with a price on my head.

SOLVEIG
I asked my way here with each turn of the climb;
They said, "Why go there?" I said, "It's my home."

PEER GYNT

Then away, away with these nails and slats!
Who needs bars against merciless thoughts?
If you can dare live in my hunter's house,
This ground will become a holy place.
Solveig! Let me look at you! Not too near!
Only to look at you! Oh, how pure and fair!
Let me lift you! But you're slender and light!
I could carry you forever and feel no weight!
I won't ever soil you. These arms, Solveig,
Will hold your lovely, warm body from me!
Who would have thought I could win your love?
Oh, the nights, the days, and the longing I've—
Look, you can see how I've built my hut;
But it's coming down; it's mean and squat——

SOLVEIG

Mean or great—it suits my mind.
It's so easy to breathe against this wind.
Down there it was stifling, closed like a trap;
That was partly what drove me up.
But here, where the firs cut the sky like gems,
What stillness and song! Here I'm at home.

PEER GYNT

Are you sure of that? For as long as you live?

SOLVEIG

The path I've chosen doesn't swerve.

PEER GYNT

Then you're mine! Go in! Let me hold the door.
Please! I'll get some roots for a fire.
In that bright warmth, that cozy glow,
You can rest content; you won't freeze now.
(*He opens the door, and* SOLVEIG *enters. He stands silent
    a moment, then laughs with joy and leaps in the air.*)
My princess! At last, she's found and won!
Now my palace will rise on a true foundation!

(He picks up his ax and starts off; at the same moment, an
OLD-LOOKING WOMAN *in a tattered green dress comes*
out of the wood; an UGLY BRAT *with a flask of beer in*
his hand limps after, holding onto her skirt.)

THE WOMAN
Good evening, Peer Lightfoot!

PEER GYNT
                                        Hello, who's there?

THE WOMAN
Old friends, Peer Gynt! Our place isn't far.
We're neighbors.

PEER GYNT
                            Oh? That's more than I knew.

THE WOMAN
As your hut built up, mine built itself too.

PEER GYNT
I'm in a rush ——

THE WOMAN
                            You always were;
But I'll track you down and get you for sure.

PEER GYNT
You've made a mistake, woman!

THE WOMAN
                                        Only once;
That time you promised me into a trance.

PEER GYNT
I promised —? What the hell kind of nonsense is that?

THE WOMAN
You've forgotten you drank at my father's one night?
You've forgotten —?

PEER GYNT
                            Yes; what I've never known.
What *is* this? When did we meet last? When?

THE WOMAN
We met last — the day we met first.

(*To the* BRAT.)

Give Daddy a drink; he suffers from thirst.

PEER GYNT

Daddy? You're drunk! Do you call him—?

THE WOMAN

You know it's bacon when you see the rind!
Where are your eyes? Don't you see, he's lame
In his leg as you're lame in your mind.

PEER GYNT

You mean to imply—?

THE WOMAN

You mean to protest—?

PEER GYNT

That gangling calf—!

THE WOMAN

He grew up fast.

PEER GYNT

You troll snout, how dare you invent—?

THE WOMAN

Listen, you're crude as an ox, Peer Gynt!

(*Crying.*)

How can I help it if I'm less beautiful
Than when you lured me on that heathery hill?
Last fall in my labor, the fiend held my back,
So it's no surprise I've a twisted look.
If you want to see me as fair as before,
Turn that female away from your door,
Tear her out of your mind and sight—
Do that, my love, and I'll lose my snout!

PEER GYNT

Get away, you witch!

THE WOMAN

Just see if I do!

PEER GYNT

I'll split your skull!

THE WOMAN
> I dare you to!
Ho-ho, Peer Gynt, I can take your blows!
I'll keep coming back till the end of your days.
I'll squint through the door and spy on you both;
And if you sit with your girl by the fire—
And start to caress—and put off your clothes—
I'll slip in between and take my share.
She and I, we'll have you by turns.
So marry her, Peer, while your pleasure burns!

PEER GYNT
You nightmare from hell!

THE WOMAN
> Oh, I nearly forgot!
My light-footed love, you can raise the brat.
There, pet, run to your daddy?

THE BRAT *(spits at him)*
> Pfft!
I'll take the ax to you—wait, just wait!

THE WOMAN *(kisses the* BRAT*)*
Oh, but there's a head on that pup!
You'll be like your father when you grow up.

PEER GYNT *(stamping)*
I could wish you as far—!

THE WOMAN
> As now we're near?

PEER GYNT *(clenching his fists)*
And all this—!

THE WOMAN
> Only for thoughts, for desire?
It's hard on you, Peer!

PEER GYNT
> Worse for another—!
Solveig, my treasure, my pure delight!

THE WOMAN
> "How the innocent suffer," said Old Nick to his mother,
> When she whacked him because his father got tight!
> > (*She plods off into the forest, followed by the* BRAT,
> > *who hurls the flask back toward* PEER.)

PEER GYNT *(after a long silence)*
> "Roundabout," said the Boyg. I have no choice—
> My palace is ruined, shivered to bits!
> There's a wall around her. We came so close—
> Now everything's foul; my happiness rots.
> Roundabout, lad! There's just no way
> Straight through to her—no, not for you.
> Straight through? Hm, there ought to be, still.
> There's a text on repentance, I seem to recall.
> But what? What is it? I forget what it said.
> Don't have the book; and there's no one to guide
> My footsteps here in this trackless wood.

> Repentance? It could run on for years
> Till I fought my way through. That's a poor life.
> To shatter what's holy and pure, what I love,
> Just to bind it together in cracks and scars?
> That can work for a fiddle, but not for a bell.
> If you want a field green, keep it free of your heel.

> But that was a lie, that with the troll snout!
> Now the corruption's all out of sight—
> Yes, out of sight, but not out of mind.
> Cringing thoughts would trail me around.
> Ingrid! And the three who danced on that crest!
> Would they appear too? Cry out, with storms
> Of laughter, like her to be hotly embraced,
> Or tenderly borne on outstretched arms?
> Roundabout, boy. Were my arms as long
> As the fir tree's root or the river's tongue,
> I know I'd be holding her still too near
> To set her down again holy and pure.

Let me work around it, this way or that,
So I manage neither to win nor lose.
Just push it away and try to forget——
> *(Goes several steps toward the hut and stops.)*
Go in after this? So foul and coarse?
Go in, with all this odor of troll?
Speak, but be silent; confess, but conceal?
> *(Throws the ax away.)*
It's a holy-day evening. For me to approach
The way I am now, would be sacrilege.

SOLVEIG *(in the doorway)*
Are you coming?

PEER GYNT *(in an undertone)*
Roundabout!

SOLVEIG
What?

PEER GYNT
You must wait.
It's dark here, and I've something heavy to get.

SOLVEIG
Wait, I'll help you. We'll share to the full.

PEER GYNT
No, stay where you are! I'll bear it all.

SOLVEIG
Please, not too far!

PEER GYNT
Be patient, my sweet;
Far or near—you must wait.

SOLVEIG *(nods to him)*
Yes, I'll wait!

> *(PEER GYNT goes down the path to the forest. SOLVEIG*
> *remains standing in the open half-door.)*

SCENE FOUR

AASE'S *hut. Evening. A log fire throws its light on the walls.*
The cat is on a chair at the foot of the bed, where AASE *lies,*
pulling restlessly at the sheets.

AASE
Lord God, why doesn't he come?
The hours drag endlessly by.
I've no way of sending to him,
And so terribly much to say.
There isn't a moment to lose!
So soon! How little we know!
If I'd thought it would end like this,
I'd never have scolded him so!

PEER GYNT *(comes in)*
Good evening.

AASE
God bless you, dear!
Oh, my boy! So you did come then!
But what are you doing down here?
Your life's at stake near town.

PEER GYNT
My life? It's not worth a hang.
I just had to see your face.

AASE
This proves that Kari was wrong;
And I can go out in peace.

PEER GYNT
Go out? What are you saying?
Where do you plan to go?

AASE
Ah, Peer, there's no denying—
It's plain that my time is due.

PEER GYNT *(writhing and pacing the floor)*
I've run from one heavy weight;

I thought at least *here* I'd be free — !
Are you cold in your hands and feet?

AASE

Yes, Peer; but it soon goes away —
When my eyes begin to glaze,
You must carefully close each lid.
And see to my coffin, please;
Take care it's the finest wood —
Oh no, I forgot —

PEER GYNT

          Be still!
There's plenty of time for that.

AASE

Yes, true. *(Looks restlessly about.)*
          You can see how little
They left. That's them, all right.

PEER GYNT *(wincing)*

Again! *(Sharply.)*
          I know I'm to blame.
But why must you hammer it in?

AASE

You? No, the demon rum;
That's what struck us down!
You know you'd been drinking, Peer;
And so your wits were dulled;
And then you'd been riding reindeer —
No wonder you acted wild!

PEER GYNT

All right, let that story drop.
Enough of that whole display.
Whatever is heavy we'll keep —
Till later — some other day.
          (Sits on the edge of the bed.)
Mother, let's talk, you and I —
But only of this and that.

    Things that are twisted and wry,
    That rankle and hurt, let's forget —
    Ah, look! It's the old cat;
    Is he really still alive?

AASE

    He screeches so in the night;
    You know what that's warning of!

PEER GYNT *(turning away)*

    What's the news of the parish?

AASE *(smiling)*

    They say there's a girl who's bent
    On the uplands with every wish —

PEER GYNT *(quickly)*

    Mads Moen, is he content?

AASE

    They say she's deafened her ears
    To her father's and mother's pleas.
    If you saw her a moment, Peer —
    You might be the one to advise —

PEER GYNT

    And Aslak, he's getting ahead?

AASE

    Don't speak of that filthy smith.
    Let me tell you the girl, instead;
    Her name's on the tip of my breath —

PEER GYNT

    No, let's talk now, you and I —
    But only of this and that.
    Things that are twisted and wry,
    That rankle and hurt, let's forget.
    You're thirsty? Do you want a drink?
    Have you room? That bed's like a toy.
    Let me see — but, yes, I think
    It's the one I had as a boy!
    Remember the evenings you sat

By my bedside when I was young
And tucked me under the coverlet
And sang me ballad and song?

AASE

Of course! And when your father
Was out, then we played sleighs.
The spread was a lap robe of fur,
And the floor was a sheet of ice.

PEER GYNT

Yes, but all else above —
You remember, Mother, too —?
The dashing horses we drove ——

AASE

Yes, don't you think I know —?
Our cat, and that other one —
Kari's; we had her on loan.

PEER GYNT

To the Castle East of the Sun
And the Castle West of the Moon,
To Soria-Moria Castle[31]
The high and the low roads wound.
You had a whip with a tassel —
It was just a stick we'd found.

AASE

I drove like a real cavalier ——

PEER GYNT

Yes, you reined the horses loose;
And you'd turn as the hoofs struck fire,
Always afraid I might freeze.
Bless you, you dear old relic,
You did have a loving soul —!
Why did you moan?

AASE

                    My back.
It's these hard boards I feel.

PEER GYNT

Here, take a better position.

There now; more comfortable?

AASE *(restlessly)*

No, I want to move on!

PEER GYNT

                    Move on?

AASE

Yes, move on for good, that's all.

PEER GYNT

Pah! Let me tuck in the coverlet.

Like so. If the night seems long,

We'll shorten it. There; I'll sit

And sing you ballad and song.

AASE

No, my Bible! I'll read the Apostle.

My thoughts are weighing me down.

PEER GYNT

In Soria-Moria Castle

There's a feast for the king and queen.

Lie back on the silken cushion;

We'll drive there over the snow.

AASE

But—have I an invitation?

PEER GYNT

Why, of course! Both of us do.

*(He throws a cord round the chair where the cat lies, picks
        up a stick, and sits on the end of the bed.)*

Gee-up! Get along, Blackie!

Mother, you're not going to freeze?

Ho, but the ride goes quickly

When Grane[32] sets the pace!

AASE

Dear heart, what is it, that ringing—?

PEER GYNT
  The silver sleighbells you heard!
AASE
  But those hollow echoes thronging?
PEER GYNT
  We're galloping over a fjord.
AASE
  I'm frightened! What is that roaring
  Like some great, hungry mouth?
PEER GYNT
  Only the night wind tearing
  Through the branches on the heath.
AASE
  Far off there, something glimmers.
  What makes that wavering blaze?
PEER GYNT
  The castle's doors and windows.
  Can you hear them dancing?
AASE

                                    Yes.
PEER GYNT
  Saint Peter stands at the main door;
  He's motioning you to come in.
AASE
  He greets me?
PEER GYNT
                      Yes, with honor,
  And pours out the sweetest wine.
AASE
  Wine! Are there cakes as well, Peer?
PEER GYNT
  In droves! The finest sort.
  And the bishop's wife, his helper,
  Makes you coffee and dessert.

AASE

My Lord, will she and I meet?

PEER GYNT

As easy and free as you like.

AASE

You mean it? Peer, what a banquet
They're giving for my poor sake!

PEER GYNT *(cracking his whip)*

Hup! Get along there, Blackie!

AASE

You're sure, dear, this is the way?

PEER GYNT *(cracks it again)*

Yes, the broad road.

AASE

I feel shaky
And weak from this racketing sleigh.

PEER GYNT

I can see the castle so close;
The race is just about run.

AASE

I'll lie back and rest my eyes
And trust it to you, my son.

PEER GYNT

Press on, Grane, my pacer!
The courtyard's filled to the brim;
They swarm to the portals and stare.
Peer Gynt and his mother have come!
Saint Peter, what did you say?
My mother may not come in?
You could look till the seas run dry
To find a worthier one!
Of myself, I won't say a word;
I can turn at the castle gate
If you stand for drinks, I'd be flattered;
If not, I won't be put out.

I've made up more lies already
Than the devil trying to preach,
And called my mother "Old Biddy"
For the way she'd cackle and scratch.
But you give her love and honor,
Make her at home in your truth.
They don't come up now any finer
From the parishes of our faith.
Ho-ho, there's God the Father!
Saint Peter, you'll get yours today!

          (In a deep voice.)

"An end to this fuss and bother—
Mother Aase can come in free!"

        (Laughs aloud and turns to AASE.*)*

Isn't *that* how I said it would break?
Now they're singing a different tune!

             (Anxiously.)

Mother! That faraway look!
It's as though your wits had flown!

       (Goes to the head of the bed.)

Don't stare! Your eyes are like china.
Mother, speak! It's me, your son!

*(Cautiously feels her forehead and hands, then throws the
      cord on the chair and says quietly.)*

So that's it. You can rest now, Grane.
The long haul is really done.

       (Closes her eyes and bends over her.)

Here's thanks for all of your days,
For the blows and the kisses I had—
But give back some little praise—

         (Presses his cheek to her mouth.)

There—that was thanks for the ride.

KARI *(entering)*

What? Peer! So then we're beyond
Our heaviest sorrow and dread!

    Dear Lord, but she's sleeping sound.
    Or is she —?

PEER GYNT

                Shh. She's dead.

    (KARI *weeps over the body;* PEER GYNT *walks slowly
    about the room, finally coming to a stop by the bed.*)

PEER GYNT

    See that she's buried worthily.
    It's time that I quit this soil.

KARI

    Are you going far?

PEER GYNT

                To the sea.

KARI

    So far?

PEER GYNT

            Yes; and farther still.

                    (*He goes out.*)

ACT FOUR

SCENE ONE

The southwest coast of Morocco. Under an awning in a palm grove, a table, on rush matting, set for dinner. Farther back, hammocks slung from the trees. A steam yacht, flying Norwegian and American flags, lies offshore. On the beach, a jolly boat. It is near sundown. PEER GYNT, *a handsome, middle-aged man in an elegant traveling suit, gold pince-nez dangling at his chest, presides at the head of the table.* MR. COTTON[33] *and* MONSIEUR BALLON,[34] *along with* HERR VON EBERKOPF[35] *and* HERR TRUMPETERSTRAALE,[36] *are finishing dinner.*

PEER GYNT

    Gentlemen, drink! If man is made

    For pleasure, then let his pleasure thrive.

    As somebody wrote: the past is dead,

    What's done is done——Now what'll you have?

TRUMPETERSTRAALE

    As a host, brother Gynt, you're enormous!

PEER GYNT

    I share that honor with my ample purse,

    My steward and my cook——

COTTON

                Very well,

    A toast to the four. Here's to them all!

BALLON

    Monsieur, you have *un goût, un ton*

    Nowadays one rarely finds

    In gentlemen living *en garçon* —

    A certain — how should I say — ?

EBERKOPF

A taste

Of free self-consciousness, a grip
On world-historical-fellowship,[37]
A vision piercing veils of mist,
The most unprejudiced of minds
Stamped by the higher criticism,
An *Ur-natur*, whose empiricism
Is raised to a total synthesis.
That was, monsieur, your intention, yes?

BALLON

Yes, probably —but with a tinge
Of beauty it could never have in French.

EBERKOPF

Ei was! That language, much too stiff—
But if we wish to seek the ground
Of the phenomenon—

PEER GYNT

That's been found.

It's because I've forsaken married life.
Gentlemen, indeed, things are
Very clear. What should a man be?
I say *himself* and nothing more.
All for *himself* and *his!* I say
Why, like a camel, should he carry
Someone else's burden of worry?

EBERKOPF

But this In-and-for-yourselfness
Has cost you a struggle, I'm sure——

PEER GYNT

Oh yes, early in my career;
But my honor was never at a loss.
Once I nearly put my leg
Into a trap that Cupid laid.
I was a gay and salty dog,

And the lady that I coveted—
She was born of royal blood——

BALLON
Of royal—?

PEER GYNT *(carelessly)*
                    Of the real old stock,
You know——

TRUMPETERSTRAALE *(slaps the table)*
                    A damned aristocrat!

PEER GYNT *(with a shrug)*
Thin-blooded snobs, the kind that take
Their pride in a family record book
Free of the least plebeian blot.

COTTON
You mean your courtship hit a snag?

BALLON
Her parents thwarted the alliance?

PEER GYNT
Quite the reverse.

BALLON
                    Ah!

PEER GYNT *(forbearingly)*
                    Well, you see,
There was a growing reason why
The marriage better be held at once.
But, to be frank, the whole business
Right from the start made me recoil.
In certain ways, I'm fastidious,
And I like an independent role.
And so, when her father came around
Insinuating his demand
That I shed my name and occupation
To dance in the puppet show of fashion,
Along with other requests as well,
Irksome, if not impossible—

Why then, gracefully, out I bowed,
Gave him his ultimatum back —
And renounced my budding bride.
          (Drumming on the table with a pious air.)
Yes, there's a Fate behind our luck!
We mortals can rely on that —
And take some comfort in the thought.

BALLON

But — was the matter really closed?

PEER GYNT

Oh no; that I discovered next.
Some meddling relatives got mixed
Up in it and violently aroused.
The worst was the family's younger set.
With seven of them I fought a duel.
It's one time I never will forget,
Although I weathered the ordeal.
It cost me blood; but that same blood
Confirmed my birthright to be great,
And boldly pointed, as I said,
To the wise governance of Fate.

EBERKOPF

You have an outlook on life's course
That ranks you with the philosophers.
For, while the common-sense observer
Views the world in scattered scenes
And gropes his stumbling way forever,
Your mind orders and combines;
All things measure to your norm.
You point up every separate rule
Until it shines forth like a beam
Of light from one Life-Principle.
And you've had no formal education?

PEER GYNT

I am — I'm happy to repeat —
A man exclusively self-taught.

My studies have had no discipline;
But fed by thought and speculation
And random reading, my mind has grown.
I started rather late in life;
And then, as you know, it's heavy stuff
Plowing your way from page to page
And prodding your memory to gorge.
History I picked up in scraps;
Never had the time for more.
And then, of course, for the evil days
One needs a faith in something sure—
So I took religion, in little sips;
It goes down easier that way.
Study should not be omnivorous,
But strictly with an eye to use —

COTTON

Now that's practical!

PEER GYNT *(lighting a cigar)*
             Dear friends,
Consider the career I've traced.
What was I when I headed west?
A ragged boy with empty hands.
I had to grub hard for everything,
And, believe me, I came near despair.
But life, my friends, life is dear,
And death, as they say, has a sting.
Well! Luck, as you know, was kind to me;
And old Fate showed liberality.
Things moved. I took them flexibly
And, step by step, rose up the ladder.
Within ten years I bore the name
Of Croesus with the Charleston traders.
Port after port declared my fame,
And fortune rode in all my hulls —

COTTON

What was the trade?

PEER GYNT
> > > I made my deals
> > Mainly in slaves for Carolina
> > And pagan images for China.

BALLON
> *Fi donc!*

TRUMPETERSTRAALE
> > > By thunder, Uncle Gynt!

PEER GYNT
> No doubt you feel that, morally,
> Traffic like that had a certain taint?
> I know the feeling thoroughly.
> I, too, found it odious.
> But, as you know, a good investment
> Isn't so easily shaken loose.
> And then it's especially difficult
> In such a prodigious operation,
> Setting thousands of men in motion,
> Once and for all, to call a halt.
> That "once and for all" I could never stand;
> But I will admit, on the other hand,
> That I've always nourished a respect
> For what they call the consequences;
> Crossing the bounds of common sense is
> Something that leaves me feeling spooked.
> Then, besides, I was getting on —
> The last of my forties running out,
> And my hair shot through with graying streaks.
> My health remained exceptional,
> But a thought kept throbbing in my skull:
> "Who knows how soon the hour may strike
> When the great judgment's handed down
> That forever parts the sheep and goats."
> > What to do? To end the trade
> With China was insupportable.
> I saw the answer, pushed ahead

With something else exportable.
In the spring I sent out idols still —
But added missionaries in the fall,
Providing them with every need,
Like stockings, Bibles, rum, and rice —

COTTON

At a profit?

PEER GYNT

       Why, naturally, yes.
Things moved. They worked like mad.
For every idol sale we closed,
They got a coolie's soul baptized;
The result — was equilibrium.
The missions' business never lacked;
For the idols came in a steady stream,
And the preachers kept them neatly checked.

COTTON

But what about the African wares?

PEER GYNT

Triumph again for my moral code.
I realized that the trade was bad
For a person of advancing age;
Death might suddenly give a nudge.
Then, too, there were the thousand snares
Of do-gooders obsessed by slaves,
As well as the hostile privateers,
The hazards of the winds and waves —
All these made me quite positive.
I thought: ah, Peter, reef your sails,
Mend your errors, prune your goals.
So I bought a piece of land down south,
Held back the last payload of meat,
Which turned out prime, a perfect lot.
They flourished well, fat and glossy,
Which tickled them as much as me.
Yes, I'll tell you the sober truth:

I was like a father to them—
And sure enough, the profits came.
I built them schools so their virtue
Could be pegged not to fall beneath
At a certain general *niveau*,
And watched its temperature like a hawk
So it wouldn't waver from that mark.
Now, moreover, I've resigned
From that whole phase of my career—
I've sold off the plantation and
All the livestock, hide and hair.
On leaving, I rolled out the keg,
And young and old had gratis grog;
The men, the women, all got stiff—
And the widows reveled in my snuff.
So now I hope—provided that
It's not untrue what I've heard said:
"Do no evil, and you've done some good—"
That my mistakes will fade from sight,
And, more than most, I'll find a rinse
Of virtue will dissolve my sins.

EBERKOPF *(clinking glasses with him)*

How inspiriting to hear
A master principle worked out,
Redeemed from theoretic doubt,
Unshaken by the world's uproar!

PEER GYNT *(who has, through the above, been steadily pulling at the bottle)*

We northmen, we know how to bear
A battle through! Yes, the key
To the art of living is simply that
Of keeping both your ears shut tight
Against an evil serpent's entry.

COTTON

And what sort of serpent, friend, is that?

PEER GYNT
> A little one, one that can twist
> A man to whatever is hard and fast.
> > *(Drinks again.)*
> What's the whole art of daring, of
> Courage in action, what is it
> But to move with uncommitted feet
> Between the pitfalls dug by life—
> To know for sure that all your days
> Aren't over on the day you fight—
> To know that behind you always lies
> A bridge secured for your retreat.
> This policy has built my name
> And colored all I've consummated.
> It's something I inherited
> From the people of my childhood home.

BALLON
> You're Norwegian?

PEER GYNT
> > Born, yes! But a
> Citizen of the world by creed.
> For the good fortune I've enjoyed,
> I have to thank America.
> I've drawn my library of books
> From the latest German scholars' works.
> From France, I took my taste in dress,
> My manners and my turn of wit—
> From England, an enterprising spirit
> And an eye for my own advantages.
> The Jews have taught me how to wait.
> From Italy, I gained a bit
> Of a flair for *dolce far niente*—
> And once, when I was in plenty
> Of trouble, I stretched my years no small
> Amount with the aid of Swedish steel.

TRUMPETERSTRAALE *(raising his glass)*
    Ah, Swedish steel—!

EBERKOPF
                  A toast instead
To the man of steel who swung the blade!
      (They clink glasses and drink with PEER,
         who begins to show the wine.)

COTTON
    What you've said is awfully nice—
    But now, sir, I'm most curious
    About your plans for all your treasure.

PEER GYNT *(smiling)*
    Hm—plans? What—?

ALL FOUR *(edging closer)*
                Yes, let's hear!

PEER GYNT
    Well, first of all, to take a cruise.
    That's why I asked you gentlemen on
    To keep me company at Gibraltar.
    I needed friends to dance a tune
    For the golden calf on his seagoing altar.

EBERKOPF
    That's clever!

COTTON
             But no one's going to raise
Canvas merely to take a sail.
You have some project, I can tell.
And that project is—

PEER GYNT
           To become emperor.

ALL FOUR
    What?

PEER GYNT *(nodding)*
      Emperor!

ALL FOUR
                    Where?

PEER GYNT
                              Of the whole earth.

BALLON
    But how, my friend—?

PEER GYNT
                          The power of money!
    The idea hasn't just entered my head;
    It's inspired me almost since birth.
    As a boy in dreams I used to journey
    Over the ocean on a cloud.
    I floated with cape and golden scabbard—
    Then fell down, barking my elbows hard.
    But, friends, my will has never swayed—
    It's been written or else been said
    Someplace, I can't remember where,
    That if you won the earth entire
    And *lost your self*,[38] what would you gain
    But a wreath on a grinning skeleton.
    That's the text—approximately;
    And it's a lot more truth than poetry.

EBERKOPF
    But what, then, is this Gyntian self?

PEER GYNT
    The world behind my brow that serves
    To set me as far from anyone else
    As God is from the devil's wiles.

TRUMPETERSTRAALE
    Now I fathom what drives you to it!

BALLON
    Sublime thinker!

EBERKOPF
                    Exalted poet!

PEER GYNT *(with rising emotion)*
    The Gyntian self—it's an army corps
    Of wishes, appetites, desires.
    The Gyntian self is a mighty sea
    Of whim, demand, proclivity—
    In short, whatever moves my soul
    And makes me live to *my* own will.
    But just as our Lord had need of clay
    To be creator of the universe,
    So I need gold if I'm to play
    The emperor's part with any force.

BALLON
    But you have the gold!

PEER GYNT
                  Poppycock!
    Yes, maybe for three days, if I ruled
    As emperor à la Lippe-Detmold.[39]
    But I have to be *myself* en bloc,
    A name in every country known—
    Sir Peter Gynt from heel to crown.

BALLON *(enraptured)*
    And possess the world's most ravishing beauties!

EBERKOPF
    Johannisberger, cellars full!

TRUMPETERSTRAALE
    And Charles the Twelfth's[40] whole arsenal!

COTTON
    But first, the right opportunities
    For profit——

PEER GYNT
              All provided for.
    It's the reason why we anchored here.
    Tonight we set a course northeast.
    Those papers brought on board were spiced
    With news that's quickened my resolve.

>   *(Rises, lifting his glass.)*
It seems that Fortune finds it normal
To help the man who helps himself —

THE FOUR
   Well? Tell us —!

PEER GYNT

>   Greece is in a turmoil.

ALL FOUR *(springing up)*
   What! The Greeks —?

PEER GYNT

>   Are out to fight.

ALL FOUR
   Hurray!

PEER GYNT

>   And the Turks are in a sweat!
>   *(Drains his glass.)*

BALLON
   To Hellas — and honor! I'll take the chance
   And help them — with French armaments!

EBERKOPF
   I'll do what I can — on long-term notes!

COTTON
   And I too — at low interest rates!

TRUMPETERSTRAALE
   Lead on! In Bender[41] let me find
   Those buckles King Charles left behind!

BALLON *(embracing PEER GYNT)*
   My friend, forgive me; for a while
   I misjudged you!

EBERKOPF *(pressing his hands)*

>   And I'm a fool;
   I'd found you almost contemptible!

COTTON
   That's too strong. Just rather simple —

TRUMPETERSTRAALE *(trying to kiss him)*
    And I, Uncle, for an example
    Of the lowest kind of Yankee rabble.
    Forgive me—!

EBERKOPF
                        We've all been led astray——

PEER GYNT
    What do you mean?

EBERKOPF
                        Now we can see
    The thronging splendor of that army corps
    Of Gyntian wishes and desires—!

BALLON *(admiringly)*
    So *that's* what it means to be Monsieur Gynt!

EBERKOPF *(in the same tone)*
    A Gynt of honor and accomplishment!

PEER GYNT
    What *is* this—?

BALLON
                        You don't comprehend?

PEER GYNT
    If I do, you're welcome to string me up!

BALLON
    Why so? Aren't you off to lend
    The Greeks your money and your ship?

PEER GYNT *(snorting)*
    Oh, no thanks! My money works
    For power; I'm lending to the Turks.

BALLON
    Absurd!

EBERKOPF
                Amusing, for a joke!

PEER GYNT *(is briefly silent, then leans against a chair and
        assumes a superior look)*
    Listen, gentlemen, it's best

We separate before the rest
Of our friendship blows away like smoke.
A man with next to nothing favors
Risk; if he owns no more of earth
Than the strip of ground his shadow covers,
He'll fling his life in the cannon's mouth.
But when your fat's well out of the fire,
As mine is, then the stakes are higher.
Go on to Greece. I'll gladly arm
You gratis and put you safe ashore.
The more you fan the flames of war,
The more propitious for my terms.
Strike for freedom and for right!
Smite the Turk! Pour on the heat —
Till all your blood and glory drenches
Down the janissary lances —
Just count *me* out.

> *(Slaps his pocket.)*
> *That's* all I want —

Money! And myself, Sir Peter Gynt!

> *(Puts up his sunshade and goes into the grove*
> *where the hammocks can be seen.)*

TRUMPETERSTRAALE
  The swine!

BALLON
      No respect for honor —!

COTTON
  Oh, honor rot! The profits —! When or
  Where can we find another chance
  Like this, if they win independence —

BALLON
  I saw myself in triumph, hidden
  By wreaths of beautiful Greek maidens!

TRUMPETERSTRAALE
  There, in my Swedish hands, I saw

Those great, heroic buckles glow!

EBERKOPF

And I saw my great fatherland's *Kultur*
Expanding on every foreign shore!

COTTON

We've lost the most financially.
Goddam![42] So help me, I could cry!
I saw Olympus all my own;
And if that mountain's what they say
There ought to be some copper mines
Still reworkable today.
And the Castalia,[43] that stream
That's talked about so much, with all
Its falls—an engineer could pull
Some thousand horsepower out of them—

TRUMPETERSTRAALE

I'm going anyway! My Swedish
Sword's worth more than Yankee cash!

COTTON

Perhaps. But fighting in the line,
Lost in those multitudes, we'd drown;
And then what profits would we have?

BALLON

Dommage! So near to Fortune's lap—
Now to be stranded on her grave!

COTTON *(shaking his fist at the yacht)*

And locked up in that coffin ship,
The gold he sweated from his blacks—!

EBERKOPF

A master stroke! Come on—! Quick!
His empire's in its final hour!

BALLON

What are you doing?

EBERKOPF

                    Seizing power!

The crew can easily be bought.
On board! I hereby annex the yacht!

COTTON

You — what — ?

EBERKOPF

Give it my protection!
(Goes to the jolly boat.)

COTTON

Self-interest tells me I ought to give
My share of that.
(Follows EBERKOPF.*)*

TRUMPETERSTRAALE

Just like a thief!

BALLON

A shameful business — ! But — *enfin!*
(Follows after.)

TRUMPETERSTRAALE

I'll have to go — but, you understand,
I protest this act to all mankind — !
(Joins the others.)

SCENE TWO

*Another part of the coast. Moonlight and driving clouds. In the
far distance, the yacht sails under full steam.* PEER GYNT *comes
running along the beach. He pinches himself on the arm, then
stares out over the sea.*

PEER GYNT

Nightmares — ! Phantoms — ! I have to wake up!
She's put out to sea! At a furious clip — !
Just phantoms! I'm sleeping! Drunk! Or mad!
(Wringing his hands.)
Impossible that I could wind up dead!

(Tearing his hair.)

A dream! I will it to be a dream!
It's terrible! Oh, but it's true, I'm afraid!
My jackass friends—! Hear me, oh God!
Thou righteous and wise—judgment on them—!

(Reaching up his arms.)

It's *me*, Peer Gynt! Are you listening, Lord?
Look after me, Father; let me be spared!
Make them turn back! Or lower the gig!
Stop thief! Oh, let the sails unrig!
Please—! Don't fuss with the world's affairs!
It'll manage itself for a while—
Damned if he's listening! Deaf! That's his style.
What a mess! A God unable to answer prayers!

(Beckoning upward.)

Hsst! I'm rid of the slave plantation!
Look what I did for the China missions!
One good turn, now isn't it worth
Another? Help me—!

(A sheet of flame leaps up from the yacht, followed by thick, billowing smoke, then the dull boom of an explosion. PEER GYNT lets out a shriek and drops to the sand. Gradually the smoke clears. The yacht has vanished.
PEER *is hushed and pale.)*

The sword of wrath!
To the bottom, sunk—every man and mouse!
What a lucky chance! Oh, infinite praise—

(With emotion.)

To chance? No, it was more than that.
I was fated to live, and they were not.
All thanks to Thee, who steadfastly loved
And shielded me, in spite of my sins—

(Draws a deep breath.)

What a feeling of peace and confidence

To know I was singled out to be saved.
But the desert! What will I drink and eat?
Oh, I'll find something. He'll provide.
Nothing to fear —
                    (In a loud, wheedling tone.)
                    He wouldn't let
A poor little sparrow like me go unfed!
Be humble in spirit. And learn to wait.
Trust in the Lord with a will of iron —
                    (Springs to his feet in terror.)
That noise in the brush, was that a lion?
                    (His teeth chattering.)
No, that was no lion.
                    (Mustering courage.)
                    A lion, all right!
Those animals, they go their own way.
They don't bite their betters. They rely
On instinct; they can feel, for instance,
That it's dangerous playing with elephants.
    All the same — I could do with a tree.
Over there, those acacias and palms;
If I climbed up, how secure I could be —
Especially if I could sing a few psalms —
                    (Clambers up.)
"Morning and evening are not alike —"[44]
Now that verse has often been analyzed.
                    (Settles himself comfortably.)
How delightful to feel one's soul upraised.
Thinking nobly is more than getting rich quick.
Trust all to Him. He knows just how full
He can portion my cup with wormwood and gall.
He does keep a fatherly eye on my fate —
                    (Glances out to sea and breathes with a sigh.)
But economical — that He's not!

SCENE THREE

_Night. A Moroccan camp on the edge of the desert. Watch fires
and lounging soldiers._

A SLAVE _(runs in and tears his hair)_
　　Gone! The Emperor's white charger, gone!
ANOTHER SLAVE _(runs in and rends his garments)_
　　The Emperor's sacred robes have been stolen!
MOORISH CAPTAIN _(coming up)_
　　Find them, or a hundred lashes will fall on
　　The bare feet of all you excuses for men!
　　(The soldiers mount horse and gallop off in all directions.)

SCENE FOUR

Daybreak. The grove of acacias and palms. Up in his tree,
PEER GYNT, _with a broken branch in his hand, is beating off a
pack of monkeys._

PEER GYNT
　　Wretched! A most disagreeable night.
　　　　　　　(Striking about him.)
　　Are you back again? Oh, hell's bells,
　　They're throwing fruit! No, it's something else—
　　The monkey is such a disgusting brute!
　　"Watch and fight," as the Scripture says,
　　But I can't do that, when I'm dull and weary.
　　　　　　　(Freshly attacked; loses patience.)
　　I'll put a spike in their repertory!
　　Let me get hold of one of those boys,
　　Hang him, skin him, and worm inside
　　Whatever's left of his shaggy hide,
　　So the others honor the family ties—
　　What is man anyway? Only a mote.

Fashion and custom can guide us a bit—
Still they come on! Swarming like locusts.
Get away! Shoo! The gibbering fools.
Oh, if I only had a false tail—
Something so I'd resemble the beasts—
Now what? That pattering overhead—!

> (*Looking up.*)

An old one—brandishing filth in his paws—!

(*Crouches apprehensively and remains still for a time.*
The ape makes a gesture; PEER GYNT *starts coaxing him,*
as if he were a dog.)

Ah—there's a boy, good old Bus!
He's reasonable. And perfectly bred.
Would he throw—? No, not on your life—
It's me! Pip-pip! We're the best of friends!
Ai-ai! There now, he understands.
Bus and I, why, we're relatives—[45]
Bus can have sugar tomorrow—! The beast!
The whole load on top of me! Ugh, horrible—!
Or could it be food? It tastes—equivocal;
But then, it's habit that forms our taste.
Who was that thinker, the one who wrote:
"Spit, and trust to the force of habit"—?
Hi, now the young!

> (*Striking about.*)

But this is crazy,
That man, who's lord of this universe,
Should have to put up with—! Help! Mercy!
The old one's foul, but the children are worse!

SCENE FIVE

Early morning. A rocky ground overlooking the desert. On one
side, a cleft in the rocks and a cave. A THIEF *and a* FENCE *in*
the cleft with the Emperor's horse and robes. The horse, rich-

*ly caparisoned, stands tied to a stone. Riders can be seen far
off.*

THE THIEF
> The tongues of the lances
> Flicker and flash—
> See, see!

THE FENCE
> They lick at my head—
> I feel them slash!
> Woe, woe!

THE THIEF *(folding his arms across his chest)*
> My father stole;
> His son must steal.

THE FENCE
> My father's a fence;
> I'm a fence as well.

THE THIEF
> You must bear your lot;
> Be the self you were taught.

THE FENCE *(listening)*
> Steps in the thicket!
> Away! But where?

THE THIEF
> The cavern is deep,
> And the Prophet near!
>
> *(They flee, leaving their stolen goods. The riders vanish in
> the distance.* PEER *comes in, cutting himself a reed pipe.)*

PEER GYNT
> What a delicious morning! How mild!
> The scarab's rolling his ball in the dust;
> The snail pokes out of his shell to feast.
> Morning! Yes, it's the purest gold—
> Just think what marvelous potency
> Nature gave to the light of day.

You feel so safe—your courage swells—
You could easily wrestle a couple of bulls—
How peaceful! Oh, the country joys—
Strange I never felt them before;
Why be penned in some crowded place,
Victim to every knock at the door—?
Ah, look at the lizards whisking their tails,
Snapping and thinking of nothing at all.
What innocence the animals have!
They each obey the Creator's will,
Hold their own features immutable,
Are themselves, themselves through joy and strife
Just as they were when He first said, "Live!"

(Puts on his pince-nez.)

A toad—in a sandstone block. The rough
Stone frames him in. Only his face is
Showing. The way he sits and gazes
At the world and is to himself—enough—

(Reflectively.)

Enough! Himself—? Now where's that from?
It must be some classic I read it in.
The prayer book was it? Or Proverbs then?
Maddening, how with passing time
My memory for dates and places dims.

(Sits down in the shade.)

Here's a cool spot for tired feet.
And look, ferns growing. Edible roots.

(Eats a little.)

This food's better fit for an animal—
But it's written, "Our nature must be molded."
And elsewhere, "Pride must have a fall."
And, "He who's humbled shall be exalted."

(Uneasily.)

Exalted? For me it will happen too—
There's just no other possible end.

Fate will guide me out of this land
And arrange it so that I come through.
This all is a trial, but I'll be spared
If only, God grant, my health's not impaired.
    (Shakes off such thoughts, lights a cigar, stretches
             out, and surveys the desert.)
What an immense, unbounded waste—
There in the distance, an ostrich strides—
What can one think was really God's
Meaning in these endless miles of dust?
This desert, lacking all sources of life;
This burnt-out cinder on the world's roof—
This patch on the map, forever blank;
This corpse since the dawn of time, that can't
Give its Maker so much as thanks—
Why was it formed—? Nature's extravagant.
Is that the sea eastward, that shimmering streak?
No, it can't be. That's a mirage.
The sea's to the west behind my back,
Dammed out from the plain by a sloping ridge.
        (A thought flashes through him.)
Dammed out? Then I could—! The hills are small.
Dammed out! A cut, that's it; a canal—
Like a river of life, the waters would run
In through the channel and flood the plain
Soon all this furnace of sand and rock
Would be as fresh as a rippling lake.
Oases would rise like desert isles,
Atlas turn green like our mountain coast;
White sails would skim, like wind-blown gulls,
Southward where once the caravans passed.
Quickening breezes would scatter the fumes
Of decay, and dew would drop from the sky;
Men will come building city on city,
And grass will grow round the swaying palms.
Beyond the Sahara the country south

Will be the new cradle of human growth.
Factories will hum in Timbuktu;
Bornu[46] will soon be colonized, while
Up through Habes[47] explorers will go
By sleeping car to the Upper Nile.
In the midst of my sea, on a rich oasis,
I'll reproduce the Nordic races.
The dalesman's blood is royal almost;
Arabian crossings will do the rest.
Within a cove, on a shelving strand,
I'll found Peeropolis, my capital.
The world's obsolete! Now the ages call.
For Gyntiana,[48] my virgin land!

(Springs up.)

Only the funding; then it's set —
A key of gold for the ocean's gate!
A crusade against Death! Let the grim miser
Spill the sack where he hoards his treasure.
In every country, freedom burns —
Like the ass in the ark,[49] I'll send a cry
Round the world and baptize in liberty
The bright shores, dreaming in their chains.
Capital! Raise it! Find a source — !
My kingdom — no, half of it — for a horse![50]

(The horse whinnies among the rocks.)

A horse! Clothing — ! Jewels — ! And a sword!

(Going closer.)

It can't be! But, yes — ! Faith is a force,
A mover of mountains, that I've heard —
But, that it also can move a horse — ?
Pah! The fact is, the horse is real —
Ab esse ad posse et cetera,[51] as well —

(Puts on the robes and regards himself.)

Sir Peter — and Turk from head to toe!
How life provides if you give it a chance —
Come on, Grane, up we go!

(Climbs into the saddle.)
And under my feet, gold stirrups now—!
You can tell great men by the style of their mounts!
(Gallops off into the desert.)

SCENE SIX

The tent of an Arab chief in an oasis. PEER GYNT, *in his eastern dress, reclines on cushions. He is drinking coffee and smoking a long pipe.* ANITRA *and a company of girls are dancing and singing to him.*

CHORUS OF GIRLS
  The Prophet has come!
  The Prophet, the Lord, the All-knowing Mind,
  Has come to us riding, to us has come
  Over the ocean of sand!
  The Prophet, the Lord, the Unfailing One,
  Has come to us sailing, to us has come
  Over the ocean of dunes!
    Sound the flute and the drum;
  The Prophet, the Prophet has come!

ANITRA
  His steed is like milk, the purest white
  That streams in the rivers of Paradise.
  Bend your knee! Cover your face!
  His eyes are stars, tender and bright.
  No child of clay can endure
  The rays of their heavenly fire.
    Out of the desert he came.
  Gold and pearls blazed on his chest.
  Where he rode, the sun passed.
  Behind him was night,
  Simoon and drought.
  He, the All-glorious, came!

Out of the desert he came,
Dressed like a son of man.
Kaaba,[52] Kaabe's a tomb —
He has enlightened his own!

CHORUS OF GIRLS
    Sound the flute and the drum;
The Prophet, the Prophet has come!

           (They dance on to quiet music.)

PEER GYNT
I've read it in print — and I'll be bound,
"No man's a prophet in his native land."
All this pleases me so much better
Than life among the Charleston traders.
There was something hollow in that affair,
Something bogus and alien there —
I never could feel myself at home,
Never really fit in with them.
What did I ever want in that crew,[53]
Rooting around in the bins of trade?
When I think it over, I hardly know —
It happened, that's all; so let it ride.
    To be yourself on a base of gold
Is the same as building your house on sand.
For a watch and a ring, the wealth you wield,
The people grovel and lick your hand;
They tip their hats to a diamond pin,
But the ring and stickpin aren't the man —
A prophet! That has a lot more point.
There, at least, you know your place.
If you're taken up, it's *yourself* they praise,
Yourself, and not your bank account.
You are what you are, and no mistake;
You owe no credit to chance or luck,
Or the support of some patent or grant —
A prophet! It's really the thing for me.
And to think it took me so unaware —

I was simply crossing the desert here
And these children of nature barred the way.
They made it plain that their prophet had come.
I really didn't try to deceive —
A lie and a prophet's reply aren't the same;
Besides, you know, I can always leave.
I'm not tied down; no cause for depression —
The deal, so to say, is thoroughly private;
I can go as I came; my horse is all set;
In short, I'm on top of the situation.

ANITRA *(approaching)*

Prophet and Lord!

PEER GYNT

                              Yes, my slave?

ANITRA

The sons of the desert are nearing thy tent;
They ask a glimpse of thy features —

PEER GYNT

                                                        Stop!

At a distance, tell them to muster up.
At a distance, let them be reverent.
And add, no man may enter this grove!
    Men, my child, are a slippery batch —
Low-minded, itchy-fingered, wild — !
Anitra, you couldn't guess how much
They've swind — I mean, have sinned, my child —
Enough of that! Dance, my maidens!
Let the Prophet forget his heavy burdens.

THE GIRLS *(dancing)*

The Prophet is good; his heart is grieved
By the evil the sons of dust have loved!
The Prophet is gentle; for this, all praise;
He raises sinners to Paradise!

PEER GYNT *(his eyes following* ANITRA *in her dance)*

Her legs go like drumsticks; faster still.
Ai! She's a succulent dish, that quail.

118

Her figure has some extravagant forms—
Hardly in line with beauty's norms;
But then, what's beauty? Convention's choice—
A coin made current by time and place.
It's such extravagances that enchant
When you've had it to here with the normal run.
Keep the legal limit, and you cheat your fun.
They're either too stout, or else too gaunt,
Disturbingly young, or grimly antique—
The ones in between make you sick—
    Her feet, they're not entirely clean;
Same with the arms; especially the one.
But that's no cause to be critical.
In fact, it's one morsel of her appeal—
    Anitra, hear me!

ANITRA *(approaching)*
                Thy handmaiden hears!

PEER GYNT
    Child, you're bewitching! Lo, you inspire
    The Prophet. If you doubt me, consider this:
    I'll make you a houri in Paradise!

ANITRA
    Impossible, Lord!

PEER GYNT
             Would I deceive?
    I'm dead serious, sure as I live!

ANITRA
    But I have no soul.

PEER GYNT
             It's what you'll get!

ANITRA
    But how, my Lord?

PEER GYNT
             I'll see to that—
    I'm taking over your education.

No soul? Yes, you are rather dumb;
It's struck me, with a certain vexation.
But, for a soul, there's always room.
Come here! Let me measure your braincase —
There's room, room enough; I *knew* there was.
It's true — you aren't ever going to go
Very deep; a *large* soul isn't for you —
But, after all, what's the difference —
You'll have enough for all your wants ——

ANITRA

    The Prophet is kind ——

PEER GYNT

                  You hesitate? Well!

ANITRA

    But I'd rather have ——

PEER GYNT

                 Come on, speak out!

ANITRA

    When it comes to a soul, I think I can wait
    But give me ——

PEER GYNT

    What?

ANITRA *(points at his turban)*

            That pretty opal!

PEER GYNT *(enraptured, giving her the jewel)*
    Anitra! Child! Eve's own daughter!
    Like a magnet drawing me — for I'm a man;
    And just as he said, that well-known writer:
    "Das Ewig-Weibliche zieht uns an!"[54]

SCENE SEVEN

A moonlit night. The palm grove outside ANITRA'S *tent.* PEER
GYNT, *with an Arabian lute in hand, sits under a tree. His beard
and hair have been trimmed; he looks noticeably younger.*

PEER GYNT *(plays and sings)*
>   I locked away my paradise
>   And carried off the key,
>   Sailed out before the northern breeze,
>   While lovely ladies spent their cries
>   Forlornly by the sea.

>   Southward, southward raced the keel
>   Across the ocean stream.
>   Where palm trees swaying proud and tall
>   Around a bay stood sentinel,
>   I put my ship to flame.

>   I climbed aboard the desert ship,
>   A ship on four swift legs.
>   It foamed beneath the lashing whip;
>   Oh, catch me on the wing! I slip,
>   A songbird, through the twigs!

>   Anitra! Nectar of the palm
>   Is how I see thee now!
>   Angora goat cheese in its prime
>   Gives hardly half so sweet a balm,
>   Anitra, dear, as thou!

(Hangs the lute over his shoulder and approaches the tent.)

Silence! Did my beauty listen?
What did she think of my little song?
Is she spying behind the curtain,
Stripped of veils and everything?
What's that? Sounds like someone tore
A cork from a bottle violently!
Again? And again! What could it be?
Sighs, perhaps? Love's melody —
No, that was a definite snore —
Sweetest music! Anitra sleeps.
Nightingale, be muted now!

Ten thousand plagues will lay you low
If you dare to match your chirps and peeps—
Oh well, as the book says, let it go!
The nightingale is a troubadour;
And, for all that, so am I.
Both of us with our music snare
Hearts that are tender, mild, and shy.
The cool of night is made for singing;
Song defines our common role.
Song is our way of remaining
Us, Peer Gynt and the nightingale.
And just that, my beauty's there asleep
Is the crowning bliss of love—
No more; only to touch my lip
To the cup, and leave the nectar safe—
But look, she's coming out at last!
Well, after all, that is the best.

ANITRA *(from the tent)*

Lord, were you calling in the night?

PEER GYNT

Yes, I was; the Prophet's calling.
I was awakened by the cat
Out hunting, with a frightful yowling.

ANITRA

Those weren't sounds of hunting, Lord;
It was something worse you heard.

PEER GYNT

What was it, then?

ANITRA

              Oh, spare me!

PEER GYNT

                    Tell!

ANITRA

Oh, I'm blushing——

PEER GYNT *(coming closer)*

                    Could it have been

That feeling that suffused me when
I made you a present of my opal?

ANITRA *(horrified)*

You compare yourself, oh earth's delight,
With an old disgusting alley cat!

PEER GYNT

Child, in love's delirium,
A prophet and a tomcat come
Out to very much the same.

ANITRA

Lord, from your lips diversion flows
Like beads of honey.

PEER GYNT

Little one —
You, like other girls, appraise
Only the surfaces of great men.
Inside me, comedy runs wild,
The more when we're alone like this.
In my position, I'm compelled
To mask it under seriousness.
The day's routine is a heavy weight;
All the worry and distress
That comes to me on every face
Makes me prophetically morose;
But only from the surface out —
No more! Away! In a tête-a-tête,
I'm what I've always been — I'm Peer.
Hi, the prophet gets his hat;
He's gone! Myself, you have me here!

(Sits under a tree and draws her to him.)

Come, Anitra, rest a while
Beneath the palm tree's emerald fan.
Let me whisper to your smile;
Later we'll change roles, and then
I'll lie and smilingly approve
Your fresh, young lips that whisper love.

123

ANITRA *(stretching out at his feet)*
>The words you speak like music fall;
>I wish I followed the meaning better.
>Master, tell me, can your daughter,
>Just by listening, gain a soul?

PEER GYNT
>The spirit's light and truth, a soul—
>Yes, you'll gain one after a spell.
>When the rose-streaked east horizon
>Reads, in gold print—"Now it's day"—
>Then, my puss, you'll have your lesson;
>You'll be tutored properly.
>But in the night's enchanted calm
>It would be stupid if my aim
>Were only, with some worn-out tags
>Of learning, to play pedagogue.
>In our lives, the soul is—once
>You see it rightly—not the key.
>It's the heart that really counts.

ANITRA
>Speak, oh Master! In your meaning
>Now I see light, like opals shining!

PEER GYNT
>Too much cunning ends in folly;
>The fruit of fear is cruelty;
>Truth, exaggerated, can
>Be wisdom written upside down.
>Yes, my child—I'd take my oath
>And swear that there's a certain class
>Of soul-inflated folk on earth
>Who won't reach clarity with ease.
>I knew a fellow just like that,[55]
>The pearl he was of all the lot;
>Yet even he mistook the point
>And lost his meaning, spouting rant.
>Around this grove, you see the wastes?

If I swung my turban to the skies,
I could make the seven seas
Pour in and drown these miles of dust.
But I'd be simply out of my mind
To go creating seas and lands.
Do you know what it means to live?[56]

ANITRA

Teach me that!

PEER GYNT

               It's just to move
Dryshod down the stream of time,
Oneself, intact, beyond all claim.
Only in full manhood can I
Be what I am, my dearest joy!
Old eagles shed their feathers,
Old beggars lag their paths,
Old fishwives lose their teeth,
Old hands of dotards wither;
All of them wither in their souls—
Youth! Oh, youth! I want to reign
Like a sultan, fiery in my pulse—
Not on Gyntiana's shores
Under vine and palm-tree arbors—
But grounded in the fresher green,
Of a maiden's pure desires.

    Now do you see, my little one,
Why I've paid you gracious court—
Why I singled out your heart
To be, as it were, the cornerstone
Of all my being's caliphate?
Over your longings, I'll be lord.
In passion, I'm an autocrat!
You must be mine, and mine alone.
I'll be always there to guard
Your charms like a jeweled cameo.
If we should part, then life is over—

Nota bene, that is, for *you!*
I want your every inch and fiber
Drained of will and, utterly
Past resistance, filled with me.
Your nest of midnight hair, your skin,
Everything lovely one could name,
Will, like the gardens of Babylon,
Beckon me to my sultan's realm.
   So it's lucky, after all,
You've kept your head so vacuous.
Those who entertain a soul
Get swallowed in self-consciousness.
Listen, while we're on this thing—
My truelove, if you like, I'll do
Your beauty proud with an ankle ring—
It's best, as well, for me and you
If *I'm* installed where your soul is hiding—
As for the rest—it's status quo.

        (ANITRA snores.)

What? Asleep! Has it gone gliding
Past her, everything I've said?
No; it shows the mark I've made,
That, borne on my passionate stream
Of speech, she's wafted into dreams.

        (Rises and lays jewels in her lap.)

Take these jewels! And here, some more!
Sleep, Anitra! Dream of Peer—
Sleep on! Your slumber is a crown
Upon your emperor's flow of wit!
Character is the cornerstone
Of the victory Peer Gynt won tonight.

SCENE EIGHT

A caravan route. The oasis far off in the distance. PEER GYNT, *on his white horse, comes galloping across the desert, with* ANITRA *in front on his saddle-bow.*

ANITRA
    Let go; I'll bite!
PEER GYNT
                Now, puss, behave!
ANITRA
    What are you up to?
PEER GYNT
                  Playing hawk and dove.
    I abduct you! And do mad tricks!
ANITRA
    Shame! An old prophet—!
PEER GYNT
                    What foolishness!
    The prophet isn't old, you goose!
    Is this a role that old age picks?
ANITRA
    Let go! You take me home!
PEER GYNT
                Coquette!
    Home? To father-in-law? How neat!
    We mad birds that fly our cages
    Can't ever go back where *he* can watch us.
    Besides, my child, it never pays
    To stay too long in any one place.
    What's won in friendship is lost in esteem—
    That's where prophets and such get caught.
    You must flash in view, then fade like a dream.
    It was time to close the visit out.
    The sons of the desert are fickle at heart—
    The prayers and incense were running short.

ANITRA

But *are* you a prophet?

PEER GYNT

      I'm your emperor!
       (Tries to kiss her.)

My, how ruffled our feathers are!

ANITRA

Give me that ring there on your finger.

PEER GYNT

Anitra dear, you can have them all!

ANITRA

Your words are songs! Sweetly they linger.

PEER GYNT

Bliss, to know that one's loved so well!
Wait! I'll lead the horse, as your slave!
   (Hands her the riding whip and gets off.)
There, my rosebud, my dainty flower;
I'll push on over the desert, move
Till I'm felled by sunstroke and expire.
I'm young, Anitra; remember that!
Don't give my highjinks too much weight.
Jokes and games are youth's own splendor!
If your mind wasn't such a languid thing,
You'd know, my fetching oleander—
That your lover jokes—*ergo*, he's young!

ANITRA

Yes, you're young. The rings, have you more?

PEER GYNT

Aren't I? Here, catch! I can leap like a deer!
If I had vineleaves, I'd crown my brow.
Hi, but I'm young! I'm dancing now!
      (Dances and sings.)
 Oh, I'm a happy rooster!
 Peck me, my little chick!

Hi! See the footwork, look—
Oh, I'm a happy rooster!

ANITRA

You're sweating, prophet; I'm afraid you'll melt—
Throw me that heavy bag at your belt.

PEER GYNT

What thoughtfulness! Keep it, child—
Hearts full of love can live without gold!

(Dances and sings again.)

Young Peer Gynt is a zany—
He doesn't know what foot he's standing on.
Ffft, says Peer—ffft, be gone—
Young Peer Gynt is a zany!

ANITRA

The dance of the prophet charms and soothes.

PEER GYNT

Stuff the prophet! Let's switch clothes!
Here! Undress!

ANITRA

Your caftan's too long;
Your waistband's too wide; your stockings, all wrong—

PEER GYNT

Eh bien! (Kneels.)
But give me a piercing sorrow—
Hearts full of love find suffering sweet!
And when you enter my castle door, you—

ANITRA

Your paradise—is it much farther yet?

PEER GYNT

Oh, a thousand miles—

ANITRA

Too far!

PEER GYNT

I swear—
You'll get the soul I promised before.

129

ANITRA

Thanks — I'll make it without a soul.

But you asked for a sorrow——

PEER GYNT *(rising)*

By heaven, yes!

Racking, but brief — for two or three days.

ANITRA

Anitra obeys the prophet! Farewell!

> *(She cuts him sharply across the knuckles and*
> *gallops away full tilt across the desert.)*

PEER GYNT *(dumbfounded)*

Well, I'll be a——

SCENE NINE

The same, an hour later. PEER GYNT, *solemn and thoughtful, is stripping his Turkish costume off piece by piece. Finally he takes his little traveling cap out of his coat pocket, puts it on, and stands once more in European dress.*

PEER GYNT *(hurling the turban far away)*

There lies the Turk, and here am I — !

Heathen existence just isn't for me.

Lucky it's only the clothes I wore,

And not burned into me like a scar —

What did I ever want in that crew?

It's best as a Christian to live in

This world, to stifle your peacock pride,

Take law and morality for your guide,

And be yourself, till at last you're given

Praise at your grave and wreaths on your coffin.

(Pacing a few steps.)

That wench — she came within a hair

Of managing to turn my head.

I'll be a troll if I can figure

What it was that made me crazy mad.
Ah well, it's done! If I'd let things progress,
I could have appeared ridiculous.
I made a mistake. But it's consolation
That what I mistook was the situation.
It wasn't my inner self that fell.
It was that prophetical way of life,
So removed from the salt of honest toil,
That took revenge in a cheap rebuff.
The prophet's role is a sorry show!
The gist of the art is to grope in mist;
And if the prophet attempts to go
Straight and act sober, the game is lost.
In that sense, I really ran true to form
To fall when that goose turned on the charm.
Still, all the same—

                    (Bursts out laughing.)

                    It piques your fancy!
To try to stop time by skipping and dancing;
To fight the current by preening and mincing!
To strum the lute, take love for a fact,
Then end like a hen—by getting plucked.
That's conduct to call prophetic frenzy—
Plucked! Oh Lord, I've been plucked all right!
Well, it's good that I kept a little out—
Some in America, and some in my pocket;
So I'll not be a beggar housed in a thicket.
And the happy medium is really best.
A coach-and-four isn't worth the cost—
Why should I travel like a patrician?
In short, I'm on top of the situation—
Now what should I choose? Such vistas call;
And choice marks the master from the fool.
My business life is a closed book;
My love game is a ragged cloak.
I'm not going crabwise, back again.

"Forward and back, it's just as far;
Out or in, it's a narrow door,"
Was written, I think, by some brilliant man.
For something new; some flight of valor;
Some end worth every effort and dollar
Spent! If I set my life story down
Complete, for guidance and imitation—?
Or, wait—! I've plenty of time on hand—
What if I went as a wandering scholar
To trace the past ages, the greed of mankind?
Yes, that's it! *There's* my place!
I always read legends as a child;
And now, with the sciences I've distilled—
I'll follow the course of the human race!
I'll float like a feather on history's stream,
Relive it all, as if in a dream—
See the heroes battle for truth and right,
But as an onlooker, safe in thought—
See thinkers perish and martyrs bleed,
See empires rise and sweep to doom,
See the world epochs sprout from seed—
In short, I'll skim off history's cream.
I must get hold of a volume of Becker[57]
And become a strict chronological seeker.
It's true—my groundwork's not very deep,
And history's mazes can be a trap—
But then sometimes the wildest notions
Can lead to the most original conclusions—
How exalting, to set up a goal
And drive right to it, like flint and steel!

                    (With quiet feeling.)

To break off every tie that binds
One to homeland and to friends—
To blow one's treasured goods to bits—
Give all to love, then call it quits—
For truth, for light from the ultimate torch—

(Brushing a tear from his eye.)
That's in the spirit of pure research!
I feel so happy, beyond compare.
Now I've unriddled my destiny here.
Now to hold out, through wealth and want!
I shouldn't be blamed for vanity if
I savor being the man Peer Gynt,
Called also the Emperor of Human Life —
The sum of the past I want to own;
Never come near the living again —
This age isn't worth the heel of my shoe.
Men have no faith, no substance now:
Souls without wings, deeds without weight —
(Shrugging his shoulders.)
And the women — pah, they're a scrubby lot!
(Goes off.)

SCENE TEN

A summer day in the far north. A hut in the forest. The door, with its large wooden bar, stands open. A reindeer horn over the doorway. A flock of goats by one wall. A MIDDLE-AGED WOMAN, *fair and still lovely, sits out in the sunlight, spinning.*

THE WOMAN *(glances down the path and sings)*
The winter may pass, and the spring disappear,
And next summer too, and the whole of the year —
But one day you'll come, I know that you will;
Then, as I promised, I'll wait for you still.
(Calls to the goats, spins, and sings again.)
God give you strength if you wander alone!
God give you joy if you stand at His throne!
I'll wait for you here till you're home again, love;
And if heaven has you, we'll meet up above!

SCENE ELEVEN

Egypt. The statue of Memnon,[58] *in the first light of dawn, surrounded by desert.* PEER GYNT *approaches on foot and studies
the scene for a while.*

PEER GYNT
    Here's a good spot for the trip to begin —
    Now, for a change, I'll be an Egyptian,
    Founded, that is, on a Gyntian core.
    Then Assyria — I'll go there.
    To start right back at the world's creation
    Would only lead me into confusion —
    I'll skip over Biblical fact and belief;
    Their secular traces will give me enough;
    And to put them under hard scrutiny
    Lies beyond both my plan and ability.
               (Sitting on a rock.)
    Now let me rest and quietly wait
    Till the statue's morning song floats out.
    After breakfast, a climb up the pyramid;
    Then, if there's time, I'll explore it inside.
    Next, round the top of the Red Sea shore;
    I might find the grave of King Potiphar —
    Now I'm Asian. I'm searching for Babylon's
    Famed hanging gardens and concubines —
    In short, for the cultural spoor of mankind.
    Next, to the walls of Troy in one bound.
    From Troy there's a sea route goes direct
    To Athens, queen city of monuments —
    There I'll explore the pass that once
    Leonidas fought and died to protect —
    I'll study the leading philosophers,
    Find Socrates' cell, where he ended his years —
    Damn! I forgot — there's a war going on — !
    Well, Hellenism I'll have to postpone.

> *(Looks at his watch.)*
>
> It's really absurd how long it takes
> For the sun to rise. I'm wasting time.
> So, after Troy — that's as far as I'd come —
>
> > *(Gets up and listens.)*
>
> What is it, that curious murmur that breaks — ?
>
> > *(Sunrise.)*

MEMNON'S STATUE *(sings)*

> From the demigod's ashes rise youth-renewing
> > birds brightly singing.
> > Zeus, the All-knowing,
> > made struggle their longing.
> > Wise Owl, among
> birds, is sleep so much safer?
> You must die or decipher
> > this riddle in song!

PEER GYNT

> Fantastic — I do think the statue expressed
> Those sounds! Music, it was, of the past.[59]
> I heard the stone voice rise and then fall —
> I'll write it up for the scholars to mull.
>
> > *(Writes in his notebook.)*
>
> "The statue sang. Heard definite tones,
> But can't quite figure what it all means.
> A hallucination, obviously.
> Nothing else worthy of note today."
>
> > *(Moves on.)*

SCENE TWELVE

Near the village of Gizeh. The Great Sphinx, carved out of rock. Far off, the spires and minarets of Cairo. PEER GYNT enters; he observes the Sphinx with some care, by turns first through his pince-nez and then through his hollowed hand.

PEER GYNT

>Where in the world did I meet up before
>With this thing, this nightmare from long ago?
>I know we've met—up north, or here.
>Was it a person? And, if so, who?
>Memnon, it came to me afterward,
>Looked like the King of the Dovre Trolls,
>The way he was sitting, stiff as a board,
>With pillars propping his bottom like stools—
>But this wonder that's neither fish nor fowl,
>This freak, this lion and woman joined—
>Is it also out of some fairy tale?
>Or something real that I've held in mind—?
>From a fairy tale? Ho, I remember the brute!
>It's the Boyg, of course, whose skull I split—
>Or dreamed I did—I was ill of fever—

>>*(Going closer.)*

>The selfsame eyes; the lips, same as ever—
>Not quite so listless, a bit more sly;
>But otherwise, one and the same to a tee.
>So that's it, Boyg; you look like a lion,
>Seen from behind by the light of day.
>You still make riddles? We can try one
>And see if you answer the same in this too—!

>>*(Calls to the Sphinx.)*

>Hi, Boyg, who are you?

A VOICE *(behind the Sphinx)*

>>*Ach, Sphinx, wer bist du?*

PEER GYNT

>What? An echo in German? How odd!

THE VOICE

>*Wer bist du?*

PEER GYNT

>>The accent, it's very good!
>This observation is new, and mine.

(Writes in his notebook.)

"Echo speaks German. Dialect—Berlin."

(BEGRIFFENFELDT *comes out from behind the Sphinx.*)

BEGRIFFENFELDT

A man!

PEER GYNT

So *he's* the explanation.

(Notes again.)

"Later came to another conclusion."

BEGRIFFENFELDT *(with agitated gestures)*

Pardon, *mein Herr*—! *Eine Lebensfrage*—!

What brought you here at just this second?

PEER GYNT

A visit. I'm greeting a childhood friend.

BEGRIFFENFELDT

The Sphinx—?

PEER GYNT *(nods)*

An early page in my saga.

BEGRIFFENFELDT

Splendid! And this after, ah, what a night!

My head is throbbing. It's ready to burst!

You know him? Speak, man! Tell me first

What is he?

PEER GYNT

What is he? Nothing to that.

He's *himself.*

BEGRIFFENFELDT *(with a bound)*

The riddle of life, in a blaze

Of light, is clear! You're sure that he *is*

Himself?

PEER GYNT

Yes; or that's what he says.

BEGRIFFENFELDT

Himself! Revolution's hour is close!

                                   (Takes off his hat.)
        Your name, *mein Herr?*
PEER GYNT

                                I was christened Peer Gynt.
BEGRIFFENFELDT *(with quiet admiration)*
        Peer Gynt! Allegorical! The One foreseen —
        Peer Gynt? Which is to say: the Unknown —
        He whose coming came to me as a portent —
PEER GYNT

        No, really! So now you're here to bring in — ?
BEGRIFFENFELDT

        Peer Gynt! Profound! Mystical! Robust!
        Each word is like a fathomless sea!
        What are you?
PEER GYNT *(modestly)*

                                I've always attempted to be
        Myself. My passport covers the rest.
BEGRIFFENFELDT

        Again the mysterious phrase intoned!
                                (Seizes his wrist.)
        To Cairo! The Interpreters' Emperor is found!
PEER GYNT

        Emperor?
BEGRIFFENFELDT

                        Come!
PEER GYNT

                                Have they heard of me?
BEGRIFFENFELDT *(pulling him along)*
        The Interpreters' Emperor — by self's decree!

                        SCENE THIRTEEN

In Cairo. A large courtyard enclosed by high walls and build-
ings. Barred windows; iron cages. THREE KEEPERS *in the yard.*
A FOURTH *enters.*

FOURTH KEEPER
   Say, Schafmann, where's the director gone?

FIRST KEEPER
   Went out this morning before it was light.

FOURTH KEEPER
   Something's gotten him all upset;
   Last night——

SECOND KEEPER
            Hsst, quiet; he's coming in!

    (BEGRIFFENFELDT enters, leading PEER GYNT, *locks
      the gate and puts the key in his pocket.)*

PEER GYNT *(to himself)*
   This man is incredibly talented;
   Nearly all he says goes over my head.
                (Looking about.)
   So here we are, in the Scholars' Club?

BEGRIFFENFELDT
   Here's where you'll find them, all that mob—
   The threescore and ten Interpreters;[60]
   Now raised by a hundred and sixty more—
          (Shouts at the KEEPERS.*)*
   Mikkel, Schlingelberg, Schafmann, Fuchs—
   Into the cages, in just two shakes!

KEEPERS
   Us?

BEGRIFFENFELDT
    Who else? Come on! Get in!
   When the world goes spinning, we have to spin.
          (Forces them into a cage.)
   He came this morning, Peer the Great—
   You can guess the rest—I'll leave it at that.
     (Locks the cage and throws the key down a well.)

PEER GYNT
   But Doctor—my dear Herr Director, please——

BEGRIFFENFELDT
>Not anymore! That's what I *was* —
>Can you keep a secret? I have a confession ——

PEER GYNT *(increasingly uneasy)*
>What's that?

BEGRIFFENFELDT
>   You think you can stand the shock?

PEER GYNT
>Well, I'll try ——

BEGRIFFENFELDT *(draws him into a corner and whispers)*
>   Absolute Reason
>Died last night at eleven o'clock.

PEER GYNT
>Good God — !

BEGRIFFENFELDT
>   Yes, it's really deplorable.
>And in *my* position, doubly horrible,
>For these grounds have been, up to this time,
>An insane asylum.[61]

PEER GYNT
>   An insane asylum!

BEGRIFFENFELDT
>But not now!

PEER GYNT *(pale and subdued)*
>   This place, now I recognize it.
>The man's gone mad — and nobody knows it!
>   *(Moves away.)*

BEGRIFFENFELDT *(following him)*
>I wouldn't want you to misunderstand.
>When I say He's dead — I'm making jokes.
>He's escaped himself. He's come unskinned
>Just like my countryman Munchausen's fox.[62]

PEER GYNT
>Excuse me ——

BEGRIFFENFELDT *(catching hold of him)*
    He was more like an eel than
A fox. That's it! Through the eye, a pin—
He writhed on the wall—

PEER GYNT
       Who can rescue me—!

BEGRIFFENFELDT
Round the neck, a slit—and whip! it's free
Of its skin!

PEER GYNT
    Crazy! He's lost his mind!

BEGRIFFENFELDT
You can't get away from it; it's clear—
This escape-from-selfing has to inspire
Complete revolution in every land.
Those persons who before were called crackbrain
At eleven last night became quite sane,
Conforming to Reason's latest phase.
And from this standpoint, it's even more
Clear that, at that identical hour,
The so-called sane lost their faculties.

PEER GYNT
You mentioned the hour; my time is short—

BEGRIFFENFELDT
Your time? That gives my thinking a spurt!
    (Opens a door and calls out.)
Come forth! The veil of the future is rent!
Reason is dead. Long live Peer Gynt!

PEER GYNT
My man, you're too kind—!
(The lunatics come, one after another, into the courtyard.)

BEGRIFFENFELDT
      Good morning! Come in.
Greet the dawning age of liberation!
Your emperor's here!

PEER GYNT
                              Emperor?
BEGRIFFENFELDT
                                    Yes!
PEER GYNT
    But the honor's too much; it's way beyond —
BEGRIFFENFELDT
    Ah, false modesty — don't let it bind
    This moment.
PEER GYNT
                         Give me some peace — !
    No, I'm not worthy! What can I say?
BEGRIFFENFELDT
    A man who brought the Sphinx to bay?
    A man who's himself?
PEER GYNT
                              But that's just it.
    I'm myself in everything I do;
    But as far as I can see, here you
    Have to be beside yourself to rate.
BEGRIFFENFELDT
    Beside yourself? What a huge mistake!
    Everyone here is himself to the gills,
    Completely himself and nothing else —
    So far in himself he can't come back.
    Everyone's shut in his cask of skin;
    He dives in the self's fermenting murk,
    Hermetically sealed by a self-made cork —
    Shrinking his staves down a well of brine.
    No one has tears for the others' griefs,
    Or feels at all for the others' beliefs.
    We're ourselves in every thought and tone,
    Ourselves to the farthest margin out —
    And so, if an emperor on a throne
    Is what we need, you're exactly right.

PEER GYNT
　　Oh, how the devil — !
BEGRIFFENFELDT
　　　　　　　　　Don't feel blue;
　　Nearly all that is once had to be new.
　　"Oneself" — here, look, I'll show you a case;
　　I'll pick at random the first that passes —
　　　　　　　　　(To a dark figure.)
　　Good day, Huhu![63] Why's there a crisis
　　Always written across your face?
HUHU
　　Can I help it when my nation
　　Dies without interpretation?
　　　　　　　　　(To PEER GYNT.*)*
　　You're a stranger; want to hear?
PEER GYNT *(bows)*
　　Why, of course!
HUHU
　　　　　　　　Then lend an ear —
　　Strung like garlands, eastward far,
　　Lie the coasts of Malabar.
　　Dutch and Portuguese have seeded
　　Culture with the goods they traded,
　　While the jungle hid their quarries —
　　Droves of native Malabaris.
　　These get by on hybrid words —
　　In that country they're the lords —
　　But the ages past belong
　　To the fierce orangoutang.
　　He, the forest's lord and master,
　　Free to fight or merely bluster —
　　Shaped direct from nature's hand,
　　How he gaped and how he whined.
　　Unrestrained he shrieked his fill;
　　He was monarch over all —

But then foreign sirens sang,
Muddling our primeval tongue,
While four centuries of sleep
Quelled the vigor of the ape—
For, you know, a night like that
Snuffs a people's spirit out.
No more forest cries are heard;
Growls and grunts now go ignored—
If we want to share our views,
Language is the crutch we use.
What a curse on every race!
Hollanders and Portuguese,
Malabaris, octaroons—
All are punished for their pains.
I have tried to keep in touch
With the old, authentic speech—
Tried to raise its corpse and strike
For the people's right to shriek—
Shriek myself and bring new fire
To the folk songs we admire.
Still, my efforts win no favor—
Now you see the way I suffer.
Thanks for lending me your ear—
How would you advise me, sir?

PEER GYNT (*to himself*)

It's been said: when wolves are howling,
Then it's wise to do some growling.

(*Aloud.*)

Friend, if I remember right,
In Morocco there's a spot
Where the apes are pining for
Poets and interpreters.
Their tongue sounded Malabaric,
Folkloristic, prehistoric!
Why don't you, like other gentry,
Emigrate to serve your country?

HUHU

    Thanks for lending me your ear—
    You have counseled; I concur.
                (With a sweeping gesture.)
    East! Thy bard has suffered wrongs!
    West! Thou hast orangoutangs!
                    (He goes.)

BEGRIFFENFELDT

    Well, was he himself? I think he was.
    Completely filled with his own distress.
    Himself in all that his thoughts involve—
    Himself by being beside himself.
    Come here! I'll show you another one
    Who found last night he was truly sane.
        (To a FELLAH *carrying a mummy on his back.)*[64]
    King Apis, how goes my noble lord?

FELLAH *(wildly, to* PEER GYNT*)*

    Am I King Apis?

PEER GYNT *(shrinking behind the doctor)*

                Well, it's hard
    To say; I don't know the situation.
    But if I were judging by your passion——

FELLAH

    Now you're lying too.

BEGRIFFENFELDT

                     Your Highness should tell
    How matters stand.

FELLAH

                As you will.
                (Turning to PEER GYNT*.)*
    You see him, there on my shoulders?
    His name was Apis, the King.
    Now he goes by the name of a mummy,
    And he's dead to everything.
        He built the pyramids skyward

And carved out the mighty Sphinx,
And fought, as the Doctor puts it,
With the Turk both *rechts* and *links*.

For this the people of Egypt
Hailed him a god over all,
And raised him up in the temples
In the likeness of a bull.[65]

But *I* am this same King Apis,
I see that as plain as day;
And if you can't understand me,
I'll clear it up right away.

King Apis, you see, was out hunting
When suddenly nature called,
And he got off his horse and retired
To part of my ancestor's field.

But the field that King Apis manured
Has nourished *me* with its corn;
And if more proof is required,
Well — I have an invisible horn.

Now isn't it quite outrageous
That no one bows down to my might!
By birth, I'm Apis, the pharaoh,
But a fellah in other men's sight.

If you see my course of action,
Please put it to me straight —
The thing is, what can I do now
To be like King Apis the Great?

PEER GYNT

Build pyramids, your Highness,
And carve out a mightier Sphinx,
And fight, as the Doctor puts it,
With the Turk both *rechts* and *links*.

FELLAH

Yes, that's very high-spoken!
A fellah! A hungry louse!
It's enough just keeping my hovel

Empty of rats and mice.
   Quick, man — find something better,
A greatness firm as a rock
To make me the spitting image
Of Apis here on my back!

PEER GYNT

What if you hanged your Highness
And then, in the earth's deep bed
And the coffin's natural confines,
Behaved like one totally dead?

FELLAH

I'll do it! My life for a gallows!
A rope to hold my weight!
At first there'll be some difference,
But time will even that out.

     (Goes off and prepares to hang himself.)

BEGRIFFENFELDT

Now that's personality, *mein Herr* —
A man of method —

PEER GYNT

         Oh yes, I'm sure —
But he's really hanging himself! God in heaven!
I feel sick — ! My brain's like an oven!

BEGRIFFENFELDT

A state of transition; it won't last long.

PEER GYNT

Transition? To what? Sorry — I'm going —

BEGRIFFENFELDT *(holding him)*

Are you mad?

PEER GYNT

     Not yet. Mad? Good Lord!

  (Commotion. HUSSEIN, *a cabinet minister,*[66] *pushes
his way through the crowd.)*

HUSSEIN

They tell me an emperor came today.

147

(To PEER GYNT.*)*

　　Is it you?

PEER GYNT *(in despair)*

　　　　　It's turning out that way!

HUSSEIN

　　Good. You have dispatches to be answered?

PEER GYNT *(tearing his hair)*

　　Yes! Why not? The madder, the better!

HUSSEIN

　　Would you honor me, sire, with a dip for your letter?

　　　　　　(Bowing low.)

　　I am a pen.

PEER GYNT *(bows lower still)*

　　　　　And I'm a sorry

　　Scrap of imperial stationery.

HUSSEIN

　　My story, sire, I can put in one line:

　　They call me a blotter, but I'm a pen.

PEER GYNT

　　My story, Sir Pen, is quickly spun:

　　I'm a blank sheet of paper, unwritten on.

HUSSEIN

　　Nobody knows my true potential—

　　They want me to soak up ink, that's all!

PEER GYNT

　　For a woman, I was a silver-clasped book;

　　Either mad or sane is a printer's mistake.

HUSSEIN

　　Imagine—what a meaningless life—

　　For a pen not to taste the edge of a knife!

PEER GYNT *(with a high leap)*

　　Imagine—a reindeer, falling free—

　　With never the hard earth under me!

HUSSEIN

　　A knife! Cut me! Carve me! I'm blunt!

The world will end if I lose my point!

PEER GYNT

How sad for the world, when all that's self-made
Was found by our Lord to be so well made.

BEGRIFFENFELDT

Here's a knife!

HUSSEIN *(seizing it)*

Ah! To lap ink the better,
What pleasure to slash oneself!

BEGRIFFENFELDT *(jumping aside)*

Don't spatter.

PEER GYNT *(in mounting terror)*

Hold him!

HUSSEIN

Yes, hold me ! Do what's proper!
Hold! Hold the pen! Set me to paper!

(Falls.)

I'm worn out. The postscript—bear it in mind:
He lived and died in other men's hands!

PEER GYNT *(reeling)*

What should I—! What am I? Oh Thou—take hold!
I'm whatever you want—a Turk, a sinner,
A hill troll—but help—somewhere it's failed—!

(Cries out.)

I can't remember your name for the world,
Thou—comfort of madmen, sustainer!

(Falls in a faint. BEGRIFFENFELDT, *a wreath of straw in
his hand, leaps to sit astride him.)*

BEGRIFFENFELDT

Hah! Look at him, enthroned in the filth—
Out of himself—! Crown him there!

(Presses the wreath down on PEER'S *head and shouts.)*

Hail, all hail the Emperor of Self!

SCHAFMANN *(in the cage)*

Es lebe hoch der grosse Peer!

ACT FIVE

SCENE ONE

On board a ship in the North Sea, off the Norwegian coast. Sunset. Stormy weather. PEER GYNT, *a rugged old man with grizzled hair and beard, stands on the poop. He is partly dressed as a seaman, with pea jacket and high boots. His clothes are rather worn; he himself is weather-beaten, and his face appears harder. The* CAPTAIN *and the helmsman are at the wheel. The crew is forward.* PEER *leans on the ship's rail and gazes toward land.*

PEER GYNT
    That's Hallingskarv in his winter coat,
    Lording it there in the evening light,
    And Jøkel,[67] his brother, next in line;
    He still has his ice-green mantle on.
    And there, how lovely! It's Folgefonnen,[68]
    Dressed like a maid in the whitest linen.
    No cutting up, you old characters!
    Stand where you are, like granite spires.
CAPTAIN *(calling forward)*
    Two hands to the wheel—and the lantern set!
PEER GYNT
    It's blowing up.
CAPTAIN
                Aye. Storm tonight.
PEER GYNT
    Can we see the Ronde peaks from here?
CAPTAIN
    Not likely—they're back beyond the glacier.

PEER GYNT
    Or Blaahø?[69]
CAPTAIN
                        No; but from up the rigging
    You can see on a clear day to Galdhøpiggen.[70]
PEER GYNT
    Which way is Haarteigen?[71]
CAPTAIN *(pointing)*
                                Thereabouts.
PEER GYNT
    Ah, yes.
CAPTAIN
                You seem to know these parts.
PEER GYNT
    When I shipped out, it was down this coast;
    And the dregs, they say, leave the bottle last.
                (Spits and gazes toward shore.)
    Up in those blue ravines and notches,
    Those narrow valleys, dark as ditches—
    And below, along the open fjord—
    These people live *there*, of their own accord.
                    (Looks at the CAPTAIN.*)*
    They build wide apart up here.
CAPTAIN
                                    Aye,
    Far between and long away.[72]
PEER GYNT
    Will we land by morning?
CAPTAIN
                                About that,
    If it doesn't get too rough tonight.
PEER GYNT
    It's threatening westward.
CAPTAIN
                            It is.

PEER GYNT
                                              I hope
    You'll remind me when we settle up —
    I want to do a good turn for each
    Of the crew —

CAPTAIN
                         Thanks!

PEER GYNT
                                        It won't be much.
    I've grubbed for gold and lost the lot —
    Fate and I had a falling out.
    You know what I have in the safe below;
    That's it — the rest was the devil's due.

CAPTAIN
    It's more than enough to raise your stock
    With the home folk.

PEER GYNT
                                   I have no relatives.
    No one waiting till the old boy arrives —
    At least you miss the scene on the dock!

CAPTAIN
    Here comes the storm.

PEER GYNT
                                      So remember then —
    If anyone here is really pressed,
    I won't be niggling about the cost —

CAPTAIN
    That's fair. They're mostly hard-up men.
    They all have wives and children home,
    And the wages barely get them by —
    But if they brought in some extra pay,
    They'd praise that day for a good long time.

PEER GYNT
    What's that? They have wives and families?
    Are they married?

CAPTAIN

               Married? Aye, the whole flock.
But the one who's hardest pressed is the cook;
There's always black famine at his house.

PEER GYNT

Married? With someone there to wait,
Who's glad when they come?

CAPTAIN

                     Aye, as the poor
Do things.

PEER GYNT

      So one evening they appear—
What then?

CAPTAIN

        Oh, I guess the wife'd set
Out a special treat——

PEER GYNT

              A lamp on the table?

CAPTAIN

Maybe two—and a brandy, double.

PEER GYNT

And so they sit, snug and warm by the fire—?
Children around them—the whole room astir—
And nobody's words are heard to the end
For the joy they feel——

CAPTAIN

          You understand;
And that's why it's fair that you offered to fill
Their pockets a bit.

PEER GYNT *(pounds the railing)*

         Damned if I will!
You think I'm mad? That I'll fork out
To provide for somebody else's brats?
I've slaved like a dog to make my mint!
No one's waiting for old Peer Gynt.

CAPTAIN

Do as you please; your money's your own.

PEER GYNT

Right! It's nobody's at all but mine.
We'll settle as soon as the anchor's struck.
My cabin passage from Panama here;
A round of drinks for the crew. No more.
If I add one cent, you give me a smack!

CAPTAIN

You'll have my receipt, and not a brawl —
Excuse me; we're heading into a gale.

(*He crosses the deck forward. It has now grown dark;
lights are lit in the cabin. The sea runs higher. Fog
and thick clouds.*)

PEER GYNT

To leave a whole tribe of children behind —
To sow delight in their growing minds —
To be borne by others' thoughts on your way —!
There's no one ever who thinks of me —
A lamp on the table? I'll put it out.
Just let me think —! I'll get them tight —
Not one of the clods'll go sober ashore.
They'll break in drunk on those family groups!
They'll curse and hammer the table tops —
And stiffen their own with the breath of fear!
The wives'll scream and bolt from the house —
And the children too! Now let 'em rejoice!

(*The ship heels over; he staggers and holds
his balance with difficulty.*)

Well, that was a lively roll. The ocean
Works as if it were paid on commission.
It's still its old self by the northern skerries;
The riptide plotting its treacheries —

(*Listens.*)

What were those shouts?

THE WATCH *(forward)*

A wreck on the lee!

CAPTAIN *(amidships)*

Wheel hard starboard! Close to the wind!

THE MATE

Are there men aboard?

THE WATCH

I make out three!

PEER GYNT

Lower a boat——

CAPTAIN

She's be swamped and drowned!

(Goes forward.)

PEER GYNT

Who thinks of that?

(To several of the crew.)

You'll try, if you're men!

What the hell if you wet your skin——

THE BOATSWAIN

It can't be done in waves like those.

PEER GYNT

They're screaming again! And the wind is dying—

Cook, will you try? Quick! I'm paying——

THE COOK

For twenty pounds sterling, I'd refuse——

PEER GYNT

You curs! Cowards! Are you forgetting,

Those men have wives and children waiting

At home for them——

THE BOATSWAIN

Patience works wonders.

CAPTAIN

Bear off the breakers!

THE MATE

The wreck's gone under.

155

PEER GYNT

And in silence——

THE BOATSWAIN

If they *were* married, right this minute
The world's got three fresh-baked widows in it.

(The storm increases. PEER GYNT *moves aft.)*

PEER GYNT

There's no faith left among men anymore—
No Christian love, as it's written and taught—
Few good deeds, and still less prayer—
And no respect for the Deity's might.
In a storm like this, the Lord God rages.
Those beasts should remember, they take a chance,
That it's dangerous playing with elephants—
But instead, they're openly sacrilegious!
But *I* have no guilt, when I can prove
I was there with my money, ready to give.
And what do I get for it—? It's been said:
"A conscience at ease is a downy pillow."[73]
Oh yes, on land that can't be denied;
But on board ship, it's not worth mud
To be honest among that rabble below.
At sea, you can't be yourself at all;
You follow the crowd from deck to keel.
Let judgment strike for the bo'sun or cook,
And I go plunging down with the pack—
Personal values don't have any place—
You rate like a hog in a slaughterhouse—

It's my mistake that I've been too soft,
With nothing to show for it, only reproach.
If I were younger, my ways would shift
And I'd try playing the boss for a stretch.
There's time for it still! The parish'll hear
How Peer came swaggering home from afar!
I'll win back the farm by hook or crook,
Rebuild it, give it a regal look

Like a castle. Ah, but they can't come in!
They can stand at the gate, cap in hand,
Begging and pleading—*that* I don't mind;
But they won't get a penny of mine, not one—
If *I've* howled under the whips of Fate,
Trust me to find people I can beat—

> (*A* STRANGE PASSENGER[74] *appears in the dark at*
> PEER GYNT'S *side and greets him amiably.*)

THE PASSENGER
Good evening!

PEER GYNT
Good evening! What—? Who are you?

THE PASSENGER
Your servant—and fellow passenger.

PEER GYNT
Odd? I thought I was all alone here.

THE PASSENGER
A false impression. It's over now.

PEER GYNT
But it's certainly strange that I see you tonight
For the very first time—

THE PASSENGER
I don't go out days.

PEER GYNT
Have you been sick? You're white as a sheet—

THE PASSENGER
Not at all. I'm in perfect health, otherwise.

PEER GYNT
What a storm!

THE PASSENGER
Yes, what a blessing, man!

PEER GYNT
Blessing?

THE PASSENGER
The waves are as big as houses.

It's simply mouth-watering! Ah, can
You imagine, on a night like this, the losses
In shipwrecks, and the men that go down!

PEER GYNT

My God!

THE PASSENGER

                    Ever seen a man who's choked —
Or been hanged — or drowned?

PEER GYNT

                                        What a subject!

THE PASSENGER

The corpses laugh. But that laughter's wrung
From them; most have bit off a tongue.

PEER GYNT

Get away from me — !

THE PASSENGER

                        One question. Wait!
Suppose, for example, we struck a reef
And went down in the dark —

PEER GYNT

                                Do you think we might?

THE PASSENGER

I hardly know what answer to give.
But let's say I float, and you sink like a stone —

PEER GYNT

Oh, rubbish —

THE PASSENGER

                    Just something to speculate on.
But when a man has one foot in the grave,
He's more disposed to do a small favor —

PEER GYNT *(reaching in his pocket)*

Ho, money!

THE PASSENGER

                No; I'd be satisfied if
You'd make me a gift of your cadaver — ?

PEER GYNT

  Now this is too much!

THE PASSENGER

                Just the corpse, you know!

  For my scientific research —

PEER GYNT

              Will you go!

THE PASSENGER

  But, my dear sir, think — how you'll benefit!
  You'll be opened up and brought to light.
  I'm investigating the source of dreams,
  But I'll also go into your joints and seams —

PEER GYNT

  Get away!

THE PASSENGER

        But, friend — a dripping stiff — !

PEER GYNT

  Blasphemer! You've helped the storm enough!
  It's madness! In all this wind and rain
  And roaring sea, with every sign
  That terrible things are due for this ship —
  You have to tempt them to hurry up!

THE PASSENGER

  I see you're not in a mood for discussion;
  But time may force another conclusion —

           (With a friendly nod.)

  We'll meet when you're sinking, if not before;
  Perhaps then you'll be in better humor.

           (Goes into the cabin.)

PEER GYNT

  Bizarre companions, these scientists!
  Damned freethinkers —

        (To the BOATSWAIN, *passing by.)*

          A word, mine host!

  That passenger? Who is that lunatic?

THE BOATSWAIN
    There's nobody else but you coming back.
PEER GYNT
    Nobody else? That's certainly queer.
                    (*To a* YOUNG SAILOR, *leaving the cabin.*)
    Who just went inside?
THE SAILOR
                        The ship's dog, sir!
                        (*Passes on.*)
THE WATCH (*crying out*)
    Land dead ahead!
PEER GYNT
                    My box! My trunk!
    All baggage on deck!
THE BOATSWAIN
                    You want us to sink?
    We're busy.
PEER GYNT
                Captain! I was carrying on —
    Joking; but by God, now I'll help the cook —!
CAPTAIN
    The jib has sprung!
THE MATE
                    The foresail's gone!
THE BOATSWAIN (*screaming from the bow*)
    Breakers under us!
THE CAPTAIN
                She's going to strike!
            (*The ship grounds. Noise and confusion.*)

SCENE TWO

Close to land, among surf and skerries. The ship is sinking.
Through the fog, glimpses of a boat with two men. A heavy

sea breaks over it; it overturns; a shriek is heard, then silence. After a moment the boat reappears, bottom up. PEER GYNT *comes to the surface nearby.*

PEER GYNT
Help! A boat! Help me! I'll die!
God have mercy—as the Scriptures say!
(*Clutches the keel.*)

THE COOK (*comes up on the other side*)
Lord! Oh, God! For my babies' sake—
Be merciful! To my rescue! Quick!
(*Clings to the keel.*)

PEER GYNT
Let go!

THE COOK
Lay off!

PEER GYNT
I'll smack you!

THE COOK
Try!

PEER GYNT
I'll smash you to pieces, wait and see!
Let go ! She'll carry one; no more!

THE COOK
I know that! Swim for it!

PEER GYNT
You swim!

THE COOK
Sure!

(*They fight; one of the* COOK'S *hands is injured; he hangs on tight with the other.*)

PEER GYNT
Let go that hand!

THE COOK
Spare me, please!
Think of my children, what they'll lose!

PEER GYNT

    I'm more in need of life than you;

    I haven't had children up till now.

THE COOK

    Let go! You've lived, and I'm still young!

PEER GYNT

    Hurry up, sink — we're foundering.

THE COOK

    Have mercy! Swim it, in heaven's name!

    You break no hearts if you don't get home —

                (He screams and slips under.)

    I'm drowning — !

PEER GYNT *(seizing him)*

               I've got you by the hair

    Of your head; say a "Lord's Prayer"!

THE COOK

    I can't remember — it's turning black ——

PEER GYNT

    Just the essentials! Say it, quick!

THE COOK

    Give us this day — !

PEER GYNT

             Oh, cook, come on;

    Whatever you need, you'll have it soon.

THE COOK

    Give us this day ——

PEER GYNT

            The same old song!

    It's obvious you've been a cook too long ——

              (His hold loosens.)

THE COOK *(sinking)*

    Give us this day our ——

            (Goes under.)

PEER GYNT

          Amen, friend!

You were yourself, right to the end —
> *(Draws himself up on the keel.)*

Where there's life, there's always hope —

THE STRANGE PASSENGER *(takes hold of the boat)*

Good morning!

PEER GYNT

         Ai!

THE PASSENGER

         I heard a whoop —

Funny I should be meeting you.

Well? Did my prophecy come true?

PEER GYNT

Let go! There's hardly room for one!

THE PASSENGER

I'll swim with my left leg and hang on

By my fingertips over this cleat

On the keel of the boat. How's that?

But, apropos your corpse —

PEER GYNT

         Shh!

THE PASSENGER

The rest of you reeks like a rotten fish.

PEER GYNT

Shut your mouth!

THE PASSENGER

         If you prefer that.
> *(Silence.)*

PEER GYNT

Well?

THE PASSENGER

         I'm speechless.

PEER GYNT

         Satan's bait —

What now?

THE PASSENGER
>   I'm waiting.
PEER GYNT *(tearing his hair)*
>   I'll go mad!
>   Who are you?
THE PASSENGER *(with a nod)*
>   Friendly.
PEER GYNT
>   What, beside?
THE PASSENGER
>   What do *you* think? Know any other who's
>   Akin to me?
PEER GYNT
>   The devil is—!
THE PASSENGER *(softly)*
>   But is it his way to illuminate
>   Life's dark journey by means of fright?
PEER GYNT
>   Oh, I see! I suppose it's your claim
>   That a messenger of light has come?
THE PASSENGER
>   Even *once* in a half year, can it be said
>   You've been shaken to the roots by dread?
PEER GYNT
>   Sure, anyone's frightened when danger lunges.
>   But all your words are set on hinges—
THE PASSENGER
>   My friend, have you even *once* in your life
>   Known the victory only dread can give?
PEER GYNT *(looking at him)*
>   If you came to open me a door
>   It's stupid you didn't come before.
>   This is absurd, to choose a time
>   When the ocean's swallowing me like foam.

THE PASSENGER
    Would the victory be more likely, then,
    By the fireside in your drowsy den?
PEER GYNT
    All right—but your words were laughable.
    How could you think they'd stir my soul?
THE PASSENGER
    Where I come from they value smiles
    As high as all the pathetic styles.
PEER GYNT
    Each in its time; the barber thrives
    On what puts bishops into their graves.
THE PASSENGER
    The souls in funeral urns don't try
    On weekdays to dress for tragedy.
PEER GYNT
    Clear off, you monster! Get away!
    I won't die! It's the land for me!
THE PASSENGER
    You needn't worry in *that* respect—
    No one dies halfway through the last act.
                    (Glides away.)
PEER GYNT
    There, he got it out at last—
    He was a tedious moralist.

SCENE THREE

A churchyard high in the mountains. A funeral in progress. The
PASTOR *and the mourners are just singing the final verse of a*
hymn. PEER GYNT *is passing by on the road.*

PEER GYNT
    Here's another who's gone our mortal way.

Thanks be to God, it isn't me.

(*Enters the churchyard.*)

THE PASTOR (*over the grave*)

Now, as the soul goes out to meet its doom
And leaves the dust here, hollow as a drum—
Now, dear friends, we must set a few things forth
About this dead man's pilgrimage on earth.

He wasn't rich, nor could you call him wise;
His voice lacked force; his bearing, manliness;
What thoughts he spoke were hesitant and tame;
He scarcely seemed the master of his home;
And when he entered church, he'd sidle in
As if he begged his place with other men.

From Gudbrandsdal he came, over the wicked
Winding roads, as a boy; and he remained.
And you remember how, to the very end,
He always hid his right hand in his pocket.

That hand thrust in his pocket is the thing
That, in one's memory, stands pre-eminent—
That and a certain diffidence, a shrinking
Look, that marked him everywhere he went.

But, though his chosen path in life was lonely,
And he kept himself a stranger to our breed,
We all knew what he struggled so to hide—
The hand he covered had four fingers only—

I well remember, many years ago,
A morning down at Lunde. Conscripts had
Been called; a war was on; all talk was stayed
On Norway's griefs and the fate of those we knew.

I watched the drafting. At a table sat
A captain, flanked by sergeants, and the mayor.[75]
Boy after boy was summoned to their fire,
Measured, questioned, signed as a new recruit.
The room was full; and outside on the square,
Loud laughter rang from the young folk gathered there.
Another name was called. We saw approach

One who was pale as snow on the glacier's edge.
They told him to step up; and as he neared,
We saw his right hand bandaged in a clout.
He gulped and swallowed hard; he groped for words,
And yet, despite their bidding, stood there mute.
Ah, yes, at last! With burning cheeks, in a voice
That failed at times, then caught up with his breath,
He mumbled of some accident, a scythe
That cut his finger right off at the base.

    Then suddenly the room was deathly still.
Glances were exchanged; men set their jaws;
They stoned the boy with silence in their eyes.
He felt the hailstorm, though he never saw it fall.
And then the captain rose and, pointing to
The door, spat and rapped out one word, "Go!"

    And so he went. On both sides men drew back
And made a kind of gantlet to be run.
He reached the door; and then his courage broke —
He fled — up and up the wooded slope
Past the rockslides, treacherous and steep.
He had his home high in the mountains then —

    Some six months later, he came here to us
With mother and betrothed and baby child.
He rented land beyond the ridge, a field
Toward Lom where the tracts of wasteland rise.
He married just as soon as possible.
He built a house; he fought the stubborn soil
And made it yield, his efforts bravely shown,
Between the rocks, in the sway of yellow grain.
In church he kept his right hand in his pocket —
But at home, I'd say his fingers, though but nine,
Slaved just as hard as other peoples' ten.
One spring the torrent struck his farm and took it.

    They got out with their skins. A ruined man,
He started in anew to clear the land;
And by that fall, the smoke rose up again

Over a farmhouse built on safer ground.
Safer? Yes, from flood—but not from glaciers.
Within two years, a snow-slide crushed his labors.

    And yet no avalanche could crush his spirit.
He dug, he raked, he swept, he carted trash—
Till he could see, as winter's first snow flurried,
His house raised up a third time, clean and fresh.

    Three sons he had, three clever, active boys;
Time came for school, which lay a long way off—
To reach the parish road, they'd have to squeeze
Down snow-banked ledges clinging to the cliffs.
What did he do? He let the eldest shift
As best he could; but where no man would walk,
He'd lead the boy, tied by a line, and lift
The others in his arms and on his back.

    So year by year he toiled, and they grew up.
Some help from them now seemed a decent hope.
In the New World, three wealthy businessmen
Forgot their father here and all he'd done.

    Shortsighted, he was that. He had no eyes
For anything beyond his family's call.
He found as meaningless as sounding brass
Words that ought to pierce the heart like steel.
This land, our people, all the shining dreams,
Weighed less to him than mist on mountain streams.

    Yet he was humble, humble as men come;
That day in Lunde stripped his conscience naked—
As certain as his cheeks that burned with shame
And those four fingers hiding in his pocket.

    Lost to his country's laws? Yes, if you want.
But one true light above the law prevails,
As sure as over Glittertind's[76] white tent
The piling clouds build higher mountains still.
No patriot, this man. For church as well as state,
A barren tree. But up where the wasteland shelves,
In his family circle where he saw his lot,

There he was great, because he was himself.
His inborn note was steadfast as a star.
His life was music, like a muted bell.
So, peace be with you, silent warrior,
Who fought the peasant's little fight, and fell.
    It's not our place to sift the heart and soul—
That's not for dust, but for the Judge of all—
Still I believe—and here it must be said:
This man stands now no cripple to his God!

     (The mourners scatter and depart.
     PEER GYNT *remains behind alone.)*

PEER GYNT

Now *that's* what I call Christianity!
Nothing unpleasant to jar the mind—
And the subject—being oneself to the end—
Brought out in the pastor's eulogy,
Has everything in it to recommend.

        (Looks down into the grave.)

Was it him, I wonder, that boy who cut
Off his finger one day not far from my hut?
Who knows? If I didn't stand with my staff
By the edge of this kindred spirit's grave,
I could almost believe it was *me* that slept
And heard in dreams my character wept.
It's really a beautiful Christian trait,
This casting of retrospective thought
In charity over the days gone by.
I wouldn't mind facing my destiny
At the hands of this excellent parish priest.
Well, I have a while, undoubtedly,
Before I'm called as the gravedigger's guest—
And as Scripture says: "It's all for the best—"
And: "Sufficient unto the day, its evil—"
And: "Don't borrow to buy the sexton a shovel—"
Ah, the church is the true consoler. Up
Till now, I've really not given it credit—

But how good it is to hear restated,
From the highest and surest authorship:
"Whatever ye sow, ye shall also reap."
We should be ourselves, that's the key;
All for yourself and your own, I say.
If your luck runs out, at least there's honor
In having lived in a principled manner.
Now homewards! What if Fortune frowns,
And the road ahead is hard and tortuous—
Old Peer Gynt will go it alone,
True to his nature: poor, but virtuous.

        (Moves on.)

SCENE FOUR

A hillside with a dried-out river bed and, beside it, a ruined mill. The ground is torn up; everything is desolate. Higher up-slope, a large farm, where an auction is taking place. A noisy crowd has gathered; many are drinking. PEER GYNT *is seated on a rubbish heap by the mill.*

PEER GYNT

Forward or back, it's just as far;
Out or in, it's a narrow door.
Time corrodes, and the stream wears out.
Remember the Boyg—and go roundabout.

A MAN IN MOURNING

Now there's only the rubbish here.[77]

      (Catches sight of PEER GYNT.*)*

And strangers too? God save you, sir!

PEER GYNT

And you! This crowd looks well amused.
A christening, or a wedding feast?

THE MAN IN MOURNING

A housewarming, I'd call it instead—

170

Except it's a bed of worms for the bride.

PEER GYNT

And the worms are fighting for rags and scraps.

THE MAN IN MOURNING

It's the end of the song; so there it stops.

PEER GYNT

They all end alike, every song;

They're old; I sang them when I was young.

A YOUTH OF TWENTY *(with a casting ladle)*

Look what I bought! An antique piece!

Peer Gynt poured silver buttons from this.

ANOTHER

See mine! Two cents for a money sack!

A THIRD.

That's nothing! Five for a peddler's pack!

PEER GYNT

Peer Gynt? Who was he?

THE MAN IN MOURNING

                        I only know Death

Was his brother-in-law. And Aslak the smith.

A MAN IN GRAY

You're forgetting me! Had too much beer?

THE MAN IN MOURNING

You're forgetting Hegstad, a storehouse door!

THE MAN IN GRAY

True; but when have you been that delicate?

THE MAN IN MOURNING

Let's see if she finds Death easy to cheat—

THE MAN IN GRAY

Come, brother! A drink, for brotherhood's sake!

THE MAN IN MOURNING

Brotherhood, hell! You've had a crock—

THE MAN IN GRAY

Nonsense! Our bloodlines don't run so faint;

We're all brothers in old Peer Gynt.

(*They go off together.*)

PEER GYNT (*softly*)

One meets acquaintances.

A BOY (*calls after* THE MAN IN MOURNING)

My dead mother

Will haunt you, Aslak, if you drink your meal.

PEER GYNT (*getting up*)

What the farmers say doesn't hold altogether:

"The deeper you dig, the better the smell."

A YOUTH (*with a bearskin*)

The Dovre-cat, look! Ready to stuff.

He routed the trolls on Christmas Eve.

A SECOND (*with reindeer horns*)

Here's that marvelous buck whose fleece

Carried Peer Gynt down Gjendin ridge.

A THIRD (*with a hammer, calls to* THE MAN IN MOURNING)

Hi, Aslak, you remember this sledge?

Is that what you used when the devil cut loose?

A FOURTH (*empty-handed*)

Mads Moen, here's the invisible cloak

That Peer Gynt and Ingrid flew with, look!

PEER GYNT

Some brandy, boys! I'm feeling old —

Let's have a beggar's auction held!

A YOUTH

What have you to sell?

PEER GYNT

I have a castle —

It lies in the Ronde, tough as your muscle.

THE YOUTH

I bid a button.

PEER GYNT

Make it a pint.

To bid any less would gall a saint.

ANOTHER YOUTH

    He's fun, the old boy!

                (A crowd flocks around.)

PEER GYNT

                 Grane, my horse —

    Who bids?

ONE OF THE CROWD

           Where is he?

PEER GYNT *(cries out)*

                Far to the west!

    In the sunset, lads! He can fly as fast —

    As fast as Peer Gynt could lie for a purse.

VOICES

    What else do you have?

PEER GYNT

               Both gold and dross!

    I bought them cheap; I'll sell at a loss.

A YOUTH

    Put up!

PEER GYNT

        One dream of a silver-clasped book.

    That you can have for a buttonhook.

THE YOUTH

    To hell with dreams!

PEER GYNT

             My empire, then!

    I'll throw it among you; catch as you can!

THE YOUTH

    Does a crown come with it?

PEER GYNT

                Of the finest straw.

    It'll fit the first man that gives it a try.

    And wait, here's more! The Prophet's beard!

    A rotten egg![78] A gray hair, snared

From a madman! All for him who can show
Me a sign in the hills saying, "Here lies the way!"
THE SHERIFF *(just arrived)*

Run on like that, my man, and you'll
Find your way takes you straight to jail.
PEER GYNT *(hat in hand)*

Most likely. But, tell me, who was Peer Gynt?
THE SHERIFF

What trash ——
PEER GYNT

Please! Just some account —!
THE SHERIFF

Oh, they say he was such a crass romancer ——
PEER GYNT

Romancer —?
THE SHERIFF

Yes, anything brave and fine
He could weave into something *he* must have done.
Excuse me — I have to be law-dispenser ——

(Goes.)

PEER GYNT

And where's this amazing fellow now?
AN ELDERLY MAN

Shipped out, he did — and went askew
In some foreign land where he never belonged.
Been a good many years since he was hanged.
PEER GYNT

Hanged? I see! Well, I'm not surprised.
Old Peer Gynt was himself to the last.

(Bows.)

Good-bye — and thanks for all your trouble!

(Goes a few steps, then pauses.)

You lovely ladies and gay young blades —
Could I repay you with a fable? [79]

SEVERAL VOICES

   Yes, you know one?

PEER GYNT

                I know hundreds—

      (Comes closer; a strange look passes over him.)

In San Francisco, I once panned for gold.

The town had more acrobats than it could hold.

One played the fiddle, using his toes;

Another fandangoed down on his knees;

A third one, I heard, wrote verse that he read

While a hole was bored in the top of his head.

For the acrobat fair, the devil came west

To try out his luck with all the rest.

His talent was this: he'd come on big,

Uttering grunts like an actual pig.

He was quite unknown, but he had a style.

Suspense ran high; the house was full.

He strode out in a cape cut sweepingly;

Man muss sich drapieren, as the Germans say.

But under his cape—which nobody guessed—

He had a live pig stowed up by his chest.

And now the representation began—

The devil, he pinched, and the pig struck a tune.

The work took the form of a fantasy

Of life through a pig's eye, from A to Z—

Till the grand crescendo, a slaughterhouse squeal;

Then the artist bowed low, and the curtain fell.

The critics weighed and discussed the results,

Defined the merits and labeled the faults—

Some found the vocal development scant;

The death-cry, for others, was mere technique—

But all were agreed in this: *qua* grunt,

The performer had laid it on much too thick.

So the devil got it; he had no sense,

Not to take stock of his audience.

*(Bows and departs. An uneasy silence
settles over the crowd.)*

SCENE FIVE

The eve of Pentecost.[80] *Deep in the forest. At a distance, in a
clearing, a hut with reindeer antlers over the door.* PEER GYNT,
on his hands and knees, picking wild onions.

PEER GYNT
    Here's one point of view. I hope, not the last—
    One tries all things and chooses the best.
    That's what I've done—up from Caesar
    And now almost down to Nebuchadnezzar.
    So I did have to go through Bible history—
    The old boy's back in his mother's custody.
    "Of earth thou art come,"[81] says Holy Writ—
    The main thing in life is to fill your gut.
    But fill it with onions? Much too coarse;
    I'll have to be clever and set some snares.
    Here's good brook water; I won't parch—
    And among the wild beasts, I'll have no match.
    When I come to die—as it has to be—
    I'll crawl in under a windfallen tree;
    Like a bear, I'll heap leaves over my tatters
    And carve in the bark, in ample letters:
    "Here lies Peer Gynt, a decent soul,
    Emperor of all the animals—"
    Emperor?

               (Laughs silently.)
        You prophet's false companion!
    You're no emperor; you're an onion.
    And I'm going to skin you, Peer, old top!
    No blubbering now; you can't escape.
        (Starts peeling an onion layer by layer.)

This outer layer, like a torn coat—
It's the shipwrecked man on the drifting boat.
Here's the passenger layer, thin as paint—
But the taste has a dash of the real Peer Gynt.
The prospector life was a run for the money;
The juice is gone—if it ever had any.
And now this rough-skinned layer—why,
That's the fur trader up at Hudson's Bay.
The next resembles a crown—no, thanks!
That we'll throw away—it's a jinx.
Here's the archaeologist, brief and brassy.
And here's the prophet, green and juicy.
He stinks, as the Scripture says, of lies,
Enough to bring tears to an honest man's eyes.
This layer that curls in softly together
Is the man of the world, living for pleasure.
The next looks sick. It has streaks of black—
Meaning priests—and slaves on the auction block.

> *(Pulls off several layers at once.)*

These layers just go endlessly on!
Shouldn't it give up its kernel soon?

> *(Pulls the whole onion apart.)*

Damned if it does! To the innermost filler,
It's nothing but layers—smaller and smaller—
Nature is witty!

> *(Throws the pieces away.)*
>
> To hell with brooding!

Go lost in thought, and you stumble for sure.
Well, *I* can make light of that foreboding,
Planted solid on all fours here.

> *(Scratches his neck.)*

How strange it is, this business—life,
As it's called! It has cards up its sleeve;
But try to play them, they disappear,
And you hold something else—or empty air.

(He has approached close to the hut,
catches sight of it and starts.)

That hut? On the moor—! Hm!

(Rubs his eyes.)

It's as though
This building is one that I used to know—
The reindeer horns under the gable—!
A mermaid, fish-shaped down from the navel—!
Lies! No mermaid—! Nails—slats—
Bars for shutting out goblin thoughts—!

SOLVEIG *(singing in the hut)*

Now the room's ready for Pentecost.
My dearest boy, in some far land—
    Will you come at last?
  If your burden is heavy,
    Then rest for a while—
    As I promised to be,
    I'll be waiting still.

PEER GYNT *(rises, hushed and deathly pale)*

One who remembered—and one who forgot.
One who squandered—and one who could wait—
Oh, life—! No second chance to play!
Oh, dread—! *Here's* where my empire lay!

(Runs down the forest path.)

SCENE SIX

Night. A moor with fir trees burnt out by forest fire. Charred tree trunks can be seen for miles around. Here and there patches of mist clinging to the earth. PEER GYNT *comes running.*

PEER GYNT

Ashes, fog, and dust, wind-driven—
There's enough to build with here!

Stench and rottenness within;
Only a whited sepulcher.
Dreams, romances, stillborn visions
Laid the pyramid's foundations;
Up from these a stonework rose
With the stairways made of lies.
"Spurn the truth; nothing's sacred."
Fly that from the highest banner;
Let the trump of judgment clamor:
Petrus Gyntus Caesar fecit.
　　　　　　　　(Listens.)
What sound is that, like children weeping?
Weeping halfway into song —
And by my feet, threadballs creeping — !
　　　　　　　(Kicks at them.)
Out of my way! You don't belong — !

THREADBALLS *(on the ground)*
We are thoughts;
You should have thought us —
Legs to walk on
You should have brought us!

PEER GYNT *(going around them)*
I brought life to *one*, in rags —
And it had twisted, bandy legs!

THREADBALLS
We should have soared
In a blending choir —
Instead we roll
Like threadballs here.

PEER GYNT *(stumbling)*
Threadballs! Drones, you mean — ! Stop!
You want to trip your father up?
　　　　　　　　　(Flees.)

WITHERED LEAVES *(flying before the wind)*
We are watchwords

You should have spoken!
See, while you dozed,
We were stripped and broken.
The worm has eaten us
Down to the root;
We'll never spread out
To garland fruit.

PEER GYNT

You've lived in vain, is that your fear?
Lie still; you'll make a good manure.

A SIGHING IN THE AIR

We are songs
You should have sung!
A thousand times
You bit your tongue.
Deep in your heart
We waited for you —
You never called.
We're poison now!

PEER GYNT

Then poison yourselves, right at the source!
What time did I have to waste on verse?

(Tries a shortcut.)

DEWDROPS (dripping from the branches)

We are tears
That were never shed.
Barbed ice that wounds
We could have thawed.
Now the barb is fixed
In the marrowbone;
The wound is closed;
Our strength is gone.

PEER GYNT

Thanks — I wept in the Ronde hall
And still I got it in the tail!

BROKEN STRAW
>We are deeds
>That you should have done!
>The strangler, Doubt,
>Has struck us down.
>In the crack of doom,
>We'll arrive like chaff
>And state your case—
>Till you cry, "Enough!"

PEER GYNT
>Filthy tricks! You can't believe
>I ought to be blamed for what's *negative?*[82]
>>*(Hurries away.)*

AASE'S VOICE *(far off)*
>Ai, what a driver!
>Hoo, I'm upset
>In the new-fallen snow—
>I'm chilled and wet—
>Peer, where's the castle?
>You've turned the wrong way.
>The devil misled you;
>He's guided the sleigh!

PEER GYNT
>It's time a poor fellow picks up and runs.
>If I had to carry the devil's sins,
>I'd soon be flat on the ground for sure—
>One's own are heavy enough to bear.
>>*(Runs off.)*

SCENE SEVEN

Another part of the moor.

PEER GYNT *(singing)*
>A sexton, a sexton! Where's the throng?

Open your bleating mouths and sing;
To rim your hats, a mourning band—
I've many dead to walk behind!
(*The* BUTTON-MOLDER, *with a box of tools and a large
          casting ladle, comes from a side path.*)

THE BUTTON-MOLDER

Greetings, old man!

PEER GYNT

                    Good evening, friend!

BUTTON-MOLDER

You're in a hurry. Where are you bound?

PEER GYNT

A funeral.

BUTTON-MOLDER

                Really? My eyesight's poor—
Excuse me—but is your name Peer?

PEER GYNT

I'm called Peer Gynt.

BUTTON-MOLDER

                        What a stroke of luck!
It's precisely Peer Gynt I've come to take.

PEER GYNT

To take? What for?

BUTTON-MOLDER

                    That's an easy guess.
I'm a button-molder; you go in this.

PEER GYNT

Why should I go?

BUTTON-MOLDER

                To be melted down.

PEER GYNT

Melted—?

BUTTON-MOLDER

            The ladle's empty and clean.
Your grave is dug; your coffin's made;

The worms in your body'll be well fed —
But the Master has instructed me
To bring in your soul without delay.

PEER GYNT

You can't—! Like this? Without a warning—!

BUTTON-MOLDER

It's a well-known ancient custom, concerning
Wakes and christenings, to keep the banner
Day a secret from the guest of honor.

PEER GYNT

Yes, that's so. These thoughts—they bewilder
Me. Are you—?

BUTTON-MOLDER

You heard. A button-molder.

PEER GYNT

I see! A pet child has many nicknames.
So, Peer, *that's* where you land, it seems.
But, listen, this is a rotten trick!
I know I deserve a better shake —
I'm not as bad as maybe you think —
I've done lots of good on earth; to be frank,
My offenses, at worst, have all been minor—
I could never be called a major sinner.

BUTTON-MOLDER

But, my friend, that precisely *is* your offense.
You aren't a sinner in the larger sense;
That's why you're let off the fiery griddle
And go, like the rest, in the casting ladle.

PEER GYNT

Oh, ladle or pit—what do I care?
Lager and bock are, both of them, beer.
Behind me, Satan!

BUTTON-MOLDER

You're not such an oaf
As to think I trot on a cloven hoof?

183

PEER GYNT

    Be it horse's hoof or fox's claw—
    Pack out! And mind you obey the law!

BUTTON-MOLDER

    My friend, you're making a big mistake.
    We're both in a hurry; so for clarity's sake,
    I'll explain your case as quick as I can.
    As you said yourself, you're scarcely one
    Who's made a name for exceptional sinning—
    You barely break even—

PEER GYNT

                Now you're beginning
    To talk some sense—

BUTTON-MOLDER

             Not so fast there—
    But to call you virtuous wouldn't be right—

PEER GYNT

    I never laid any claim to that.

BUTTON-MOLDER

    You're average then, just middling fair.
    A sinner in the old flamboyant style
    One meets with nowadays hardly at all.
    There's more to sin than making a mess;
    A sin calls for vigor and seriousness.

PEER GYNT

    That's true enough; you can't be a piker.
    You have to plunge in like an old berserker.[83]

BUTTON-MOLDER

    But you, my friend, you took sin lightly:

PEER GYNT

    Like a splash of mud; something unsightly.

BUTTON-MOLDER

    Now we're agreeing. The sulfur pit
    Is hardly for those who dabble in smut—

PEER GYNT

And, therefore, friend, I can go as I came?

BUTTON-MOLDER

No, therefore, friend, it's melting time.

PEER GYNT

What are these tricks you've hit upon
Back here at home while I've been gone?

BUTTON-MOLDER

The custom's as old as the serpent's creation;
It follows the laws of conservation.
You've worked at the craft—so you know how
A casting often turns out with a flaw.
Suppose, say, a button was missing a loop;
What did you do?

PEER GYNT

                          I threw it out.

BUTTON-MOLDER

Ah yes, Jon Gynt was a waster all right,
As long as his wallet was well filled up.
But the Master, you see, is thrifty, he is;
And that's why he's grown so prosperous.
He throws out nothing as unrepairable
That still can be used for raw material.
Now *you* were planned as a shining button
On the vest of the world, but your loop gave way;
So you'll have to go into the rubbish carton
And merge with the masses, as people say.

PEER GYNT

But you can't mean to melt me together now
With Tom, Dick, and Harry into something new?

BUTTON-MOLDER

Yes, so help me, it's just what I mean.
We've done it to others, time and again.
It's what they do with coins at the mint
When the image has worn away too faint.

PEER GYNT

But why be so wretched miserly!
My dear good friend, let me go free —
A loopless button, a worn-out coin —
What's that to your Master, so great a man!

BUTTON-MOLDER

Oh, as long as there's spirit in you, it'll
Lend you some value as casting metal.

PEER GYNT

No, I say! No! Tooth and nail,
I'll fight against it! I won't, that's all!

BUTTON-MOLDER

But what else? Use the brain you were given.
You're hardly buoyant enough for heaven ——

PEER GYNT

I'm easily pleased. I don't aim so high —
But I won't give one jot of myself away.
Let the old-time judgment settle my life!
Send me a while to Him with the Hoof —
Say a hundred years, if it comes to that;
I know I could manage to bear it out —
The torture is moral, so it must be gentle;
At least it could hardly be monumental.
It's a transition, as the adage goes,
And as the fox said. [84] One waits; the news
Of deliverance will come; one can pull back
And hope, in the meantime, for better luck.
But this other — simply to disappear
Like a mote in a stranger's blood, to forswear
Being Gynt for a ladle-existence, to melt —
It makes my innermost soul revolt!

BUTTON-MOLDER

But, my dear Peer, why all the fuss
Over a technical point like this?
Yourself is just what you've never been —
So what difference to you to get melted down?

PEER GYNT

    I've never been—? That's a funny thought!
    Peer Gynt's been somebody else, no doubt!
    No, button-molder, you judge in the dark.
    If you could see into me, straight to the mark,
    You'd discover then that I'm solid Peer,
    And nothing but Peer, to the very core.

BUTTON-MOLDER

    Not so. Here in my orders, you're named.
    See, where it's written: "Peer Gynt; to be claimed
    For setting his life's definition at odds;
    Consigned to the ladle as damaged goods."

PEER GYNT

    What rot! It's some other person they mean.
    Does it really say Peer? Not Rasmus or Jon?

BUTTON-MOLDER

    I melted them down a long while back.
    Come quietly now, and no more talk!

PEER GYNT

    Damned if I will! Oh, that'd be nice
    If you heard tomorrow you'd made a wrong choice.
    Better be careful, my excellent man!
    Consider the burden you're taking on——

BUTTON-MOLDER

    I have it in writing——

PEER GYNT

                    Just a little more time!

BUTTON-MOLDER

    What would you do then?

PEER GYNT

                    Get some proof
    That I've been myself all of my life—
    Since it's there that we're at odds, it would seem.

BUTTON-MOLDER

    Proof? Of what sort?

PEER GYNT

                          Statements sworn—
Witnesses—

BUTTON-MOLDER

               The Master, I fear, would decline.

PEER GYNT

Impossible! Well, sufficient unto the day—
My friend, allow me the loan of myself;
I'll come back soon. We're born only once;
And it's hard for creatures like us to dissolve.
Yes; you agree?

BUTTON-MOLDER

               All right; one chance—
But at the next crossroads, there we'll see.

                (PEER GYNT *runs off.*)

SCENE EIGHT

Farther along on the moor.

PEER GYNT *(running full tilt)*

Time is money, as the Gospel says.
If only I knew where the crossroad lies!
It could be far, or it could be near—
The earth's like a red-hot iron floor.
A witness! A witness! Wherever one is!
It looks hopeless, almost, in this wilderness.
The world's botched up. It stuns your wits
That a man has to prove his obvious rights!

       (A bent OLD MAN, *with a staff in his hand and a
          bag on his back, trudges in front of him.*)

THE OLD MAN *(stopping)*

Good sir—a few coins for a homeless man?

PEER GYNT
>Sorry — but I'm terribly short of funds.

THE OLD MAN
>Prince Peer! Ah no; so we meet again — ?

PEER GYNT
>But who — ?

THE OLD MAN
>He's forgotten his Ronde friends?

PEER GYNT
>But you can't be — ?

THE OLD MAN
>The Troll King, yes!

PEER GYNT
>The Troll King? Really? The Troll King! Speak!

TROLL KING
>Oh, but I'm miserably down on my luck — !

PEER GYNT
>Ruined?

TROLL KING
>Stripped to my very self.
>A tramp on the highway, starved as a wolf.

PEER GYNT
>Hurrah! Such witnesses don't grow on trees!

TROLL KING
>But your Lordship's also gray as a squirrel.

PEER GYNT
>Dear father-in-law, the years leave scars.
>Ah, well; let's pass over our private affairs —
>And please, above all, no family quarrels.
>I was headstrong then —

TROLL KING
>Yes; ah, yes —
>The Prince was young. And the things youth does!
>But your Lordship was wise in leaving his bride;

She'd only have brought him shame and bother;
For later, she went completely bad——

PEER GYNT

She did!

TROLL KING

It's wretched, the life she's had.
Just think—she and Trond are living together.

PEER GYNT

Trond who?

TROLL KING

Of the Valfjeld.

PEER GYNT

Oh, yes, him!
The one I took those herd girls from.

TROLL KING

But my grandson's grown up fat and strong,
With strapping children all over the land—

PEER GYNT

Yes, my dear man, but we can't talk long—
There's something quite different on my mind—
I'm caught in a rather awkward spot
Where I need a character affidavit—
You'd help me greatly if you could give it.
I'll dig up some change, and we'll down a shot——

TROLL KING

Oh, really; could I help the Prince?
Then maybe you'd give me a reference?

PEER GYNT

Gladly. It's just that I'm pinched for cash
And have to be careful more than I'd wish.
But now, here's the thing. You must recall
The night I courted your daughter well——

TROLL KING

Of course, your Lordship!

PEER GYNT

                   You can drop the title!
All right. By force, you were going to drill
My eyes and adjust my vision a little
And turn me from Peer Gynt into a troll.
But what did I do? I put up a fight—
Swore I'd stand on my own two feet;
I gave up love and power and glory
Since being myself was more necessary.
I want you to swear to that in court—

TROLL KING

    No, but I can't!

PEER GYNT

          What do you mean?

TROLL KING

    You want me to play the liar's part?
Remember, you put our troll gear on,
And tasted the mead—?

PEER GYNT

                 You set the trap;
But I never took the ultimate step.
And a man's made of just that kind of thing.
It's the final verse that makes the song.

TROLL KING

    But, Peer, it's closing quite differently.

PEER GYNT

    What rot is that?

TROLL KING

           When you went away,
You'd cut our motto in your coat of arms.

PEER GYNT

    Motto?

TROLL KING

        That shrewd and severing term.

PEER GYNT
    What term?

TROLL KING

                    The one that parts human life
    From trolldom: Troll, to yourself be enough!

PEER GYNT *(recoils a step)*
    Enough!

TROLL KING

                Since then you've lived to serve
    Our realm with every straining nerve.

PEER GYNT
    I! Peer Gynt!

TROLL KING *(weeping)*

                    It's so ungrateful!
    You've lived as a troll, secret, deceitful—
    You used the word I taught you to win
    Your place as a well-established man—
    And now you come back to me and sneer
    At the motto you ought to be thankful for.

PEER GYNT
    Enough! A hill troll! An egoist!
    It must be nonsense; I know it must!

TROLL KING *(pulls out a bundle of old newspapers)*
    Aren't you aware that we read our papers?
    Here, look; you can see it in black and red,
    How the *Bloksberg Post* accords you all proper
    Praise; and the *Heklefjeld Times*[85] has played
    Up your story from the winter you went abroad—
    Want to read them, Peer? I'll give you leave.
    Here's an article, signed by "Stallion-hoof."
    And another, "On Troll Nationalism."
    The writer demonstrates that a simple
    And natural trollish enthusiasm
    Is worth far more than horns and a tail.
    "Our *enough*," he says, "gives the mark of the troll

To man"—and you're his conclusive example.

PEER GYNT

    A hill troll? Me?

TROLL KING

                It's perfectly clear.

PEER GYNT

    I might just as well have stayed on here,
    Snug in the Ronde mountains, right?
    Spared toil and trouble and tired feet!
    Peer Gynt—a troll? You lunatic, you!
    Good-bye! Here's something to buy tobacco.

TROLL KING

    No, Prince!

PEER GYNT

            Let go! You're out of your skull,
  Or senile. Be off! Find a hospital!

TROLL KING

    Ah, just the cure for my pains and aches.
    But, as I told you, my grandson's brats
    Have been taking over hereabouts;
    And they're saying I only exist in books.
    Your relatives always treat you worst:
    I've heard that said, and I've learned it's true.
    It's hard being only a legend now—

PEER GYNT

    So many have been in that way cursed.

TROLL KING

    And we trolls, we have no pension plan,
    No mutual savings, or home relief—
    In the Ronde they'd hardly be in line.

PEER GYNT

    Thanks to that damned, "To yourself be enough"!

TROLL KING

    Oh, the Prince doesn't have any cause for complaint.
    And now, if somehow or other you could—

193

PEER GYNT

My man, you're sniffing on the wrong scent;
As it stands with me, I haven't a shred —

TROLL KING

Is it really true? His Highness, a beggar?

PEER GYNT

To the core. My princely ego spoils
In hock. It's your fault, you hellish trolls!
That shows what low company can augur.

TROLL KING

There goes another one of my hopes!
Farewell! It's not far to town, I'd judge —

PEER GYNT

What will you do there?

TROLL KING

                                    Go on the stage.
The papers are calling for national types —

PEER GYNT

Good luck on your journey. Greet them from me.
If I can break loose, I'll go the same way.
I'll write them a farce, half gall, half candy,
And call it, *"Sic transit gloria mundi."*

> (*Runs off down the road, as the* TROLL KING
> *shouts after him.*)

SCENE NINE

At a crossroads.

PEER GYNT

Now you're in for it, Peer — and then some!
The trolls' *enough* has sealed your doom.
The ship is wrecked. Cling to the spars!
Try anything; melting has to be worse!

BUTTON-MOLDER *(at the crossroads)*
　　Well, where's your affidavit, Peer?
PEER GYNT
　　Is this the crossroads? Here, so soon?
BUTTON-MOLDER
　　I can see spelled out on your face like a sign
　　How the message goes; I've read it before.
PEER GYNT
　　I'm tired of running—it does no good——
BUTTON-MOLDER
　　Yes; and besides, where does it lead?
PEER GYNT
　　True. To a forest, in the dead of night——
BUTTON-MOLDER
　　But there's an old tramp. Shall we have him wait?
PEER GYNT
　　No, let him go. He's been drinking, man!
BUTTON-MOLDER
　　But perhaps——
PEER GYNT
　　　　　　　　　Shh; no—leave him alone!
BUTTON-MOLDER
　　Then, shall we start?
PEER GYNT
　　　　　　　　　　　One question only.
　　What is it, "to be yourself," in truth?
BUTTON-MOLDER
　　A curious question out of the mouth
　　Of someone who recently——
PEER GYNT
　　　　　　　　　　　　Answer me plainly.
BUTTON-MOLDER
　　To be yourself is to slay yourself.[86]
　　But on you, that answer's sure to fail;

So let's say: to make your life evolve
From the Master's meaning to the last detail.

PEER GYNT

But suppose a man never gets to know
What the Master meant with him?

BUTTON-MOLDER

He must use intuition.

PEER GYNT

Intuitions can often be wrong and draw
A man *ad undas* in his profession.

BUTTON-MOLDER

Of course, Peer Gynt; but closing them out
Gives Him with the Hoof the choicest bait.

PEER GYNT

This affair is complicated at best—
All right; that I've been myself, I'll waive—
It's maybe too difficult to prove.
I'll accept that part of the case as lost.
But just now, walking the dew and drench,
I felt the shoes of my conscience pinch,
And I said to myself: yes, you have sins—

BUTTON-MOLDER

You're not going to start all over again—

PEER GYNT

No, not at all; great ones, I mean.
Not only in deeds, but thoughts and plans.
Abroad, I lived in dissipation—

BUTTON-MOLDER

Perhaps; but I have to see the list.

PEER GYNT

Well, give me time; I'll find a priest,
Confess, and bring you a declaration.

BUTTON-MOLDER

Yes, bring me that, and I can promise
You won't have the casting ladle to face.

But my orders, Peer —

PEER GYNT

That paper's old;
I'm sure it's already obsolete —
I played the prophet and trusted in Fate.
Well, may I try?

BUTTON-MOLDER

But — !

PEER GYNT

My dear, good man —
You can't have so much that needs to be done.
Here in this district, the air's so sweet,
It makes the people age more slowly.
You know what the Justedal pastor[87] wrote:
"It's rare that anyone dies in this valley."

BUTTON-MOLDER

To the next crossroads; not a step beyond.

PEER GYNT

A priest, if he has to be tied and bound!

(Runs off.)

SCENE TEN

A hillside with heather, and a path winding over the ridge.

PEER GYNT

"This could be useful for many a thing,"
Said Espen, finding the magpie's wing.[88]
Who would have thought the sins I've done
Would save me when the night came on.
Well, it's a ticklish matter, I'm sure,
To go from the frying pan into the fire —
Still there's a precept you can't escape —
Namely, that as long as there's life, there's hope.

(A LEAN PERSON, *dressed in a priest's cassock kilted up*
high and carrying a fowling net over his shoulder, comes
hurrying along the slope.)

Who's that? A priest with a fowling net!
Hi! I'm Fortune's child, all right!
Good evening, Pastor! This path is foul——

THE LEAN ONE

It is; the things one does for a soul.

PEER GYNT

Ah, someone's soon for heaven?

THE LEAN ONE

                        No;
There's another route I hope he'll go.

PEER GYNT

Could I walk with you, Pastor, a little way?

THE LEAN ONE

With pleasure; I'm fond of company.

PEER GYNT

I'm quite disturbed—

THE LEAN ONE

               Heraus! Explain!

PEER GYNT

You see here before you a decent man.
I've always obeyed our country's laws;
Never been booked in a station house—
But a man can sometimes lose his foothold
And stumble——

THE LEAN ONE

            Yes, even the best have failed.

PEER GYNT

You know, small things——

THE LEAN ONE

            Just trifles?

PEER GYNT

                   Yes;

When it comes to sinning in bulk, I pass.

THE LEAN ONE

Then, my dear man, find someone else;
I'm not what you seem to think I am —
You stare at my fingers; What about them?

PEER GYNT

You have such developed fingernails.

THE LEAN ONE

And now at my feet? Do you disapprove?

PEER GYNT *(pointing)*

Is that hoof natural?[89]

THE LEAN ONE

So I believe.

PEER GYNT *(raising his hat)*

I could have sworn that you were a priest;
And now I've the honor — Well, all for the best.
When the front door's open, avoid the back way;
When the king appears, bid the help good-by.

THE LEAN ONE

Shake hands! You seem unprejudiced.
Well, friend, what can I do to assist?
Now please, don't ask for money or power;
I haven't got them to give any more.
It's shameful how business has fallen off;
There's not enough market to feed a dwarf —
Souls aren't moving; just now and again,
A stray —

PEER GYNT

Has the race advanced so far?

THE LEAN ONE

On the contrary; no, it's slipping lower.
The majority end in a melting spoon.

PEER GYNT

Oh yes — I heard about that one time.
In fact, it's the reason why I've come.

THE LEAN ONE
  Speak out!
PEER GYNT
                  If it wouldn't be immodest,
  I'd be so glad —
THE LEAN ONE
                        For a lodging place?
PEER GYNT
  You guessed what I need exactly, yes.
  Business, you say, is declining fast;
  So maybe you might relax a rule —
THE LEAN ONE
  But, friend —
PEER GYNT
                    My demands are very small.
  A salary is hardly necessary;
  Just pleasant companions, if that's the story —
THE LEAN ONE
  A heated room?
PEER GYNT
                      Not *overly* warmed —
  Mainly the chance to leave unharmed —
  The right, as they say, to transfer out
  If a better position comes to light.
THE LEAN ONE
  This makes me truly sorry, friend —
  But you can't imagine how many requests
  Of a similar type I've heard expressed
  By those departing their mortal round.
PEER GYNT
  But when I think over my former life,
  I know that I'm highly qualified —
THE LEAN ONE
  They were only trifles —

PEER GYNT
That's what I said;
But now I remember, I traded in slaves —

THE LEAN ONE
There are men who've traded in minds and wills,
But done it badly, and lost their appeals.

PEER GYNT
I've packed out idols to the Orient.

THE LEAN ONE
Mere quibbles! Pure divertissement.
People pack idols of a viler sort
Into sermons, literature, and art —
And they stay outside —

PEER GYNT
But the worst of it
You couldn't guess — I played a prophet!

THE LEAN ONE
Abroad? Humbug! The end of most subtle
Sehen ins Blaue is the casting ladle.
If that's all you have to support your case,
With the best good will, I'll have to refuse.

PEER GYNT
But wait; in a shipwreck — I clung to a boat —
"Drowning men clutch at straws" — there's proof;
And, "It's every man for himself" — I quote —
Well, I halfway robbed a cook of his life.

THE LEAN ONE
I couldn't care if you'd half-robbed a pretty
Kitchenmaid of her virginity.
What kind of stuff is this "halfway" talk?
Begging your pardon, but I wish you'd tell
Me who's going to waste expensive fuel,
In times likes these, on such poppycock?
Now don't get mad; it's your sins I'm attacking,
Not you; forgive this bold way of speaking.

Listen, my friend, don't be absurd;
Resign yourself to the melting spoon.
What would you gain by my bed and board?
Consider; you're a sensible man.
Well, you'd have memory, that's for certain—
But in the country of memory, the scene
Would offer both your mind and your brain,
As the Swedes would put it, "Mighty poor sport."
You'd have nothing to rouse a moan or a laugh;
Nothing to fill you with joy or grief;
Nothing to make you run cold or hot;[90]
Just barely enough to irritate.

PEER GYNT

As they say: it isn't that easy to know
Where the shoe hurts when it's not on you.

THE LEAN ONE

That's the truth. Thanks to so-and-so
I've no need for more than a single shoe.
But it's fortunate one of us brought up shoes;
It reminds me I have to be hurrying on—
I'm fetching a roast that's far from lean;
And I can't stand around, shooting the breeze —

PEER GYNT

May I ask what fodder of sin you used
To fatten the man?

THE LEAN ONE

I was advised
That he'd been himself in every respect;
And that, after all, is the crucial fact.

PEER GYNT

Himself! Tell me, is *that* group yours?

THE LEAN ONE

It depends. Some find their way in downstairs.
Remember, there are two ways that a man
Is himself; two sides, right and wrong, to a coat.
You know they've discovered in Paris of late

How to make portraits by means of the sun.
The picture comes either direct and alive,
Or else in the form of a negative.
In the latter the lights and shadows reverse;
The casual eye will find it coarse—
But the likeness is there for all of that,
And it only remains to bring it out.
Now if, in the path of its life, a soul
Records itself in the negative way,
The plate doesn't go in the rubbish pile—
Rather, it's simply turned over to me.
I take it and treat it in suitable fashion
And gradually work a transformation.
I steam and I dip, I burn and rinse
With sulfur and other ingredients,
Till it has the image it ought to have—
Or as people call it, the positive.
But with someone like you that's half erased,
Sulfur and lye just go to waste.

PEER GYNT

So one has to come to you black as a crow
To become a white grouse? May I ask you now
What name is under this negative portrait
That you're going to change to the positive state?

THE LEAN ONE

The name's Peter Gynt.

PEER GYNT

Peter Gynt? Ah, yes!

Is he himself?

THE LEAN ONE

He swears that he is.

PEER GYNT

Well, he can be trusted, this same Herr Peter.

THE LEAN ONE

You know him perhaps?

PEER GYNT

                              Oh, just a smatter —
    One knows so many ——
THE LEAN ONE

                              I've got to skip;
    Where'd you see him last?
PEER GYNT

                              Down by the Cape.

THE LEAN ONE
    Di buona speranza?
PEER GYNT

                              Yes, but I'd guess
    He'd be sailing soon, if I'm not amiss.
THE LEAN ONE
    Then I'd better be heading down there quick.
    If I only can catch him now in a hurry!
    That Cape of Good Hope, it makes me sick —
    It's been ruined by Stavanger[91] missionaries.
                    (Rushes off southwards.)

PEER GYNT
    The stupid dog! There he's racing off
    With his tongue hanging out. That's a laugh.
    What a pleasure it is to fool such an ass
    With his precious airs and his solemn face!
    He thinks he has something to swagger about!
    His job's not likely to make him fat —
    He'll fall from his perch, with all that's his.
    Hm! I'm not that secure in *my* own nest,
    Expelled, as it were, from the *self*-possessed.
            (A falling star is seen. He nods after it.)
    Here's from Peer Gynt, Brother Shooting-Star!
    Shine, flash down, and disappear —
    *(Pulls himself together apprehensively and goes deeper
        into the mists; silence for a moment; then he cries:)*

Is there no one, no one to hear me even—
No one in darkness, no one in heaven—!
*(Re-emerges farther down, throws his hat on the path and
tears at his hair. Gradually a stillness comes over him.)*
So unspeakably poor, then, a soul can go
Back to nothingness, in the misty gray.
You beautiful earth, don't be annoyed
That I've left no sign I walked your grass.
You beautiful sun, in vain you've shed
Your glorious light on an empty house.
There was no one within to cheer and warm—
The owner, they tell me, was never at home.
Beautiful sun and beautiful earth,
All you gave to my mother went to beg.
Nature is lavish; the spirit is mean.
How costly to pay with your life for your birth!
I want to climb up on the highest crag
And see the sunrise once again
And stare myself blind at the promised land;
Then let me be covered by drifting snows;
Scratch on a rock, "Here No One lies."
And afterwards—then—! Ah, never mind.

CHURCHGOERS *(singing on the forest path)*
O blessed morn,
When the tongues of God
Struck the earth like flaming steel!
From the earth reborn
Now the sons of God
Raise songs to praise His will.

PEER GYNT *(shrinking in fright)*
Don't look! It's desert there inside—
I fear I was dead long before I died.

*(Tries to creep into the bushes, but stumbles out
onto the crossroads.)*

BUTTON-MOLDER

Good morning, Peer! Where's your list of sins?

PEER GYNT

Don't you think I've been turning stones
For all I'm worth?

BUTTON-MOLDER

You met no one here?

PEER GYNT

Only a traveling photographer.

BUTTON-MOLDER

Well, your time is up.

PEER GYNT

Everything's up.
The owl smells a rat. He hoots in his sleep.

BUTTON-MOLDER

That's the matin's bell —

PEER GYNT *(pointing)*

What's that shining?

BUTTON-MOLDER

Just light in a hut.

PEER GYNT

That sound growing louder?

BUTTON-MOLDER

Just a woman's song.

PEER GYNT

Yes, *there's* the meaning
To all my sins.

BUTTON-MOLDER *(seizing him)*

Put your house in order![92]

*(They have come out of the wood and
stand near the hut.)*

PEER GYNT

Put my house in order? That's it! Go on!
Pack out! If your ladle was big as a chest —
It still couldn't hold both me and my list!

BUTTON-MOLDER

>To the third crossroads, Peer; but *then* — !
>>*(Turns aside and goes.)*

PEER GYNT *(approaching the hut)*

>Forward and back, it's just as far.
>Out or in, it's a narrow door.
>>*(Stops.)*
>No! Like an endless, wild lament,
>It tells me: return, go in where you went.
>>*(Takes several steps, but stops again.)*
>Roundabout, said the Boyg!
>>*(Hears singing in the hut.)*
>>>No! This time
>Straight through, no matter how steep the climb!
>*(He runs toward the hut. At the same moment,* SOLVEIG
>*appears in the doorway, dressed for church, with a hymn-*
>*book wrapped in a kerchief and a staff in her hand. She*
>*stands there, erect and mild.* PEER GYNT *throws himself*
>>*down on the threshold.)*
>Lay judgment on a sinner's head!

SOLVEIG

>It's him! It's him! Praise be to God!
>>*(Gropes toward him.)*

PEER GYNT

>Cry out how sinfully I've gone astray!

SOLVEIG

>You've sinned in nothing, my only boy!
>>*(Groping again and finding him.)*

BUTTON-MOLDER *(behind the hut)*

>The list, Peer Gynt?

PEER GYNT

>>Cry out my wrongs!

SOLVEIG *(sitting down beside him)*

>You've made my whole life a beautiful song.

    Bless you now that you've come at last!
    And bless our meeting this Pentecost!

PEER GYNT

    So then I'm lost!

SOLVEIG

                That's for One to settle.

PEER GYNT *(with a laugh)*

    Lost! Unless you can solve a riddle!

SOLVEIG

    Ask me.

PEER GYNT

           Ask you? Yes! Tell me where
    Peer Gynt has been this many a year?

SOLVEIG

    Been?

PEER GYNT

        With his destiny on him, just
    As when he first sprang from the mind of God!
    Can you tell me that? If not, I'm afraid
    I'll go down forever in the land of mist.[93]

SOLVEIG *(smiling)*

    O that riddle's easy.

PEER GYNT

              What reply can you give!
    Where have I been myself, whole and true?
    Where have I been, with God's mark on my brow?

SOLVEIG

    In my faith, in my hope, and in my love.

PEER GYNT *(starting back)*

    What are you saying—? Don't play with words!
    To the boy inside you're mother and nurse.

SOLVEIG

    I am, yes—but who is his father?
    It's He who grants the prayers of the mother.

PEER GYNT *(a light breaks over him; he cries out:)*
  My mother; my wife! You innocent woman—!
  O, hide me, hide me within![94]
        (Clings to her, covering his face in her lap.
        A long silence. The sun rises.)[95]
SOLVEIG *(singing softly)*
  Sleep, my dear, my dearest boy,
  Here in my arms! I'll watch over thee——

  The boy has sat on his mother's lap.
  In play, they've used their life's day up.

  The boy's been safe at his mother's breast
  His whole life's day. May his life be blessed!

  The boy has lain so near to my heart
  His whole life's day. Now he's tired out.

  Sleep, my dear, my dearest boy,
  Here in my arms! I'll watch over thee!

BUTTON-MOLDER'S VOICE *(from behind the hut)*
  We'll meet at the final crossroads, Peer;
  And *then* we'll see——I won't say more.
SOLVEIG *(her voice rising in the early light)*
  Sleep in my arms; I'll watch over thee—
  Sleep and dream, my dearest boy!

NOTES

NOTES

With proper names and place-names, I have followed as far as possible the spellings of Ibsen's nineteenth-century Dano-Norwegian, rather than the later revisions of the language reformers he regarded with such suspicious concern. In a few cases I have made or kept transliterations where euphony in English or precedents of usage seemed to recommend them: Boyg, for instance, for Bøyg in the original.

For a number of other instances, in which the original forms have been retained, some guide to Norwegian pronunciation might be useful. The phoneme *aa* (the modern *å* recommended by the Nordic Orthographic Congress, Stockholm, 1869, to which Ibsen was a delegate) is sounded like the *aw* in "flaw"; and the final *e* is pronounced: thus *Aase* is "AW-suh." The double *ee* has the *ai* sound in "chair"; and *y* is equivalent to German *ü*: thus *Peer Gynt* is "PAIR GÜNT." The *a* has its full sound as in "fall"; and *j* is pronounced as *y*: thus *Valfjeld* is "VOL-f(yell)d." *Ei* has the sound of *ay* in "play"; final *g* is mute: thus *Solveig* is "SOHL-vay." Among the vowels, *i* is pronounced *ee* (*Kari*, "KAHR-ee"), and *ø* has the sound of German *ö*. As in Danish, the letter *d* within a word is often not pronounced: *Mads Moen* is "MAHSS MOAN." The above are only approximations, but they should allow an actor or reader to find intonations that have some flavor of the original.

1. *Gjendin ridge:* A precipitous mountain edge between Lake Bygdin and Lake Gjendin in Jotunheimen, Norway.

2. *Where are the snows of yesteryear:* This expression, though originating in Villon's *"Où sont les neiges d'antan?"* had become assimilated in Norwegian and Danish.

3. *loafing in the chimney-corner home:* The hero of Norse fairy tales from at least as far back as the Middle Ages is the Askeladd, the male counterpart of Cinderella. Usually the youngest of three brothers, he holds the most menial position in the household and is assumed to be lazy, stupid, and incompetent. When he escapes from the narrow and humiliating conditions at home, however, he proves that, without difficulty, he can master any task set before him. He vanquishes trolls, confounds the king, and wins the princess and half the kingdom. Aase's denunciation is in part her hope that Peer will live out the Askeladd's destiny.

4. *Lunde:* A common name for a farm throughout Norway; so probably a large farm, consisting of as many as twenty-five to thirty buildings, virtually on the scale of a small village.

5. *changeling:* An ugly, malformed, or imbecilic child, thought to be the offspring of gnomes or evil spirits and substituted by them for a normal human child. One way that the mother could recover her own was to beat the changeling soundly, whereupon it would vanish through the air and the true child would reappear in the cradle.

6. *Engelland:* An old form, found in ballads and nursery rhymes, for England. Logeman observes that the name connotes the country of angels (Engel-land), suggesting that it must be taken as a vague, cloud-borne realm of chivalry and high romance.

7. *the halling:* The most acrobatic of the Norwegian folk dances, performed only by men, who dance alone, frequently to show off their agility before a girl.

8. *Master of Ceremonies:* Literally, the chief cook, but in function a kind of master of ceremonies at a country wedding feast.

9. *It's high to this ceiling:* In the halling, it is considered a great feat for the dancer to kick the rafters. Here, in the open air, the young man is saying, his leaps will be even more spectacular.

10. *Hedal:* Near the Sperillen lake in Valdres.

11. *the kerchief she carried her prayer book in:* Peasant women had the custom, when going to church, of carrying their hymnbooks wrapped in their kerchiefs. Solveig's parents thus show their expectation that the wedding will be a solemn and religious one.

12. *I'm just confirmed:* About fifteen or sixteen years old.

13. *The soul of piety:* Solveig's father belongs to a sect of pietists, possibly that begun in the early nineteenth century by H. N. Hauge, whose followers were known as "the awakened ones"; therefore he would regard most forms of pleasure as sinful and to be avoided.

14. *draug:* "an apparition of a headless man (often in a half-boat), which appears to somebody destined to die soon, especially by drowning." Haugen, *Norwegian-English Dictionary.* Exactly how a headless apparition screams is a fine point for pneumatologists; but Aase, in her distraction, is clearly beyond such considerations.

15. *Three Herd Girls:* Literally, three *seter* girls, the *seter* being the alpine meadows where the cattle were driven to pasture for the summer months, watched over by dairy maids, who lived an isolated life in the outfarms, or *seter*-huts.

16. *a three-headed troll:* Trolls came not only in the two- and three-headed varieties, but also with four, five, six, eight, nine, and twelve heads. But these hardly bore comparison with the

Devil's grandmother, who, according to report, had three hundred.

17. *We won't have a bed lying empty now:* "Now," in the original, reads "this Saturday night." On Saturday evening, when the week's farmwork was done, the unmarried girls would retire, usually to the *stabbur* or storehouse, and the young men would meet them in bed, although decorum dictated that the strict rules of bundling must be observed. This was often the only way for young people to get to know one another, since it was considered effeminate for a young man openly to seek a girl's company.

18. *The Ronde Mountains:* A mountain group on the southeastern edge of the Dovre range.

19. *A Woman in Green:* Cf. Asbjørnsen, "Reindeer Hunt at Ronde," in which a hunter named Klomsrud falls in with fourteen green-clad women, green because they belong to the race of the *underjordiske*, those who live under the green sod and are thought to incorporate the souls of the dead.

20. *drawing his finger across his throat:* Probably with the implication of Polonius (*Hamlet*, II, 2), who points to his head and shoulders, saying, "Take this from this, if this be otherwise."

21. *The Royal Hall of the King of the Dovre Mountains:* Much of the basic material for this scene has been freely adapted from H. C. Andersen's charming tale, "Elf Hill" ("Elverhøj").

22. *Same as with us:* cf. Holberg, *Ulysses von Ithacia*, II, 2. Ulysses' servant Chilian, encountering a Trojan, questions him about life on the other side of the lines and, to every disclosure of folly and corruption, can rightly reply, with a score

of minor variations of the phrase, "Same as with us." Ibsen puts the quotation to ironic use: Whereas Chilian realistically perceives the universality of human nature everywhere and thus the supreme folly of misunderstanding and war, Peer is spiritually blind to the very real difference between the complacent self-satisfaction of the trolls and the striving toward self-realization of the truly human being.

23. *to yourself be—enough:* Herman Weigand finds the conceptual equivalent of this phrase in Augustine's *De Civitate Dei*, Book XIV, Ch. 13. In discussing the fall of man, Augustine states that man's fundamental sin consists in *"sibi sufficere,"* i.e., falling away from God, the source of all being. *"Sibi sufficere,"* Weigand suggests, may have filtered down to the theological language of Ibsen's time in sermons or the catechism, to be exactly rendered, then, in the phrasing of the troll's motto.

24. *Our simple, domestic way of life:* "Under the figure of the trolls, the party in Norway which demands commercial isolation and monopoly for home products is most acutely satirized." Edmund Gosse, *Northern Studies.*

25. *food and drink:* The act of eating or joining with others in a common meal has a sacramental and binding character in many myths and rituals, e.g., the seven pomegranate seeds that condemned Persephone to three months each year in the Underworld.

26. *our tails:* Trolls are most easily recognized by their tails, which link them both to prehuman existence and to the family and domain of Satan. The outward symbol of certain inward traits, the tail falls off of itself when the *huldre* (literally, one of the "hidden people," from Germanic *haljō,* "concealed place," whence also Old Norse *Hel,* "the underworld"),

through marriage with a human being, is consecrated by the priest.

27. *Blackfrock's cows:* A reference to the cassock of the priest. The trolls identify the church bells, which they cannot abide, with cow bells.

28. *King Saul killed hundreds:* Cf. *I Samuel* 18:7. "Saul has slain his thousands, And David his ten thousands." Peer might be identifying with David in another context as well, casting the Boyg as his Goliath.

29. *The Great Boyg:* The enigma of this symbolic presence has called forth a wide spectrum of interpretations. In Asbjørnsen's original folk tale, it is an invisible, apparently enormous troll. The word *bøyg* is related to the German *beugen*: to curve, meander, bend. Thus, some have identified the Boyg with the Midgardsorm of the Eddas, the world serpent coiled, like Okeanos, about the earth. Others have suggested that this voice speaking out of the darkness may be taken to be a voice out of the depth of Peer's own being. Groddeck describes it as "the self, the objective self, the opposite to the ego." On this point, as with everything else in the poem, readers had best follow the Button-molder's advice and subordinate the commentators to what, intuitively, they feel is meaningful to them.

30. *the wingbeats of great birds:* Probably the sound of witches in flight, cf. Asbjørnsen, "Tales of a Sexton." Or possibly, the spirits of the dead, which also are often reincarnated in birds (cf. *New Golden Bough*, II: "Taboo and the Perils of the Soul," 151, and Add. Note). When the saga hero Sigurd killed the dragon Fafnir and tasted his heart's blood, he acquired a knowledge of the language of birds. But Peer, already partly in the trolls' power, by closing out the hero's mission he was born for, makes the birds his enemies.

31. *Soria-Moria Castle:* The name "Soria-Moria" comes from the Arabic and refers to a group of small islands outside the Red Sea which the Arabs believe to be the Isles of the Blessed.

32. *Grane:* The legendary horse belonging to Sigurd Fafnirs-bane.

33. *Mr. Cotton:* In his poem "Abraham Lincoln's Death" Ibsen designates John Bull as "the cotton magnate." And elsewhere, in an early piece of drama criticism, he comments on "a complete Englishman, who is willing enough to help his friend, but by no means loses sight of his cotton interests."

34. *Ballon:* The surname "balloon" evokes the airiness of French politesse, with possibly an allusion to vacillating policies of the Emperor Napoleon III.

35. *Eberkopf:* In German, "boar's head," an image suggesting recent Prussian aggressions against Austria and Denmark.

36. *Trumpeterstraale:* Literally, "trumpet blast," a barbed thrust at Swedish nonintervention in the Prusso-Danish War.

37. *world-historical-fellowship:* In the original, *verdenborger-domsforpagtning*—a far-fetched example of German agglutinated words.

38. *if you won the earth entire, and lost your self:* Cf. *Luke* 9:25; *Matthew* 16:26; *Mark* 8:36.

39. *Lippe-Detmold:* A small Westphalian principality, later incorporated in 1870 in the German Empire.

40. *Charles the Twelfth:* The Swedish warrior-king (1682-1718) who led campaigns against Denmark, Norway, Poland, Russia, and Turkey.

41. *Bender:* The town in which Charles XII is said to have torn the caftan of the Turkish vizier with his spurs for betraying his ambitions by concluding a truce with Russia.

42. *Goddam:* Ibsen inserts this old form of the oath, in English, in his Norwegian text. As far back as the fifteenth century, Joan of Arc had called the English soldiers in France "the Goddams" for their effusive swearing.

43. *Castalia:* Not a stream, but the celebrated fountain sacred in antiquity to Apollo and the Muses. It is situated on Mount Parnassus, not Olympus, as Cotton seems to believe.

44. *Morning and evening are not alike:* Probably an allusion to *Psalms* 90:6, although there is also a recall of the Troll King's words in Act Two.

45. *Bus and I, why, we're relatives:* Darwin's theories had been introduced into Norway by way of thorough and intelligent expositions appearing in the magazine *Budstikken* for February and March, 1861.

46. *Bornu:* A region in the Sudan, south of the desert.

47. *Habes:* Or Habesch, the Arabic word for Abyssinia.

48. *Gyntiana:* In 1852, Ole Bull, the celebrated violinist, had founded a Norwegian colony in America, modeled after those of the French socialists, which he named "Oleana." The name and the fantastic claims advanced by the founder—here echoed by Peer—survive today in the well-known folk song.

49. *The ass in the ark:* Probably alludes to a venerable conundrum: Q. What ass brayed so loud that everyone in the world could hear it? A. The ass on Noah's ark.

50. *My kingdom . . . for a horse:* Cf. Shakespeare, *Richard III*, V, 4.

51. *Ab esse ad posse:* The axiom in logic, *ab esse ad posse valet, ab posse ad esse non valet consequentia.* It is permissible to argue from fact to possibility, but not the reverse.

52. *Kaaba:* A small, cubical building in the court of the Great Mosque in Mecca, which contains the famous Black Stone, believed to have been given the prophet Abraham by the angel Gabriel.

53. *What did I ever want in that crew:* Cf. Molière, *Les Fourberies de Scapin*, II, 11, "*Que diable allait-il faire dans cette galère?*" Ibsen had staged *Scapins skalkestykker* at Det Norske Theater in Christiania in March, 1859.

54. *Das Ewig-Weibliche zieht uns an:* An intentional misquotation of the concluding lines of *Faust:* "*Das Ewig-Weibliche zieht uns hinan.*" Goethe's "The Eternal Feminine draws us upward," filtered through the Gyntian soul, becomes "The Eternal Feminine lures us on."

Ibsen's series of pointed references to Shakespeare, Molière, Holberg, and Goethe may be taken both as an *hommage* to his great predecessors, their influence and inspiration, and as a discreet bid to be considered in their company.

55. *I knew a fellow just like that:* Frances Bull makes the interesting suggestion about this otherwise obscure passage that the soul-inflated man who lost his meaning, spouting rant, was Brand. If so, Peer sees his antithesis through a degree of self-projection.

56. *do you know what it means to live:* Peer's reply to his rhetorical question should be compared with Ibsen's own

answer, phrased in a famous quatrain:

> What is life—but to fight
> In heart and mind with trolls?
> And poetry? That's to write
> The last judgment of our souls.

57. *Becker:* K. F. Becker's *Weltgeschichte*, a popular textbook published 1801-1809, and translated into Danish in 1851.

58. *The statue of Memnon:* Memnon was the son of the dawn, king of the Ethiopians, and lived in the extreme east, on the shore of Ocean. He and his warriors fought for Troy, where he was slain by Achilles. On his death, his mother Eos (Dawn) begged Zeus to grant him honor and immortality. Zeus did so by turning the sparks of his funeral pyre into birds, which rose, divided into two flocks, and fought until they turned back into ashes. Every year the battle of these birds, called Memnonides, is re-enacted. The enormous stone seated figure by the Nile at Thebes is said to give forth a sound like the breaking of a lyre string each morning at sunrise, which supposedly is Memnon greeting Eos. Ovid relates the story in Book 13 of the *Metamorphoses*.

The owl of wisdom was the emblem of the University of Christiania; so that, in the midst of Peer's historical phase, in a land burdened by a dead past, Ibsen would seem to be accusing the academics in his own country of doting on the dead past, rather than perpetuating and renewing their culture through song (poetry) and struggle (healthy controversy).

59. *Music . . . of the past:* An allusion to the *Zukunftsmusik* of Richard Wagner, whose book, *The Art Work of the Future*, had appeared in 1849.

60. *threescore and ten Interpreters:* The authors of the Greek version of the New Testament known as the Septuagint.

No satisfactory explanation has been offered for the 160 more.

61. *An insane asylum:* Ibsen follows the tradition of Dante in the Inferno of *The Divine Comedy* and Goethe in the Walpurgisnacht scenes of *Faust*, by elaborating a symbolic setting that will fitly contain, characterize, and condemn the definitive evils of the time. The dawning age of a deranged future over which Peer Gynt is to reign would appear to be a complete and self-centered transvaluation of values of the sort that the later Ibsen was often, if falsely, accused of abetting.

62. *my countryman Munchausen's fox:* Cf. Ch. 2, *The Adventures of Baron Munchausen*. The Baron, out hunting in a Russian forest, encounters a black fox whose skin is too fine to spoil by gunshot. He skewers the fox's tail to a tree with a spike nail, and flogs him with his whip till he leaps out of his skin.

63. *Huhu:* A caricature of the *Maalstrevere*, the ultranationalist group of language reformers, and particularly, Logeman notes, an attack on A. O. Vinje. As a result of Ivar Aasen's publications, beginning in 1848, demonstrating the continuity of local Norwegian dialects with Old Norse, and led by him and Vinje, the *maalstrevere* faction agitated against Dano-Norwegian in favor of return to the old language, the *Landsmål* which Aasen codified, eventually renamed *Nynorsk* or "New Norwegian" in 1929. *Foreign sirens* refers to the cultural domination of the Danes, who had ruled the country from the end of the fourteenth to the beginning of the nineteenth centuries. The *orangoutangs* are the Norse vikings, whose "growls and grunts" must be fostered in the latter-day, peasant Malabaris.

64. *a Fellah carrying a mummy on his back:* A satire on the cult of the heroic Charles XII among the Swedes, who had

proved themselves like their venerated "royal mummy," during the events in 1864, only in the lifelessness of their responses.

Of more general importance here is the fact that Ibsen is showing two forms of the self-preoccupied withdrawal from and distortion of reality that arises out of living in and for an irrecoverable past, first as it affects words, then as it affects deeds.

65. *In the likeness of a bull:* The sacred bull worshiped in Ptolemaic times as the earthly incarnation of the Egyptian god of the underworld, Serapis (Osiris-Apis).

66. *Hussein, a cabinet minister:* An allusion to the Swedish Foreign Secretary, Count Manderström, who had thought to deter Prussian aggression with a flurry of diplomatic notes. F. L. Lucas aptly compares him to Neville Chamberlain.

67. *Hallingskarv, Jøkel:* A mountain and a glacier, respectively, in the Hardanger district, along which the ship is coasting.

68. *Folgefonnen:* An immense glacier between the Hardanger Fjord and its branch, the Sør Fjord.

69. *Blaahø:* Literally, in Norwegian dialect, "bluetop," the name of several peaks in Jotunheim.

70. *Galdhøpiggen:* The highest mountain (8097 ft.) in Scandinavia, near the end of the Sogne Fjord in Jotunheim.

71. *Haarteigen:* A mountain east of Odda in Hardanger.

72. *Far between and long away:* In 1886, Ibsen wrote to a German friend: ". . . he who would know me fully must know Norway. The grand but austere nature with which

people are surrounded in the North, the lonely, isolated life —
their homes often lie many miles apart — compel them to be in-
different to other people and to care only about their own
concerns; therefore they become ruminative and serious-
minded; they ponder and doubt; and they often despair. With
us every other man is a philosopher. Then there are the long
dark winters, with the thick fog about the houses — oh, they
long for the sun!"

73. *A conscience at ease is a downy pillow:* The proverb
appears both in Norwegian and German: *Ein gutes Gewissen
ist ein sanftes Ruhekissen.*

74. *The Strange Passenger:* This personification of Peer's
destiny as guide has been variously interpreted — as Peer's
double, as an emissary from the supernatural world, as the
Devil, as Lord Byron, and as a projection of Kierkegaardian
dread.

75. *mayor:* i.e., *lensmann,* rural mayor (Brynildsen, *Norsk-
Engelsk Ordbok*), that is, the chief civil authority in a district.
The titles of functionaries, being intrinsically bound up with
the particular social system of a country, are the translator's
despair.

76. *Glittertind:* A peak almost as high as its close neighbor,
Galdhøpiggen. Its summit is covered by a snow mantle nearly
one hundred feet thick.

77. *Now there's only the rubbish here:* In this scene, relationships that have developed during Peer's long absence are
made to surface and disappear in such obscurity that some explanation seems called for. Both Hegstad and Ingrid have
apparently gone downhill since Peer's bride-rape. Aslak (The
Man in Mourning) has married her; he shows, however, no
great love for her, perhaps because her ways have become too

225

free and easy even for him, though Mads Moen (The Man in Gray) observes that Aslak has never been overly delicate. Their conversation degenerates into a coarse joke that Ingrid may yet cheat Death: i.e., Death has been the last of her several lovers. Considering the time lapse, the boy is hardly Peer's child, as some have conjectured, but Aslak's or, perhaps, Mads Moen's.

78. *A rotten egg:* In the original, a wind egg, i.e., one which has lost power of development and become putrid.

79. *a fable:* Peer's adventure in San Francisco is adapted directly out of Phaedrus, *Fabulae*, V, 5, "Scurra et Rusticus." In the original fable, after the buffoon has won the prize for the realism of his grunts, the countryman produces the real pig from under his cloak, rebuking his audience with the words: "Look, this shows what sort of judges you are."

80. *The eve of Pentecost:* The feast of Pentecost, being the ceremony of the descent of the Spirit, is central to the emphases Ibsen wishes to develop, as against the more familiar and orthodox Christian Easter symbolism in such works as *The Divine Comedy* and *Faust*.

81. *Of earth thou art come:* Cf. *Genesis* 3:19 (or *Eccles.* 12:7), characteristically misquoted by Peer.

82. *What's negative:* A play upon Hegelian terminology, in which "the negative"—that which opposes the primary thesis —creates the opportunity in turn for the higher concept, the synthesis.

83. *an old berserker:* One of a class of legendary warriors, who, in battle, fought in a frenzied rage, howled, bit their shields, foamed at the mouth, and were generally thought

invulnerable. Peer briefly imitates their spirit in the Boyg scene when he bites his own arm.

84. *as the fox said:* A reference to the proverb: "This is a change," said the fox as they flayed him.

85. *Bloksberg . . . Heklefjeld:* The Blocksberg, where German as well as Norwegian witches gathered for their great sabbaths on the Eve of May Day (Walpurgis Night) and Midsummer Eve, is commonly identified with the Brocken, the highest peak of the Harz Mountains. The Hekla Mountain in Iceland is another similar trysting place.

86. *To be yourself is to slay yourself:* This prescription has overtones of *Matthew* 16:25-26, but more directly concerns the choice first stated and now recently revived by the Troll King, namely, to kill one's self-sufficiency in order to become the open, full, and true self. The nature of the latter is eloquently indicated by Ibsen's French translator, Count Prozor, as follows: "*Être soi-même, ce n'est pas être Peer Gynt ou un autre, c'est être homme, c'est tuer en soi ce que Peer appelle orgueilleusement le moi Gyntien pour y faire vivre le moi humain.*"

87. *the Justedal pastor:* Matthias Foss (1714-1792) became the parish priest of Justedal in 1742 and, eight years later, wrote a "short description of Justedal" in which this claim is advanced.

88. *Espen, finding the magpie's wing:* Refers to the folk tale "The Princess That No One Could Silence," in which Espen Askeladd finds a cringle, then a potsherd, and finally a dead magpie, and these apparently worthless things enable him to win "the princess and half the kingdom."

89. *Is that hoof natural:* The Devil in Norwegian folklore is represented as having a single hoof.

90. *Nothing to make you run cold or hot:* Cf. *Revelation* 3:15-16.

91. *Stavanger:* The Norwegian Missionary Society, founded in 1842, had its headquarters in Stavanger.

92. *Put your house in order:* Cf. *Isaiah* 38:1.

93. *the land of mist:* According to the Eddas, there was once no heaven above nor earth beneath, but only a bottomless deep, and a world of mist in which flowed a fountain that froze into rivers of ice. The world of mist was contrasted with the world of light lying to the south.

94. *hide me within:* Cf. *John* 3:3-7.

95. *The sun rises:* Ibsen may have been thinking of the belief, in folk tales, that the troll monster can only remain abroad until dawn, whereupon this primeval mountain spirit is changed back ("stone thou wast, to stone returnest") into its element, symbolically vanquished, as when the first rays of the Light of the World were shed on it. The hope of the ending is that the troll within Peer Gynt is immobilized at last.

APPENDIXES

APPENDIX I

A classic is classic not because it conforms to certain structural rules, or fits certain definitions (of which its author had quite probably never heard). It is classic because of a certain eternal and irrepressible freshness.

EZRA POUND

THE TEXT

In the ordinary and generally held view, the form and the meaning of a text are separable, and the latter may readily be detached from the former for purposes of analysis, argument, rejection, or assent. The form comprises the vessel; the meanings are the contents. When the work is shaped by a first-rate poetic imagination, however, form *is* meaning, down to its least and subtlest elaboration. If the work is the product of a first-rate intellect as well, those meanings infused into and expressed by the form will have not merely limited biographical and psychological reference, but also philosophical and historical implications, since even the minutiae of form take their stamp from the conscious or unconscious quest of the individual writer for an intelligible, personally significant order inevitably conditioned by the dominant world-view of the age. Ibsen's *Peer Gynt*, in this regard, is no different from other masterpieces, some greater, some lesser, composed on its same high level of capacious awareness.

That the form of *Peer Gynt* is as crucial to its entire meaning as anything specifically stated within the drama must be the essential premise of any valid approach to the text, to its translation, and to its abridgment into an effective script for

231

theatrical performance. This ground rule is amply demonstrated by certain authors in the mainstream of Western tradition
that particularly interested Ibsen during the period immediately before *Peer Gynt* was written in 1867. Dante was one of
these. Twice, in May and again in October of 1865, Ibsen bor-
rowed *The Divine Comedy*, in C. K. F. Molbech's Danish translation, from the library of the Scandinavian club in Rome; and
in 1872 he wrote a translator of Horace's *Ars Poetica*, remon-
strating that Molbech's attempt to convey the texture of
Dante's verse through the exclusive use of feminine rhymes
had been misguided, for Danish, unlike Italian, was amply provided with masculine endings.[1] The fact of the matter, he con-
cluded, is that "a translator should employ the style which the
original author would have used if he had written in the language of those who are to read him in translation."[2] In short,
those ingredients of a text which in translation prevent the
genius of the host language from being itself can be regarded as
accidental and expendable.

On the other hand, however, there are textual components
intrinsic to the conception of the original, without which *it*
cannot be itself, that are ignored and abandoned only at severe
cost to the very essence of the work. Among these are the formal elements that register the largest context of meaning, the
writer's apprehension of the world-view of his age, a consideration Ibsen was acutely conscious of. For, he writes, "is not
each generation born with the marks of its age? Have you
never noticed in a collection of portraits of some past century
a curious family resemblance among persons of the same period? It is the same in spiritual [*åndelige*, e.g., intellectual, artis-
tic] matters." Thus, the verse form invented by Dante, *terza
rima*, is, in miniature, a regularly recurring reminder of the
total intent of the *Commedia*. Archibald MacAllister has noted
that "Dante lived in a Catholic world or, rather, universe, in
which every slightest thing was encompassed in the will and
knowledge of an omnipotent and omniscient Deity, and that
the supreme attribute of that Deity was the mystery of his

Trinity and Unity."[3] The Trinity is figured in both the stanzaic progression of tercets as well as the recurring triple rhymes; but beyond these obvious numerological correspondences, the prosodic unit of the *terza rima*, endlessly reiterating a sequence of a b a, b c b, c d c, mimes the generation of the Son and the Holy Spirit out of the Father, a movement wherein the Trinity at the same time both is and proceeds from the mystery of its Unity. As the medieval soul is never more than an instant's remove from the potentiality of its salvation, the vast matter of Dante's poem, even in the most scabrous and blasphemous *bolgia* of the *Inferno*, is never more than a line's beat away from the formal principle, the divine, redemptive order that bounds and rules the universe.

What is true in the case of Dante's inspired choice of a symbolic narrative verse holds equally for the poet of the theater: a prosodic structure attuned to the central tendencies and preoccupations of the age leads the artist heuristically beyond himself to a scope of achievement that would have proved impossible had some other, less resonant form been chosen. For evidence, one need look no further than the contrasting examples of Molière and Goethe, playwrights with whom Ibsen had a particular affinity. References to Molière abound in Ibsen's drama criticism of the 1850s and early 1860s, including at one point a detailed analysis of the final scene of *Tartuffe*. The Alexandrine couplets that supply the structural building blocks for that play and others of its kind convey more than a social ideal of classically balanced antitheses as a barrier and a corrective against excess piled upon baroque excess, and epigrammatic polish and concision as weapons of wit against hypocritical corruption. With their clockwork precision, they reflect as well a century obsessed by the revelations of mathematics and astronomy, from Galileo's eye trained on the symmetrically orbiting moons of Jupiter and number as the preferred vocabulary for clear and distinct Cartesian ideas to the eventual triumphs of Newtonian mechanics. The rational majesty of a watchmaker God whose creation turns on jeweled bearings is mirrored in the tiny, exquisite metrical engine with its balance spring (a a, b b, c c) that ticks off a constant reminder that the cosmos itself subsists on order, design, moderation, and good sense.

Faust, for the main and critical part, is a decidedly different story. Couplets reappear in the rhyme scheme, though nowhere as commandingly as with Molière; and in further reaction from French neoclassicism, the lines no longer are uniformly duodecasyllabic. In fact, as if the poem, like its protagonist, sought to encompass the whole range of human possibility, the work has become an omnivorous anthology of previous Western verse forms. The dominant *Knittelvers*, the freely elastic four-stress verse adapted by Goethe out of Hans Sachs, with its intermittently defective lines, accords with a cosmos that has now come to resemble the quirky variability and a-symmetry of a living organism, as against the modular artifice of a perfected machine. The play, like the poet, is in a process of becoming; self-created-and-creating in the image of a God who is itself *das Werdende das immer wirkt und lebt.* To his officious Boswell, Johan Paulson, Ibsen once remarked that he would prefer the destruction of Germany to that of *Faust*, and, in a less ark-torpedoing mood, that he had studied Goethe more closely than anyone suspected. Indeed, in both 1865 and 1866 he took out copies of *Faust* from the Scandinavian Club library; its influence on the gestation and shaping of *Peer Gynt* can hardly be overestimated.

Several years after its appearance Ibsen expressed misgivings that, of all his works, *Peer Gynt* was least likely to be understood outside the Scandinavian countries. From the standpoint of the compelling humanity of its characters and the perennial relevance of its theme, he need scarcely have concerned himself on that score. But in addition, as these brief notations on the background figures of Dante, Molière, and Goethe indicate, his determined efforts to "Europeanize" his imagination carried him securely beyond the parochialism of his origins. Having set himself to school with the masters of the Western tradition, he could well assert in a letter to his publisher in Copenhagen, Frederick Hegel, that *Peer Gynt* had been written "with mature consideration." One cannot be documentably certain that among the lessons learned from paradigms like *The Divine Comedy, Tartuffe,* and *Faust* was the superior expressive force of a poetic form reverberant with the spirit of the age; such recognitions tend, in any event, to be quietly intuitive with artists of acute sensibility. What *is* plainly apparent is, on the one hand, Ibsen's propensity — in its turn an outgrowth of the widespread historicism of the latter nineteenth century — to view the history of civilization as a spiritual evolution falling into clearly defined, dialectically contrasted phases; along with, on the other hand, his detailed technical interest and practiced fluency, until his mid-forties, in the resources of verse composition. And, most important as always, there is the ultimate testimony of the text itself, which bears within its form the imprint of its time.

The most obvious constituent of that form, the classically Greek, five-act structure of *Peer Gynt*, is further subdivided into a typically Elizabethan deployment of thirty-eight loosely connected scenes, one more than most polyscenic of Shakespeare's dramas, *Anthony and Cleopatra*. As noted by William and Charles Archer — of all previous English translators of the play, the only ones to give its versification anything like an adequate, explicit analysis — thirty of these thirty-eight scenes are composed predominantly in a supple, irregular accentual verse containing four stresses variably apportioned in the line according to emphases of meaning.[4] Immediately, the prototype of Goethe's *Faust* comes to mind, the attraction of its organically shifting meter reinforced by the perhaps not incidental circumstance that the fictional career of Faust extends as a kind of via media between the polarities represented by Brand and Peer Gynt. But if Goethe's *Faust*-verse is a conspicuous antecedent of the poetic style of *Peer Gynt*, another factor deserves more attention. To paraphrase Wagner on Beethoven's

Seventh Symphony, the text of Ibsen's dramatic poem could well be termed an apotheosis of the ballad.

The ballad meter that finds its way through innumerable modifications into *Peer Gynt* is, of course, not the so-called common measure, the a b c b quatrains of alternating four- and three-stress lines familiar from such traditional English ballads as "Sir Patrick Spens" and "Barbara Allen," but rather the long measure liberally represented in the *folkeviser* or folk songs of the Norse Middle Ages—a regular tetrameter progression in the pattern a b a b, or a a, b b, c c, etc. Apart from providing a stable, vernacular prosodic base, there is much in the ballad form that might attract an ambitious playwright: its use of strong dramatic contrasts; its paratactic advance through abrupt transitions, encouraging composition in terms of vivid individual scenes rather than the lesser, or larger, units of well-crafted dialogue or fully articulated acts; its unvaried or incremental repetition of refrain phrases or lines, particularly apposite to the thematic role of repetition in *Peer Gynt*; and its fruitful tension between powerful, primitive emotions and a generally detached, impersonal point of view.

More germane to the present context, the ballad was subtly and intrinsically expressive of the central tendencies and spirit of the age that *Peer Gynt* reflects, the approximate half-century from the early 1800s to the 1860s that represents the full flowering and Indian summer of the romantic movement in literary Northern Europe. The enthusiastic revival of interest in traditional ballads among the romantics attained a singular intensity in Norway. Here the treasury of native folk ballads was prized as the most vital, and virtually the only, unbroken strand of national identity bridging the long subjugation (1380-1814) of Norway to Danish administration and culture. Ibsen, although vehemently opposed to the compensatory extremism of certain of his ultrapatriotic contemporaries (witness the satiric portrait of Huhu in Act IV), nevertheless found in the popular ballad tradition the means of making an

austere, exalted vision of human life and destiny both humanly
moving and theatrically effective. Toward these ends we find
him unreservedly commending the most influential collection
of the day, M. B. Landstad's *Norwegian Ballads*, in a lengthy,
seminal article titled "On the Heroic Ballad and Its Significance for Serious Poetry."

This statement, published ten years before *Peer Gynt* in
1857, is the best clue we possess to the aesthetic underlying
the years of experimentation with poetic drama that culmina-
ted in his final masterpiece in the form.[5] The following notes
represent what I take to be its most important points, re-
phrased slightly to render more explicit its implications for
dramatic art. The sequence of ideas diverges somewhat from
Ibsen's, since my purpose is to clarify the bearing of his
thought on the text of *Peer Gynt*. Parenthetically, I have
added some commentary to bring out, not merely that later
connection, but as well the relevance of his concerns to the
modern movement of drama into our own time.

[1]

Folk poetry, and specifically the heroic ballad, must be
understood as created, not by any one individual, but by the
poetic energies of an entire people. As such, it has enjoyed almost alone a strong, healthy, continuous life in the consciousness of the people, basically for two reasons: (a) It expresses
the inner spiritual content of their collective awareness; and
(b) It does so objectively, untainted by the literary subjectivity
of the poet intruding his own private autobiography.

[The character of Peer Gynt, derived from folk creation,
may be read as an "objective correlative" of the collective
awareness of the present age, a kind of spiritual barometer
registering the inner weather of the people's psychic health.]

[2]

By contrast, contemporary theatergoers are interested

solely in short-lived novelty, demanding always new situations, new intrigues. By catering to this appetite, the theater restricts its audience to a relatively small, educated, and by implication jaded minority, thereby cutting itself off from the larger life of the people.

[Ibsen's observation applies equally to the taste for Scribean melodrama and to an endemic problem of modern, and modernist, theater.]

[3]

To make the new inviting to the people, it must be identified with something old, something forgotten but now rediscovered, steeped in memories, like a family heirloom from the national past. Only by such means will the masses be reached and the audience expanded for high art (*Kunstpoesie*).

[Peer Gynt, who finds himself confronted by the new in the form, economically, of the industrialized, international, capitalistic business world and, philosophically, of evolutionary, Hegelian concepts of history and existential, Kierkegaardian redefinitions of the self, is depicted as stemming from and subsiding back into a dying, rural, agrarian order, a nostalgically recalled hinterland of *rosemaling* and lintel-mounted reindeer horns, ornamented silver buttons and colorful country wedding costumes.]

[4]

This salutary expansion of the audience can be accomplished in two ways:

(a) The poet must draw the raw material for his art out of the people themselves.

[Accordingly, in 1862 Ibsen traveled through the Norwegian countryside, collecting folk songs and tales, among them the germinal story of Peer Gynt and the Boyg.]

(b) The poet must give scope in his work to the craving of the people for independent activity; because unlike the Latin races, those of the North desire, not finished art passively consumed, but rather to complete the artwork through their own active imaginations. The Northerner does not want the way pointed out to the center of the work; he wants to seek the center himself, in his own individualistic way.

[Thus ironically, Peer, the self-proclaimed Northman who contends he knows how to bear a battle through, is depicted as attempting repeatedly to seek the center of his own *magnum opus*, his individuality, only to discover his failure at last in the metaphoric onion.

Ibsen's insistence on the active role of the audience is remarkably Brechtean. It is tempting to view the open-ended conclusions and provocatively discussable aspects of the later prose play cycle as a direct extension of this principle of active audience involvement.]

[5]

Realistically, however, it must be admitted that the rising level of civilization and the inroads of print culture have rendered the living oral tradition of the ballad moribund. What had once sprung exuberantly out of the abundance of its age, in a diminished time has come to resemble cut flowers in a vase, retaining freshness for a while, but incapable of propagation.

[Similarly, Peer Gynt, who has within himself the vivacity of folk creation, has dwindled into a "crass romancer," incapable of more than parroting the legendary exploits of others. Regarding the incursions of print culture, one notes that even the trolls now publish newspapers, printed distinctively in black and red.]

[6]

But in one real aspect, the death of the ballad is more apparent than real: as with anything that retains a momentum of cultural vitality (*aandigt Livsmoment*), it holds potentialities for a new and higher existence. Indeed, just as drama is known to be the higher synthesis of the lyric and the epic forms, ballad poetry can furnish the lyrical component for a revivified dramatic art.

[In Ibsen's Hegelian aesthetic, that heirloom from the national past, its treasury of lyric ballads richly stocked with objectified emotion and collective spiritual inwardness, must be productively united with the epic consciousness of great events and vast historical forces to yield a drama worthy of the time.

More specifically, the world that Peer Gynt is poised to enter, the world of the future, of financiers and deals, international trade and mass exploitation, is epic, is history on the move; the world he tries to leave behind, the world of the past, of simple verities and home truths, small minds and smaller opportunities, is lyrical, a grieving celebration of lost possibilities. The unaccomplished synthesis of the two is one version of the dramatic conflict.]

[7]

Historically, the true significance and potential of the ballad was unripe for recognition until the development of the romantic movement in Germany and its initial influences on the artistic consciousness of Scandinavia, which took place after the debut of the Danish poet and dramatist Oehlenschläger.

[The date Ibsen has in mind is the year of the appearance of Oehlenschläger's "Guldhornene" ("The Golden Horns"), namely, 1802. The lifespan of Peer Gynt is thus depicted as precisely parallel to the advent and reign of literary romanticism and the consequent revived appreciation of ballad poetry in the Northern countries. The folk tale source, indeterminately set in mythic time ("in the old days"), has been synchronized, and shaped in resonance, with the chief tendencies and preoccupations of the age.]

[8]

Oehlenschläger grounded his plays, however, in the native source that, at the time, was already ripened and prepared by research for use: the great, cold, complete, and closed-in epic form of the saga. But the saga is intractable to synthesis into drama, since it is totally devoid of lyricism, so much so that introduction of lyrical elements stands out as something intrusively imposed and aesthetically unsettling, like a statue tinted with naturalistic colors.

By contrast, the ballad is far better suited to dramatic use, as prosody and plot, as well as content and theme. For example, it will assuredly be recognized in time that iambic pentameter is by no means the most congenial meter for treating Scandinavian themes. Only through use of native *forms*, such as four-stress ballad verse (*vor nationale Metrik*), can native *experience* achieve full expression.

[Ibsen had employed blank verse in his first dramas, *Cataline* and *The Burial Mound*. Now, in this declaration of prosodic independence, he throws off, as alien constraint, the chosen meter of that demigod of the romantic movement, Shakespeare. Likewise, sixty years later, Ezra Pound would declare, as the paramount need for modern poetry, "to break the pentameter."]

[9]

Moreover, building upon the lyric flexibility of ballad verse permits the dramatic poet to reflect the age and the events he is treating more exactly and intimately, and to phrase a freer, more natural dialogue.

[The compound dividends accruing from this principle are unmistakable in *Peer Gynt*. Although critics were reluctant to acknowledge it, Ibsen had solved, at least in this sovereign instance, the problem of poetic drama since the seventeenth century: that of fashioning a verse language for actors, supple and gestural, which could be minutely responsive to observed fact while capable, at the same time, of ranging to the outer limits of human experience.]

[10]

Whereas the poetry of the sagas — the latter term to be explicitly understood as including the materials of myth as well — is essentially pagan, inviting dramatization in the ancient Greek style, the heroic ballad is essentially Christian. And whereas the figures and stories of the Aesir, the pantheon of Norse mythology, are supernatural throughout, romanticism, the poetic emanation of Christianity, grants rationality its rightful place and due validity, while perceiving beside, through and above it, the mysterious, the inexplicable, the Christian regarded as a mystery, in a universe which is at once natural *and* supernatural.

[The details of Ibsen's thought become somewhat muddied and inconsistent at this point, e.g., the Nordic mythic narratives, pervaded by the supernatural, are compared to the fable, which denied the supernatural. There is, however, no misconstruing the exceptional pertinence of these ideas both to *Peer Gynt* and to the body of plays from *Emperor and Galilean* on. The cosmos that contains Solveig *and* the Troll Princess, Aslak *and* the Strange Passenger, the Sphinx *and* the Boyg, the Pastor *and* the Button-molder is conceived as both natural and supernatural. Under the internal laws of its creation, neither explains, much less explains away, the other. Each stands as an aspect of the truth. The later "realistic" plays proceed to affirm the same duality: existence is the photographic studio run by the prosaically rational Gina Ekdal, at the same time that it is the mysterious loft pervaded by the enigmatic presence of the wild duck.]

[11]

On closer examination, masked beneath the figures of the warrior knights and the chivalric exploits of the ballads, one can discern the primaeval gods and heroes and cosmogonic events of the Aesir. Disguised and reincarnated in this manner, the old mythic spirits have continued to live in the consciousness and faith of the people right down to our own time. Their vitality has been preserved as well by the Christian priests' representation of the Aesir as evil powers, hostile and dangerous to the new religion.

[In terms of its subsequent implications, this phase of Ibsen's argument is probably the richest and most remarkable. The collective poetic genius of the people (cf. Sect. 1) has modeled the characters and plots of the heroic ballads over more primitive mythic prototypes—one is reminded of Arnold Rubek, in *When We Dead Awaken*, sculpting his portrait busts over the brutish visages of animals, or James Joyce molding the Dubliners of *Ulysses* over the archaic figures and motifs of the *Odyssey*. From this primary level of folk creation, the theater poet learns the lesson he needs to channel the evolution of forms, that being to combine dialectically (i.e., sublate) the deeply interiorized, still potent, saga-related, mythic material from pagan antiquity with the more recent, Christianized, individually defined heroes and heroines that people the lyric form of the ballad, thereby actualizing that dramatic synthesis of both old and new, both ancient roots and unprecedented challenges, that a truly national theater must be capable of to adequately reach, represent, and guide the people. What Ibsen appears to be evolving here, though still in a rudimentary state, is a mythopoeic method of playwriting designed to cope with the pressures of history and the dilemmas of the contemporary self, a method which is tempered and honed to a fine edge in the cycle of major prose plays.[6] There, the lyrical component becomes the modern individual objectively presented in his or her precisely denoted context of revelatory things; and the subsurface force of persisting myth breaks through the veneer of bourgeois comfort and propriety when it is least expected.

By the time of *Peer Gynt*, ten maturing years later, Ibsen's

243

stay in Rome and his immersion in Mediterranean civilization had modified the insularity of his earlier exclusive reliance on Norse myth in favor of a more cosmopolitan frame of reference. Hence one can detect overtones in Peer of the classic myths of Oedipus and Odysseus, in his encounter with the Sphinx and his return after long, fantastic wanderings to a faithful Penelope; though he also bears within him the anathematized presence of the Aesir gods in his resemblance to Loki, the trickster, the shape-shifter, and the thief.]

[12]

More specifically, the content of the ballads concentrates on themes and motifs dealing with (a) chivalry, (b) the taking and avenging of women, (c) battles with dragons and serpents, (d) fantastic journeys to the home of the trolls, thought to lie in the far North, and (e) struggles with trolls and dwarfs who reside in mountains and hills and rule over incalculable treasures.

[All these elements, which amount to an anatomy of medieval Norse versions of the quest-myth, are duplicated in the text of *Peer Gynt*: (a) as the hillside dream of Engelland, and the characteristic cast of Peer's imagery and rhetoric throughout, e.g., in Act III, iii, his distancing transformation of Solveig into a princess, (b) as the Ingrid/Woman in Green/Anitra complex, (c) as the Boyg motif throughout, (d) as the journeys to Hegstad, to the Dovre King's Hall, and to the Cairo asylum, and (e) as the struggles with the Hegstad peasants, Dovre trolls, and asylum inmates over the incalculable treasure of the self.]

[13]

What led the people into the field of ballad composition was not external compulsions, but the stimulation of its own unconscious artistic sense. That need responded to the felt need to transmute poetry in the old pagan mode into the, then

new, romantic and Christian art form. In this process of transformation, the poet finds his task: to perceive clearly and to
waken into conscious life what lies dreaming and fermenting
within the people.

[Within scarcely more than a decade, Ibsen would broaden
and redefine this subsumption of the Norse pagan era in its
successor as the world-historical passage of the First (Greco-
Roman) Empire into the Second (Judeo-Christian) Empire.
Exactly as the anonymous ballad poets accomplished the essential cultural task of their time, so the theater poet of today
must articulate the inchoate, dreaming, and fermenting forms
of the Third Empire, the next great age of civilization struggling to be born. The tragic aspect of Peer Gynt, the poet
manquè, is the waste of his enormous gifts through his lack of
inner self-determination. He fails to think the thoughts, speak
the watchwords, voice the songs, feel deeply and act greatly to
bring his potentially unique selfhood, which includes his portion of the dreaming and fermenting unconscious of his people
at this moment of historic time, into expression. This is in no
way a sin, as the Button-molder patiently explains; merely the
standard evasion of the Master's meaning which, in turn, is the
normal cause for being melted down.]

[14]

Let no one object that the world of the ballad is a world of
poetic fictions that have nothing to do with reality. The poetry of the people is its philosophy as well; it is the form wherein the people expresses its own intuitions about the concrete
existence of the spirit. Like all artistic creations, it naturally
seeks to unfold and develop out of real life, out of history, out
of active experience, and out of the enveloping context of
nature.

[Brief as it is, Ibsen's effective peroration on the significance of the heroic ballad for high poetic art is unmistakably a
profession of personal faith and a sworn pledge of commitment

to his own future vocation as the theater poet called forth to engage the crisis of the times. *He* will articulate the inner spiritual content of his people, and do so with the necessary objectivity. *He* will gather up and reshape the dying forms of the national past into the drama of the new age—a drama constituted not out of fictions, but out of reality; a drama equivalent to philosophy, embodying those intuitions about the concrete life of the spirit that the Button-molder declares crucial for realizing the Master's meaning; a drama that generates its metaphorical structures out of the real life of society, the whole of Western history, the experience of the self as action, and the great cycles of nature. As an ascending sequence of stages moving from a largely unconscious, primitive ground upward through ever-widening and more inclusive realms of consciousness, Ibsen's ambitious program can be charted in a table that may help to clarify the relationship of its elements, although certain of these—the items bracketed—only crystallized over the next two decades of his authorship:

ART FORM	ELEMENTS OF FORM	CONCRETE CONTENT	STAGE OF CIVILIZATION
New national poetic drama	Drama ╱ ╲ Epic—Lyric	"The new" [The individual emergent in evolving history, with mythic substrate]	[Third Empire]
Heroic Ballad	Epic—Lyric	"The old" Warrior knights: Christianized (i.e., disguised) pagan myths	[Second Empire]

ART FORM	ELEMENTS OF FORM	CONCRETE CONTENT	STAGE OF CIVILIZATION
Saga	Epic	"The old" Norse gods and heroes of pagan myth	[First Empire]

The article on the heroic ballad ranges discursively beyond the key points condensed and paraphrased above: the discussion of the resistance of the saga form to dramatic treatment is more extended; there is a complementary deprecation of scaldic poetry as a seed-ground for the ballad; and the last quarter of the paper is given over to an euhemeristic account of Norse myth designed to prove the origins of the heroic ballad in prehistoric *Völkerwanderungen* from Eastern Europe. However this last may have excited the chauvinistic curiosity of his contemporary listeners and readers, it sheds scant light on the prehistory of Ibsen's later masterpieces. Certainly, one can find stock ideas of romanticism interlacing the argument of the piece; echoes of Herder and Schelling, for example, not to mention Hegel. Nevertheless, "On the Heroic Ballad and Its Significance for Serious Poetry" is a remarkable affirmation for a young man of twenty-nine whose progress in the theater had been decidedly uneven to say the least, and it establishes how far from happy accident or caprice Ibsen's choice was, in *Peer Gynt*, of ballad meter for four-fifths of its scenes. Given the communal matrix of a people and a nation distracted by foreign cultural influences while seeking their own identity, in reciprocity with a dramatic poet striving to answer the sphinx-riddle of his own vocation through a response to that collective dilemma, the choice of verse form was an organic and inevitable outgrowth of the drama's central thematic conflict: that of being true to one's self, as against being enough to one's self.

247

Of the remaining, subordinate verse forms in *Peer Gynt*, certain of the scenes or extended passages find their rationale in this theme, while others are variations within the ballad convention having the function of controlling heightened emotions or further defining a speaker. For example, the dominant tetrameter, identified so pervasively with the Gyntian condition of falling short of being a true self, is bounded at one extreme by the nervous antiphony in dimeter of the Thief and the Fence (Act IV, v) and, at the other, by the diapason of the entire poem in the majestic pentameter of the Pastor's graveside eulogy (Act V, iii). Of all the human characters, the Thief and the Fence represent the least developed selfhood, the mere static repetition of role from generation to generation, hardly more than the desert lizards "snapping and thinking of nothing at all." Appropriately, they are accorded the most restricted span of poetic expression. The Pastor, on the other hand, speaks out of a selfhood grounded in the fullness of faith as he recounts the "pilgrimage on earth" of a self-mutilated man, a coward and a misfit, who overcomes obstacle after obstacle, inwardly and outwardly, to win through to an entelechy of spirit; correspondingly, the verse expands to the larger measure and meaning of what a human life can become.

Elsewhere, in the opening scenes of Acts I and II, in Act IV, vii, and in Huhu's speech (Act IV, xiii), Ibsen reins in the loose-gaited, four-beat line to strictly tallied trochaic feet. The clipped, tautly energetic trochees provide a textural foil for the main tenor of the scenes: Peer's exuberant, imaginary reindeer ride; the bitter mutual recriminations of Ingrid and her once ardent, now bored lover; and the lush role-playing of the would-be sultan and his sensual and cagy odalisque. (Conversely, and still more brilliantly, obeying a kind of prosodic Boyle's Law, the contraction of the verse to trimeter in Act II, iv, Peer's drunken, post-coital rhapsody in the Ronde mountains, and Act III, iv, Aase's death, propels the content all the more powerfully forward in a rush of intensified feeling.)

Huhu's seriocomic tirade demonstrates another expressive re-
source in the trochaic mode: by tuning the verse to a metro-
nomic cadence, Ibsen admirably reinforces his portrayal of the
monomaniacal rigidity and barely contained hysteria of the
born fanatic.

The ingeniously varied rhyme patterns in *Peer Gynt*, though
not as closely tied to local meaning in the text, are even more
resourcefully developed than the metrical changes. In general,
apart from the interpolated songs with their own distinctive
stanzaic structures, the text divides between passages in couplets and more open distributions, ranging from a relatively
tight a b a b to elaborately extended concatinations of end-
rhymes wherein the closure of couplet or tercet may be de-
layed over six or eight lines. The sustained passages in couplets
frequently project a mesmerizing vision or narrative (Peer's
daydream on the hillside, the anecdote of the Devil and the
pig), an episode of intense concentration (the search for the
lost Peer in Act II, ii, or Huhu's diatribe), defiance (Peer's
scorn of his pursuers, Act II, iii), or stichomythic exchange
(Peer and the Woman in Green) — in short, moments when the
language is gripped by a unifying purpose. Conversely, the
more excursive rhyme schemes usually evoke the wayward im-
pulses, vagrant longings and fraying resolves within the protagonist, for which the play's variability of setting and incident
is the external counterpart.

This basic tension between cohering intention and diffusing
possibility is carried through into the specifics of diction. Ibsen's choice of rhyme-words ranges from the simplest, most
elemental referents in Norwegian, the irreducible bedrock of
physical and psychological reality (*moer/bord, drøm/døm*), to
exotic combinations that manifest the extravagant play of
Gyntian fantasy (*tetatet'en/profeten, bibelhistorien/spor igen,
sanger/orangutanger, sandt er/elefanter, fotograferet/kasseret*).
These pairings inevitably suggest the precedent of Byron's *Don
Juan*; and indeed, in the letter of 1872 already cited, while

disclaiming wide acquaintance with Byron's writings, Ibsen prescribed them as an antidote to the moral prejudices hobbling aesthetic judgment in Norway.[7] Considered by itself, the virtuosity of the rhyming in *Peer Gynt* is reminiscent of one of those color organs that once were fixtures in exhibitions of avant-garde art, in which the constant shifting of hues reiterated a gamut from hard-edge, prismatic purity to chromatic fugues and shimmering auroras of unexpected conjunction.

When on publication, the text of *Peer Gynt* was raked by critical fire, its author countered with his now well-known rejoinder that, "My book *is* poetry; and if it isn't, it shall be. The concept of poetry in our country, in Norway, will come to conform to the book." Time and the shock of recognition among those few that ultimately shape literary judgment have proved Ibsen right. His last and greatest verse drama is a model of organic form, once defined by Herbert Read as a work that has "its own inherent laws, originating with its very invention and fusing into one vital unity both structure and content." Unfortunately, *Peer Gynt*'s formal achievement as a dramatic poem is not so readily demonstrated in languages other than the poet's own.

THE TRANSLATION

Translation, like politics, is the art of the possible. The rightful function of both is to reconcile competing claims, giving priority in each instance to the most legitimate and pressing. If the project at hand is a verse drama of the stature of *Peer Gynt*, the number of claims at stake would be sufficient to daunt anyone not intoxicated by the hubris of making a personal appropriation of past greatness as a necessary enlargement of life. Not often enough talked or written about, it is in good part from this buccaneering spirit of adventure, of discovery, of the incommunicable spoils of conquest and possession that the translator begins.

But then, and repeatedly after that, madness has to submit to, and learn, method. Each compositional unit—the line, the sentence, the module of rhyme, the verse paragraph—has to be individually assayed into its controlling elements, which, no matter how tenaciously the conscious mind works to compound them, can only, finally, be resolved in a flash of intuited cohesion. Of these elements, there is first of all the metrical configuration that needs to be synchronized between the texts. There are the harmonies of the rhyming, a variable that has within it a whole spectrum of subdifficulties. There is the constantly changing texture of the diction, involving the ratio of short words to long, of gutturals to labials to sibilants, of the commensurability of metaphors and proverbs between the original and the host language, and so on. Modifying all the above, there is the character speaking to be considered, his or her distinctive rhythms and patterns of speech, and how these may alter under the stress of action. Lastly, and not to be minimized, is the fact that every tone and trope of the verse is dialogue for actors and must be eminently sayable, dense and taut with appropriate histrionic values, neither too much nor too little like the dramatic classics of one's native tradition, but rather memorably itself, the paradoxical mimesis of an inimitable voice. Even such major elements as these fail to exhaust all the competing claims on a translator's attention, which include such further concerns as the degree of fidelity possible to period or regional expressions, and adequate sensitivity to the catch phrases and ruling ideas of the age.

Obviously, all these components, organically fused in the original, cannot be served in equal measure in translation; and so the translator of *Peer Gynt* finds himself in the ironic position of applying a delicate balance of compromises to a work dedicated to exposing compromise as a way of life. Mercifully, Ibsen himself understood the problem. "It is difficult to translate well," he wrote. "It is not simply a question of rendering the meaning, but also, to a certain extent, of remodeling the expression and the metaphors, of accommodating the outward form to the structure and requirements of the language into which one is translating."

But how much is "to a certain extent"? The precedents among even the best of contemporary translators vary sizably. John Ciardi has noted that, in the preliminary stages of translating *The Divine Comedy*, he found the relatively rhyme-poor English language incapable of unforcedly supplying, as Dante's Italian could, the third, right, word choice to complete the *terza rima* stanza. His solution was to adopt a tercet wherein a bracketing couplet enclosed an unrhymed, flexible middle line (a x a, b x b).[8] One could maintain that a symbolic form intrinsic to the poem's meaning was violated by that decision. One could equally contend that, to most knowledgeable readers, the integral *terza rima* form persists as a phantom subtext beneath the translator's simplifying and liberating expedient. What can scarcely be argued, however, is the greater naturalness, vigor, and grace Ciardi's solution attains over versions of the *Commedia* that have kept strict fidelity to the triple rhymes of the original.

By contrast, Richard Wilbur's verse translations of Molière retain their rhymed couplets intact, but the meter has been contracted from the classic Alexandrines to pentameter. The loss is subtle, but not inconsequential. The recurrent medial cesura in Molière's line, breaking it in equal segments, gives the dramatic poetry a Mozartian balance and equanimity. The regularity of that proportioning is, one could say, the fingerprint of the *Zeitgeist*. Pentameter, however, cannot be equally divided. Wilbur's

> Brother, I don't pretend to be a sage,
> Nor have I all the wisdom of the age

is both metrically and ideologically a reduction from Molière's

> Je ne suis point, mon frère ‖ un docteur révéré,
> Et le savoir chez moi ‖ n'est pas tout retiré.

Yet, again, who would wish to argue that a Molière in English Alexandrines, dragging their slow, serpentine lengths along, could hold its own against Wilbur's nimbly felicitous solution for our own theater and time?

If these are translators' hard tactical decisions that surrender vital territory in order to ensure an ultimate victory, there are also tactical errors that result in insupportable losses and a greater or lesser measure of defeat. William and Charles Archer, in projecting their joint translation of *Peer Gynt*, wisely determined to follow Ibsen's injunction that the play only be brought across as poetry, rather than prose paraphrase. They then settled upon two principles of procedure: first, that the translation would adhere as strictly as possible to the original meters, and, second, that all attempt at rhyming would be suppressed. These led in turn to a fatal third principle: that since the major concession of abandoning all rhyme had been allowed, no further liberty whatsoever was permissible. The ground was thus prepared for what in fact ensued, a repeated capture of the letter and forfeit of the spirit throughout the translation. The Archers' *Peer Gynt* is, with some fifty or so minor transpositions, a line-for-line rendering of Ibsen's text (approximately the same can be said for the present translation)—but with no echo of the deft music, the harmonic jeu d'esprit of Ibsen's rhymes, it must be seriously questioned whether a dramatic *poem* has been conveyed at all. Especially so, when the cost is added in of the procrustean commitment to the exact original meters, prompting such lines as Peer's "Keen the blast towards me swept" (where "towards" must be awkwardly sounded as a disyllable), or Aase's "Right proudly I perked on the box-seat," or again, Peer's "Dearest payment cheap I'll reckon." These are among the more extreme examples, but the stiff inadequacy of the Archers' *Peer Gynt* was clearly recognized and censured almost immediately on its publication; the critic for *The Dial*, reviewing its use in performance by Richard Mansfield in 1906, called it a "hybrid composition" that had proved "very unsatisfactory."

Nevertheless, this first text in English of Ibsen's masterpiece defined the inescapable issues that every subsequent close translation and loose adaptation has had to address. Some of these, substituting a meticulous fidelity to the rhymes for the Archers' programmatic abandonment, have turned the poetry into jingles. Others have substantially jettisoned, not merely the rhyme, but the meter as well; the result, even if crudely lined out, has been exactly that prose paraphrase that Ibsen categorically repudiated. The broad diversity of the prior approaches demands a statement of the principles underlying this present translation; I would only hope that they have ensured the justifying paradox of a successful failure to match the original.

The premise from which all else proceeds is, that if indeed form is meaning down to its least and subtlest elaboration, then the meaning of the text can never be adequately conveyed in translation unless every aspect of its form is representatively reflected to the fullest degree possible. The compromises must be shared proportionately, for to concentrate them in one competing claim alone spells disaster.

Toward this end, the accommodating elasticity of the dominant four-stress verse is, in English, as gratefully plastic a medium as in Norwegian. Where, as in Virgil's *Aeneid* or Shakespeare, there is an occasional broken-end passage, the defective line has not been filled out, as in some other versions, but permitted to stand as Ibsen left it. The rare, rogue three-stress line has been taken as a warrant, in other locations, but with I trust comparable rarity, to avoid verbal padding by the same means. The real difficulties arise, however, as they did for the Archers, in the metrically strict speeches and scenes, particularly those in regular trochees. In one instance, Huhu's tirade, that versification has been retained without the least deviation, as the inspired expression of a psychotic rigidity. In other scenes, cited earlier, I have been fairly free in using anacrusis or hypermeter rather than truncate a meaning or mangle a natural speech cadence. The trochee, after all, is a more accustomed mode of utterance in Norwegian than in English, which gravitates toward iambs. Norwegian, for example, suffixes the definite article to the noun, (*dágĕn*, vs. the dáy); and, as in Chaucer's Middle English, many words have a terminal, sounded -e (*hérrĕ, kómmĕ*) that in English are monosyllabic (lord, come). Acknowledging and compensating for such root distinctions between languages, as Ibsen counseled in bringing Dante's Italian into Danish, is finally more accurate translation than blind obedience to original meters. The alternative is to be lured, like the Archers, into archaisms ("sleepeth," "dareth"), syncope (" 'twill," " 'mid") and stilted inversions ("Peeps she from behind her curtain") in the effort to stretch the living bones of speech on a metrical rack.

If rendering the meters of *Peer Gynt* called for a more relaxed responsiveness to the original within a familiar convention, then indicating the rhymes, I discovered, required inventive exploration within a new one. The contribution of the rhyme toward projecting the total meaning of the play could hardly be ignored. Nevertheless, styles and tastes in theater change; and rhymed verse drama is no longer a form that audiences feel comfortable with. In Molière, the glittering wit, the barbed politesse, the social artifice, the sententious concision all conspire to make a texture of precisely rhymed couplets theatrically acceptable, as the Wilbur translations have demonstrated. But an outsized, mid-nineteenth century, late romantic critique of romanticism could display, in today's theater, no more than a modicum of moon-June chime-rhyming without risking disqualification as one of the world's master visions of psychological and philosophical penetration. One might as well seek to rewrite *Hamlet* in the idiom of the Player King.[9]

Fortunately, a solution presented itself in the writings of another mid-nineteenth century poet who was Ibsen's match in indomitable independence: Emily Dickenson. The practice of slant rhyming that she pioneered was informed, in the words of her editor and biographer Thomas H. Johnson, by an "evident belief that verse which limits itself to exact rhyme is denied the possible enrichment that other kinds can bring." That belief cost her heavily. As Johnson continues: "Her way of poetry was to prove far lonelier than she expected, for it denied her in her lifetime all public recognition. The metric innovations might have been tolerated, but in her day no critic of English would have been willing to accept her rhymes. Milton had proved that English verse could be great with no rhymes at all. No one in 1860, reader or critic, was ready to let it be supple and varied."[10] Although some conservative quarters still appear unwilling or unable to recognize it, perhaps now, over one hundred years later, slant rhyme can be enfranchised as a legitimate and invaluable tool for the translator. Its singular expressiveness is amply confirmed by Emily Dickinson's own art. Consider, for instance, the masterfully uncertain hovering in tension between longed-for confession and stoic resolve caught by the half-rhyme of "tell" and "steel" in the following:

> How many times these low feet staggered —
> Only the soldered mouth can tell —
> Try — can you stir the awful rivet —
> Try — can you lift the hasps of steel!

Since this and other such quatrains, contemporary with the composition of *Peer Gynt*, numerous poets have made eloquent capital of slant rhyming, among them Yeats, Wilfred Owen, Auden, and Dylan Thomas. All seem to have appreciated intuitively the double meaning one might choose to find in their forerunner's lines: "Tell all the truth but tell it slant — / Success in circuit lies. . . ."

For the translator of *Peer Gynt*, parched by that rhyme-poor aridity complained of by Ciardi in the otherwise prodigal English language, the luxuriant oasis of slant rhyme is irresistible. It offers the opportunity of making Ibsen's kaleidoscopically shifting rhyme patterns continuously and unobtrusively present to eye, ear, and mind, without the sing-song overtone of Gilbert-and-Sullivanian patter that our age has left behind. Moreover, slant or consonantal rhyming can avail itself of parallel gamuts of word choice based on nineteen different vowel sounds as against the single scale of options allowed by a perfect rhyme, a fact that opens up a plenitude of additional

combinations of sense and sound; and this in turn frees and en-
livens the remainder of the line anchored to that decisive terminal rhyme. True rhyme can still be reserved for passages of
heightened emotion, purpose, or significance; and as a compensation for other losses, I have endeavored to use it to that
effect. A further inducement to slant rhyming resides in the
large number of close cognates in Norwegian and English that
could not retain their original rhyme (Berlin/min) and place-
ment unless the resulting rift in vowel sounds (Berlin/mine)
was bridged by a more liberal prosodic policy.

The other basis for a solution of off-rhyming for the translation of *Peer Gynt* derives not from the tradition of what Ibsen calls *Kunstpoesie*, or "art poetry," (e.g., Emily Dickenson),
but from the work's status as a vastly expanded, elaborately
orchestrated folk ballad. From the anonymous Scots Border
ballads down to Woody Guthrie and the Beatles, the best in
popular and folk song has always had its own way with the
niceties of exact rhyme:

> 'How old are you, my pretty little miss?
> How old are you, my honey?'
> 'If I don't die of a broken heart,
> I'll be sixteen come Sunday.'

The pert exchange in that familiar Appalachian ballad is no
more than a whistle and a stomp from Peer Gynt circulating
among the dancers, looking for a partner at Hegstad. The anonymous balladeer, one notes, has paired "honey" and "Sunday" without the slightest detectable twinge of prosodic guilt.
Accordingly I have not hesitated to employ such common-
places of the ballad convention, where the alternative would
be rhyme-forced, as singular-plural rhymes (flame/dreams),
light rhyming of masculine and feminine endings (lie/twenty),
as well as the kind of assonantal rhyming exemplified in the
quatrain above (Father/answer). In rare instances even these
devices were insufficient to release a meaning impounded by
the intricate rhyme patterns of the original, and in such cases

I have reordered that pattern slightly, trusting that its larger skein of complexity remained evident.

Brian Johnston has aptly observed that the range of physical actions given Peer Gynt exceeds that of any other major fictional hero with the possible exception of Odysseus (one might also include Rabelais's Pantagruel). Peer walks, runs, leaps, carries his mother, wrestles, mimes an imaginary reindeer ride, climbs, fights, chops wood, abducts a bride, a troll princess, and an Arabian girl, dresses, undresses, dances, has sex, rides various steeds, swims, crawls on all fours, and, finally exhausted, falls asleep in Solveig's arms. Such a prodigy of vitality demands nothing less from the literary forms and techniques that body forth his world. Ibsen has provided them; and it is up to the translator to follow suit, not with some anemically correct facsimile, but by recreating, responsibly and to the best of his talents, that same vitality, independence, and shaping élan. To quote the translator of Valèry, Jackson Matthews, "One thing seems clear: to translate a poem whole is to compose another poem. A whole translation will be faithful to the *matter* and it will 'approximate the form' of the original, and it will have a life of its own, which is the voice of the translator. . . . the final test of a translated poem must be *does it speak, does it sing?*"[11] And as well, if the translated poem is a verse drama, *does it play?* That, however, can be determined only when gifted actors, directors, and designers have the imaginative courage and initiative to risk its life on the stage.

THE SCRIPT

Any producer or director whose imagination is captured by the challenge of realizing *Peer Gynt* in the theater will face, needless to say, a more than usual array of critical choices. Apart from the sine qua non, the availability of a Peer whose versatility, magnetism, and stamina can carry off the role, no question will have greater consequence than the determination of the script,[12] which parses into the initial dilemma of whether to cut the play at all (an option that includes minimal, cosmetic surgery), or whether to cut fairly extensively, thereby raising the related subquestions of how much, where, and by what principle, or process, of elimination.

The full text of *Peer Gynt* is 4302 lines. By comparison, the longest Shakespearian drama, *Hamlet*, runs to 3776 lines, with the average of the thirty-seven plays approximating 2700, the span of *Twelfth Night*. In translation, *Oedipus Rex* has a line-count of 1530, while *Everyman* weighs in at 931, perhaps proving only that, as in Olympic boxing, international champions come in all sizes and categories. But if that perennial heavyweight contender, *Hamlet*, is almost always considerably cut to bring it down to fighting trim, *Peer Gynt* has understandably been regarded as bloated to excess. A practical theater person with an instinct for possibilities is likely to conclude, long before putting matters to a line-count, that somewhere in this seemingly massive verse drama a much thinner stage play is signaling to be let out.

But to what degree is that estimate actually justified? The point bears some examination. The length, the line-count, the sheer heft of *Peer Gynt* is deceptive. The work, first of all, is composed in tetrameter, not pentameter, the amputated metrical foot signifying that, line for line, the quantity of dialogue is up to twenty percent less than a Shakespearian text. Furthermore, *Peer Gynt* contains no prose passages extending the dialogue to the margins of the page, as against the average twenty-seven percent component of prose in Shakespeare. When one adds in the fact that Ibsen's ballad-based, four-stress line can be more rapidly delivered (and comprehended) than Elizabethan blank verse, one arrives at a text that is not longer, but in reality appreciably shorter, than *Hamlet* and more on the scale of *The Taming of the Shrew* or *The Merchant of Venice*.

The comparison with Shakespeare is useful because the

producer or artistic director interested in *Peer Gynt* has most likely had some experience staging Shakespearian drama as a standard of reference. Useful, indeed; but is it appropriate? We know that Shakespeare, the enterprising actor-manager, conceived and wrote every one of his plays for performance. But was the form and diction of *Peer Gynt* intended for the stage, or does it, rather, represent a closet-drama detour for its creator, a text for the armchair on a par with Wordsworth's *The Borderers* or Hardy's *The Dynasts*?

Fourteen years after its composition, Ibsen wrote his German translator Ludwig Passarge that *Peer Gynt* was "in no way designed to be performed." He appears to have forgotten his earlier ambivalence during the actual composing process, when he asked his friend Wilhelm Bergsøe if he thought audiences would accept on stage a man with an enormous casting ladle, large enough to hold a human being. Ultimately, of course, an artist's comments, vexed by all manner of personal misgivings, are of dubious worth in assessing the performability, or even the real content, of his work. Otherwise, conductors could reasonably decline to program Brahms' Fourth Symphony on the basis that the composer himself had dismissed it as merely a few entr'actes thrown together. Such instances of artists' uncertainty about work to which they are so uniquely and intimately related are legion. What can, I think, be legitimately inferred is that in *Peer Gynt*, as well as in *Brand* and *Emperor and Galilean*, Ibsen was writing primarily for a theater of the mind whose praxis was non-existent until Dickson and Edison invented the cinematograph, and Appia and Craig dissolved the old, halting, laborious, mechanical set changes into a virtually continuous musical flow of scenic images. The revelatory application of the new stagecraft to what Ibsen at the time could only hope to designate "A Dramatic Poem" has disclosed it to be not only the late culmination of dramatic romanticism, but a work adventurously ahead of its time that has had to wait for, and to an extent inspire, the scenography necessary for its expression.

That same new stagecraft, by streamlining the cumbersome mechanics of production, made less cutting of the text needful and more of the play available within a long, but still feasible evening in the theater.[13] In fact, the advances and innovations in theatrical expertise and technology over the century since the 1876 premiere of *Peer Gynt* (Christiania Theater, staged by Ludvig Josephson, with Henrik Klaussen as Peer, Sofie Parelius as Aase, and Thora Neelsen as Solveig) could effectively be measured in terms of the progressive conforming of the stage to the fluidity and cohesion of Ibsen's vision. The international production history, so far as it can be pieced together from scattered sources, is a compendium of the stylistic influences and ideologies that have swept successively over the Western theater during that restless era. Each cadre of innovators has shaped a somewhat different script from the text in line with its own emphases, although one production element, peculiar to the play's advent in the theatrical repertory, has exercised until lately an almost gyroscopic power of momentum in setting the course of performance interpretation. That element is the famous incidental music by Edvard Grieg.

An evocative and at times movingly eloquent commentary on the action from a quintessentially romantic point of view, the Grieg score was commissioned, at Ibsen's instigation, for the premiere as a series of (in this case, not misnomered) entr'actes long enough to mask the noisy shifting of the realistic sets. As the appended American production list attests, for three-quarters of a century a presentation of *Peer Gynt* was unthinkable without the accompaniment of Grieg; the two went together, as Peer would say, "like a leg for a trouser; like hair for a comb."

Thus Grieg was taken to be an indispensable adjunct to that production which, perhaps more than any other, canonized the play for the English-speaking stage—directed by Tyrone Guthrie amid and despite the privations of wartime London (The Old Vic, August 31, 1944, with Ralph Richardson as Peer, Sybil Thorndike as Aase, Joyce Redman as Solveig,

Margaret Leighton as the Woman in Green, and Lawrence Olivier as the Button-molder). At the time of its successful run, Guthrie had regrets only that war conditions had compelled considerable cuts in Ibsen's text and in Grieg's score. Less than two years later, his attitude had altered radically: "If I ever have the opportunity of staging *Peer Gynt* again, I shall hope to feel free to jettison Grieg, to jettison any 'realistic' scenery; and to spend the time thus saved on playing more of the text than is otherwise possible. . . . If it is to be presented at all, it must be with great simplicity, even austerity." The following year he amplified this position in the magazine *The Norseman* on behalf of rendering the text more intelligible and of unfettering the spirit of the work, which aims "to convey deep and serious ideas, laid out on a most ambitiously sweeping plan, by means of a witty, fanciful and essentially light style. . . . It is the fantasy which matters and the ideas that the fantasy symbolically suggests."[14]

In Norway these observations fell on fertile soil. Hans Jacob Nilsen, the newly reappointed head of the Norwegian Theater in Oslo, who had played the traditional, sentimentally blurred, romantic version of Peer Gynt as nationalistic propaganda while a refugee in Sweden during World War II, was intent on a fresh, antiromantic approach to the text. The ground swell for such a reinterpretation had risen from diverse Scandinavian sources, but Guthrie's thoughts reinforced the movement and were echoed in Nilsen's preparatory work. For him, as for Guthrie, Grieg's music was bound to the nineteenth century Victorian world that the living play had left behind, and he commissioned from the contemporary Norwegian composer Harald Saeverud an astringent score that stressed such satiric elements as the capitalist cabal on the North Moroccan coast. Using almost the complete text in a vivid, revisionist, four-and-a-half hour performance, which, by report, seemed not at all too long to those present, Nilsen's *Peer Gynt* succeeded in freeing the script from its automatic coupling with Grieg (Det Norske Teatret, March 2, 1948, with Nilsen playing Peer,

Ranghild Hald as Aase, Eva Sletto as Solveig, Lydia Opøien as the Woman in Green, and Lars Tvinde as the Button-molder). This pivotal production, by releasing the drama's wealth of ironic content, became, in Odd-Stein Anderssen's words, "an overwhelming manifestation of the forces in the play which had been lying latent and undeveloped for eighty years."[15]

Nilsen's declaration of the interpreter's freedom to search the text freshly and fundamentally, well beyond the rearrangement of nuances on an authorized model, has had widespread repercussions, exemplified by two sharply contrasted, equally impressive productions. The first of these was exceptionally well prepared, and cast with enviably lavish resources, by its director Ingmar Bergman (Malmö Stadsteater, March 8, 1957, with Max von Sydow as Peer, Naima Wifstrand as Aase, Gunnel Lindblom as Solveig, Åke Fridell as the Troll King, Ingrid Thulin as Anitra, and Toivo Pawlo as the Button-molder). A total of 220 hours was spent on rehearsals; and the finished production, which involved 130 scene changes, consisted of 90 principals and supernumeraries. Again, the directorial commitment was made to present as much of the text as possible, with cuts restricted mainly, and wisely, to Act Four. And again this intention compelled a reassessment of the place of music in the total conception. As the Stadsteater's manager, Lars-Levi Laestadius, wrote: "The modern music that Hans Jacob Nilsen invited Saeverud to compose for the notable production at Det Norske Teatret in 1947 [sic] has considerable merits, but we have found it unwarranted in the present instance to link the work with those harsh tonalities. For us the essential thing has been to present the play as it is, without expressionistic decoration and contemporary political distortion, but also without swaddling it in a romanticism that it already was dissociated from at its moment of creation."[16] As a result, a few spare phrases of Norwegian folk music served as the only accompaniment to the action. With an unlocalized and ironical Peer, an Aase wholly without illusions from the outset, and a Dovre King's domain more reminiscent of a Hieronymus Bosch inferno than a conclave of folkish Norse trolls sketched by Kittelsen, Bergman's production carried through the universalizing and deromanticizing impetus initiated by Nilsen.

Diametrically opposed to the Malmö staging was the politically engaged, brilliantly tendentious *Peer Gynt* collectively conceived in West Berlin under the supervision of Peter Stein (Schaubühne am Halleschen Ufer, April 27, 1971, with Heinrich Giskes, Michael König, Bruno Ganz, Wolf Redl, Dieter Leser, and Werner Rehm as Peer, Edith Clever as Aase, and Jutta Lampe as Solveig). Adapted to epic theater technique, the text was divided into eight scenic chapters, with six actors interchanging the protagonist's part, and each transfer of identity, like the passing of a baton in a relay race, marking a distinctive transition in Peer's circumstances and pattern of role-playing vis-à-vis the objective world. Cutting was minimal before the Fourth and Fifth Acts, the entire six-hour action transpiring over two evenings to permit the fullest development of the significance of each scene. In Hugh Rorrison's summation, Peer was conceived as "a kind of 'petit bourgeois Faust' engaged on a quest for identity which took the form of nostalgia: bourgeois longing for the restoration of times of glory in the historical past (Peer wants to be Emperor)."[17] Identifying with the reigning power elite, the successful bourgeois capitalist class, imitating its exploitative expansionism and invariably failing, Peer inevitably gravitates to the camp of the trolls, who are internalized, deformed, animalistic caricatures of the petit bourgeois mentality. The ideology of the trolls holds that shifty standards and self-deception (vile looks fair, foul looks pure) are advantageous for getting ahead in the present capitalistic society; their smug moral confusion derives from the underlying, unprincipled, and irrational reality of an economic system that is destroying itself through its own internal contradictions.

Nothing illustrates the polarity of the two interpretations so well as the striking contrast in the stagings of the closing scene. As Bergman's Peer gropes his way toward the final crossroads, all the stage properties vanish. The desolation of the final reckoning impacts on the audience out of the fathomless black scenic depths, where the Button-molder sits in a dimly lit circle bent over his bellows, his casting ladle and his doomsday book. Then, out of that same darkness Solveig steps forward, a figure of light. The final tableau confronts us with isolated, individual selves—wayward man, the messenger of judgment, the hope of loving forgiveness—set against an immense abyss of mystery, the indecipherable ground of all being.

At the Schaubühne, on the other hand, the final scene is played out, after epic practice, in a uniform and matter-of-fact light. Workers in overalls have moved in to clear and disinfect the historic scene. Peer, curled up in fetal position on the lap of Solveig, is trundled forward and photographed by an old-fashioned, tripod-based portrait camera, so that posterity can study this quaint and obsolete species of anarchic individualism. At one point, the plan was then to set up an assembly line on stage and wrap little icons of the Peer-Solveig pietá in cellophane to distribute, like dashboard madonnas, to the audience. In this production concept, clearly mystery is irrelevant. Judgment resides in the sovereign rationality of the audience, in its capacity to recognize a potentially dangerous style of behavior, an ideal of egocentric expansionism that crested in the latter nineteenth century at the historic moment when it called forth the critical consciousness that could oppose and limit it.

The point here is not that either interpretation of the text is superior to the other. The four productions described—one British, one Norwegian, one Swedish, one German—represent what, from this vantage, appear to be the landmark achievements in the staging of *Peer Gynt* during the approximate middle third of the twentieth century. Each displayed a singular integrity of vision—Guthrie's neo-Craigian and lyrical, Nilsen's deromanticized and ironic, Bergman's existential and metaphysical, Stein's Marxist and epic—and each vision discovered another stage play in the verse drama, another script in the text. As the exploration of possibilities continues today in the English-speaking theater, it has become obvious through this heritage that there can now be any number of potentially valid *Peer Gynts*, if no longer a conventionally "definitive" one.

In this recognition lies the only answer to the initial questions, whether to cut the text minimally or extensively, exactly how much, where, and by what principle. For the richest ultimate harvest of meanings, the first approach to the text should most probably be to suspend all preconceived notions in the resolve, as Laestadius put it, simply "to present the play as it is." Without further qualification, that axiomatic openness has to lead, logically and inevitably, either to a presentation of the text entire and intact, or else to the adoption of any number up to a thousand lines of "neutral" cuts, which I have found, in working with directors, can be made merely as clarification of the main lines of action and thought with no threat to the essential structure. But sooner or later a thematic point of view is bound to assert itself, preferably emerging from rather than imposed upon the material; and that germinating production concept, by restoring certain neutral cuts if necessary and excising other matter, will eventually shape the working script. Such a concept, dedicated to exploring either the manifest content of Ibsen's world-view or latent, textually supportable variants of it, is the sole determinant that can settle the vexing question, from line to line, of whether to cut or not to cut.

The corollary procedure, which occasional misbegotten productions have disastrously abandoned, is to have a clear idea in mind of what *cannot* be cut. Certain scenes, passages, metaphors, and lines are too inextricably part of the essential form of the work to be removed. Even Richard Mansfield, whose feeling for the play was exemplary, who deserves immeasurable credit for venturing the first professional English-language production, and who garnered superlatives from reviewers in the title role, was widely censured by the more knowledgeable critics for the surprising insensitivity of his cuts. After the first three acts, which were presented virtually complete, the Darwinian encounter with the Barbary apes was dropped, Anitra and her dance were presented without an establishing context, followed by the omissions of Memnon, the Sphinx, the struggle with the cook in the water, the graveyard eulogy, the onion scene, and the accusations of the threadballs, leaves, dewdrops, and straw. (As partial compensation Mansfield did, however, offer what one reviewer hailed as "the most realistic storm scene ever produced on the American stage.") Today, any such mayhem wrought by a director or producer would be roundly, and rightly, condemned as mutilation of the very substance of the play's identity. Between the inviolable core of *Peer Gynt* and its patches of obviously expendable prolixity and repetition lies that middle ground where the serious choices can be made, and the quality of editing can reveal the range from an interpretive artist worthy of the playwright to a butchering hack with murderous shears.

Like the cutting of the text, the doubling of parts in performance functions best when keyed thematically to a cohering perspective on all that takes place. Except in university theater productions where student actors are readily available and the teaching aim may be the widest possible distribution of roles, some doublings are almost certain to be an economic necessity. These, nevertheless, do not have to represent compromise, accident, or afterthought. At a time when an avant-garde "transformational theater" has evolved an aesthetic and a praxis of its own, that particular necessity can mother a host of inspired inventions from the fertile minds of imaginative directors, actors, designers, costumers, and maskmakers. *Peer Gynt* is thereby capable of becoming, in the course of a single presentation, its own miniature repertory company, at least in terms of the spectators' ability to delight in the versatility of a player. The one imperative is that the doubling, and redoubling, follow out the arc of a developing idea. If Peer is pursuing an anima figure in the women he successively encounters, there is sound justification for Ingrid, the Troll Princess, and Anitra to be played by the same actress. Likewise, there is considerable divergence of meaning, and optimally a conscious interpretive choice, involved between a voice of the Great Boyg which is Peer's own, taped and amplified from offstage, and one that is unmistakably that of another, alien being.

With all the challenges it has posed as text, translation, and script, *Peer Gynt* has been slow to arrive at its duly recognized place in the repertory. Like other works of Ibsen's—*A Doll House*, for example—it has too often been appreciated by the general public, and even theater professionals, for incidental rather than intrinsic reasons. Its impact has been muffled by cultural piety or an apparent satisfaction with the merely picturesque, rather than collaborative acts of penetrative understanding. To the true initiate in its world, the actor, director, designer, or translator who can see clairvoyantly before his or her mind's eye the unadulterated power and life-clarifying grace and—strange as it may sound to some—the resultant popularity of a production in which all the elements are right, the restless search always is for the opportunity of the next staging to bring more of the play's potential into realization and confound the skeptics of Ibsen's art. His scattered band of visionaries need to be reminded periodically of that maxim phrased by the philosopher Hegel: "It is in the nature of excellence to make itself known."

For Ibsen is only at the beginning of a long voyage through time. One hundred years after Shakespeare's unexampled blaze of creativity, his work was being critically patronized by Thomas Rymer and travestied on stage in bastard adaptations by Colley Cibber and Nahum Tate. Ibsen seems, in large part, to have negotiated that phase more quickly. *Peer Gynt* is now acknowledged by many of those who care about such things to rank with *Hamlet* and *Faust* among the world's supreme masterpieces of philosophical drama—philosophical as the average person employs the term, in praise of a generous scope of mind that thinks feelingly, wonderingly, and eloquently about the human destiny we all variously share. Unless the trolls of the world finally take command and silence all such humanizing endeavors, one can be confident that there will be no end to the theatrical making and remaking of *Peer Gynt* and to the perpetually startling release of its irrepressible classic freshness.

NOTES

1. Gunhild Ramm Reistad observes that Ibsen is likely to have worked with Molbech's text against the original Italian. "Om Ibsens Lesning," *Ibsenårbok* (Oslo: Universitetsforlaget, 1969), p. 52.

2. *Ibsen: Letters and Speeches*, ed. Evert Sprinchorn (New York: Hill and Wang, 1964), p. 117.

3. Archibald T. MacAllister, "Introduction," Dante Alighieri, *The Inferno*, tr. by John Ciardi (New York: New American Library, 1954), pp. 23-24.

4. William Archer, "Introduction," in *The Collected Works of Henrik Ibsen*, Vol. IV, *Peer Gynt* (New York: Charles Scribner's Sons, 1907), p. xxxiv.

5. A translation of this article appears in *The Oxford Ibsen*, Vol. I, *Early Plays*, ed. and tr. James Walter McFarlane and Graham Orton (New York: Oxford University Press, 1970), pp. 672-84; however, in some instances my preferred phrasings differ from the text given there.

6. See *Ibsen: The Complete Major Prose Plays*, tr. Rolf Fjelde (New York: Farrar Straus Giroux/New American Library, 1978).

7. Reistad, "Om Ibsens Lesning," sees evidence of the likelihood that Ibsen had encountered Byron's poetry as early as 1853.

8. "Translator's Note," in Dante Alighieri, *The Purgatorio*, tr. by John Ciardi (New York: New American Library, 1961), pp. xxiv-ix.

9. Only one Shakespearian drama, *Love's Labor's Lost*, is over half in rhymed verse. The average ratio of rhymed to blank verse in Shakespeare is 9 percent. *Lear, Hamlet,* and *Othello* are 3 percent rhymed to unrhymed pentameters, and *Macbeth* 6 percent.

10. Richard B. Sewell, *Emily Dickenson: A Collection of Critical Essays* (Englewood Cliffs, N.J.: Prentice-Hall, 1963), p. 72.

11. Jackson Matthews, "Third Thoughts on Translating Poetry," in *On Translation*, ed. Reuben A. Brower (Cambridge, Mass.: Harvard University Press, 1959), pp. 67-68.

12. The term "script," at this juncture, should be understood as meaning more than a matter of the words of the original or translation; it implies a capacity to visualize and notate their explicit or implicit cues to gesture, movement, pauses, manipulation of props, characters' entrances and exits—in short, all those physicalizations of the text that co-opt stage time and, together with the spoken words, comprise the organic totality of theatrical form that is the meaning of the work in performance.

13. Certain early productions of *Peer Gynt* and its companion piece *Brand* were, in fact, presented uncut. With their old-style set changes, however, the performances were scarcely what would be considered feasible today for an evening in the theater, such as the 6½-hour Stockholm premiere of *Brand* in 1885, which ended at 12:30 a.m. with the ladies in the audience half asleep, bodices and corsets unfastened.

14. Tyrone Guthrie, "Foreword," in Henrik Ibsen, *Peer Gynt*, English version by Norman Ginsbury (London: Hammond, Hammond and Co., 1946), p. 5. For the article in *The Norseman*, see "Selected Bibliography."

15. For Anderssen, see "Selected Bibliography." The Nilsen production is discussed at book length in Hans Midbøe, *Peer Gynt teatret og tiden: Hans Jakob Nilsen og den 'antiromantiske' revolt* (Oslo: Universitetsforlaget, 1976).

16. Program, *Peer Gynt*, Malmö Stadsteater Stora Scenen, 1957. Other material in Henrik Sjøgren, *Ingmar Bergman på teatern* (Stockholm: Almquist & Wiksell, 1968), pp. 182-93.

17. Hugh Rorrison, p. 24, see "Selected Bibliography."

APPENDIX II

This phantasmagoria, or comedy of human life, embraces all the elements of the serious, the pathetic, the tragic, the grotesque, the real and the unreal, the actualities and the dreams, the facts and the consequences, the ambitions and the disappointments, the hopes and the disillusions, and the dread and the terror, and the resurrection in love, of the human soul.

RICHARD MANSFIELD

First published: Gyldendal, Copenhagen, November 14, 1867

First performed: Christiania Theater, Christiania [Oslo], February 24, 1876

The stage history of *Peer Gynt* begins, not merely for the American theater, but for professional Anglo-American production anywhere, with Richard Mansfield. Reservations can justly be invoked regarding his premiere presentation of the play in English (see Appendix I, under "Script"), and these can appropriately be countered by the glowing tributes to his consummate interpretive artistry that filled the contemporary press. Whatever the balance that finally will be struck by historical judgment, two things are indisputable about the Mansfield *Peer Gynt*: it was big, and it was successful. The company that set out for Chicago in eleven railway cars was, by report, the largest dramatic organization ever to leave New York. Augmented on arrival, the cast and crew consisted of one stage manager and assistant, one property man and two assistants, a scenic artist, a head carpenter and three assistants, one armorer, one wig dresser, one wardrobe mistress and three assistants,

271

eight electricians, one hostler, one baggageman, one call boy, fifty-one principal artists, one hundred ninety-two people in various crowd scenes, seventy-seven stagehands, and a concert-size orchestra for the variegated incidental music.

If the census of participants was operatically imposing, the special effects were accounted nothing short of stunning, from the great boar constructed on a steel frame with real boar's hide and two men inside for locomotion, to the "steam curtains and other daring devices" that changed the sets and kept the action moving with then seemingly miraculous rapidity. "Scenically," observed one onlooker, the production was "a strange combination of every trick of the stage." And, at the apex of the support system of machines and the massive, if admittedly uneven complement of performers, was Mansfield himself, crowning his long, distinguished career in the theater with a herculean performance that courted exhaustion. Wrote the critic of the conservative literary review, *The Dial*: "He has seized the greatest opportunity offered by the dramatic literature of our time, and he has given us a characterization that outranks the best of his previous efforts." How he may have done so is suggested tantalizingly by John O'Connell Bennett, reviewer for the Chicago *Record-Herald*: "Mansfield caught what was mythical and what was elemental in his tale, and he hurled them forth." In consequence, vast audiences, we are informed, filled the Chicago Grand Opera House nightly, week after week, the majority doubtless gorging on the blend of spectacular travelogue, picturesque musical comedy, and pre-De Mille extravaganza, and the minority supping on caviar for the general, the pervasive poetry of conception and the bracing ethical conflict of self-realization pitted against self-sufficiency.

Mansfield's *Peer Gynt* typifies, with a largesse and perhaps a verve never since equaled in America, a category of production that deservedly finds a place in the historical record. This group includes all those that automatically become "major" by virtue of the producing organization or individual, in conjunction with the talent of note (actors, director, designers), who have joined forces in what can be taken to be a full-scale assault, like a carefully planned mountaineering expedition, upon the work. Anyone who has seen a certain number of these will know that there is no necessary guarantee of artistic triumph, or even creditable distinction, in the eminence of the collaborators; but the size of the endeavor usually ensures that preparation and resources will not be stinted, that discoveries will be made, and that even the mistakes will be instructive. All in all, the continuity of such storied productions remains the true heart and living tradition of an authentic theater culture that America's dispersed and still probationary performing arts institutions are as yet barely able to supply.

The other category of productions that demands inclusion may be more modest in overall achievement, but claims our due attention for its accomplishment of a single historic or aesthetic point of interest. The event may mark the first complete, uncut performance of the play in the United States (Amherst, Mass., 1940), or the American premiere of a significant new score (Madison, Wis., 1950), or the brilliant transmutation of the script into a new medium (Tatterman Marionettes, 1937). It may simply involve a rare grace of inspired invention in the handling of one or more elements of the play's stagecraft, whose contribution might be lost in obscurity without the saving reprieve of such agencies as the American College Theater Festival to bring it to wider currency.

Peer Gynt has not had many major productions in the United States—surprisingly few, in fact, compared with other countries such as England or Germany. On the other hand, when all areas of theatrical activity are considered, it has had a fairly high incidence of revival, placing it safely within the top five of Ibsen's most frequently staged works, somewhere after *A Doll House, Hedda Gabler,* and *Ghosts.* The list that follows is by no means either quantitatively or qualitatively definitive. It includes the major productions, and a representative selection of regional resident and university theater stagings. Doublings and redoublings of characters have been indicated in

273

italics. Although in the interests of a reasonable brevity some distinctly minor roles have been dropped, this expedient may prove useful in suggesting how small a cast of principals has been deemed essential to mount the play, and what patterns of doubling have been previously employed. To facilitate comparison, the designation of characters has been standardized as far as possible from their original variant listings in programs and reviews.

Like Everest or Godwin Austen, Mansfield's peak is still there, waiting for new mountaineers to ascend.

Grand Opera House (Chicago, Ill.), October 29, 1906

PRODUCER AND DIRECTOR: Richard Mansfield. MUSIC: Edvard Grieg, Paderewski, Schubert, Beethoven, Mendelsohn, and Saint-Saens.

PEER GYNT	Richard Mansfield
AASE	Emma Dunn
ASLAK	Damon Lyon
MASTER OF CEREMONIES	Frank Reynolds
MADS MOEN	Cecil Magnus
HIS FATHER	Edward Caldwell
HIS MOTHER	Sydney Cowell
NEWCOMER	James L. Carhart
HIS WIFE	Myra Brooke
SOLVEIG	Adelaide Nowak
HELGA	Ory Diamond
HEGSTAD FARMER	Walter Howe
INGRID	Adelaide Alexander
PEASANT GIRLS	Evelyn Loomis, Marguerite Lindsay, Isabel Howell, Ruby Craven, Olive Temple
WOMAN IN GREEN	Gertrude Gheen

TROLL KING	Henry Wenman
KARI	*Sydney Cowell*
TROLL BRAT	George MacDonald
COTTON	Frank Kingdon
BALLON	Marc McDermott
EBERKOPF	Gordon Mendelsohn
TRUMPETERSTRAALE	*Cecil Magnus*
ANITRA	Irene Praher
SEA CAPTAIN	*Edward Caldwell*
MATE	Lawrence C. Toole
BOATSWAIN	*Frank Reynolds*
COOK	*Marc McDermott*
STRANGE PASSENGER	Arthur Forrest
BUTTON-MOLDER	*Arthur Forrest*
LEAN ONE	*Frank Kingdon*

Tulane Theater (New Orleans, La.), October 8, 1908

PRODUCER AND DIRECTOR: Louis James.

PEER GYNT	Louis James
AASE	Laura Frankenfield
ASLAK	Norman Sweet
MADS MOEN	Arthur Weston
HIS FATHER	James Robertson
HIS MOTHER	Mary Bernard
NEWCOMER	Kraft Walton
HIS WIFE	Margaret Warren
SOLVEIG	Aphie James
HELGA	Belle Keefe
HEGSTAD FARMER	Frank C. Chapman
INGRID	Ida Werner
HERD GIRLS	Myrtle Webster, Elsie Scharff, Josephine Leon
WOMAN IN GREEN	Anne Schaeffer

TROLL KING	J. Arthur Young
BOYG	F. A. Browne
TROLL BRAT	Vera Walton
COTTON	*J. Arthur Young*
BALLON	William C. Andrews
EBERKOPF	*Kraft Walton*
TRUMPETERSTRAALE	Richard I. Scott
ANITRA	Frances Harcourt
SEA CAPTAIN	James G. Howe
BOATSWAIN	R. D. Sanderson
STRANGE PASSENGER	*William C. Andrews*
SHERIFF	Alden Jewel
BUTTON-MOLDER	*William C. Andrews*

Garrick Theater (New York, N.Y.), February 5, 1923

PRODUCER: The Theater Guild. DIRECTOR: Theodore Komisarjevsky. SETTINGS AND COSTUMES: Lee Simonson. MUSIC: Edvard Grieg.

PEER GYNT	Joseph Schildkraut
AASE	Louise Closser Hale
ASLAK	Stanley G. Wood
MADS MOEN	William Franklin
HIS FATHER	Philip Leigh
HIS MOTHER	Ellen Larned
NEWCOMER	William W. Griffith
HIS WIFE	Elizabeth Zachry
SOLVEIG	Selena Royce
HELGA	Francene Wouters
HEGSTAD FARMER	C. Porter Hall
INGRID	Bertha Broad
HERD GIRLS	Elise Bartlett, Eve Casanova, Helen Sheridan
WOMAN IN GREEN	Helen Westley

TROLL KING	Dudley Digges
COURTIER TROLL	*William Franklin*
KARI	Armina Marshall
TROLL BRAT	*Francene Wouters*
COTTON	*Stanley G. Wood*
BALLON	Albert Carroll
EBERKOPF	Edward G. Robinson
TRUMPETERSTRAALE	*Philip Leigh*
THIEF	Romney Brent
FENCE	Alfred Alexandre
ANITRA	Lillibel Ibsen
BEGRIFFENFELDT	Charles Halton
FELLAH	*William Franklin*
HUSSEIN	Stanley Howlett
BUTTON-MOLDER	*Edward G. Robinson*
LEAN ONE	*Sidney Howlett*

Seattle Repertory Playhouse (Seattle, Wash.), February 6, 1931

PRODUCER: The Playhouse. DIRECTOR: Florence Dean James. SETTINGS: Robert E. Mahaffay, Jr. MASKS: Virginia Opsvig and Walter Shaw. MUSIC: Edvard Grieg. CHOREOGRAPHY: Mary Ann Wells.

PEER GYNT	Burton W. James
AASE	Sophia Rosenstein
ASLAK	David Henderson
MASTER OF CEREMONIES	Walter Shaw
MADS MOEN	Bertram Boog
HIS FATHER	David Harris
HIS MOTHER	Maud Bracknell
NEWCOMER	Tom Gilpatrick
HIS WIFE	Margaret Hall
SOLVEIG	Helga Lund
HELGA	Gertrude Hersh

INGRID	Doris Hall
HERD GIRLS	Sally Sue White,
	Louise Hastert, Jayne Garvin
WOMAN IN GREEN	Monty Margetts
TROLL KING	J. T. Hirakawa
BOYG	*J. T. Hirakawa*
TROLL BRAT	Jimsy Boudwin
COTTON	Alex Winston
BALLON	*Tom Gilpatrick*
EBERKOPF	*Bertram Boog*
TRUMPETERSTRAALE	*David Henderson*
ANITRA	*Louise Hastert*
BEGRIFFENFELDT	Albert M. Ottenheimer
HUHU	*Bertram Boog*
FELLAH	Lloyd Schram
HUSSEIN	*David Harris*
BUTTON-MOLDER	*Albert M. Ottenheimer*

Pasadena Community Playhouse (Pasadena, Calif.), July 26, 1932

PRODUCER: Pasadena Community Playhouse Association. DIRECTOR: Gilmore Brown. SETTINGS AND COSTUMES: Reddington Sharpe. MUSIC: Edvard Grieg. CHOREOGRA-PHY: Muriel Field.

PEER GYNT	Douglas Montgomery
AASE	Lenore Shanewise
ASLAK	Frank Lydiard
MASTER OF CEREMONIES	Abner M. Kramer
MADS MOEN	Fenelon Richards
HIS FATHER	William Northrup
HIS MOTHER	Esther J. Gay
NEWCOMER	Lee J. Cobb
HIS WIFE	Ethel Caskey

SOLVEIG	Gloria Stuart
HEGSTAD FARMER	Gordon Patterson
INGRID	Virginia George
HERD GIRLS	Herma Reach, Beth Porter, Mildred Drummond
WOMAN IN GREEN	Evelyn Knowles Bates
TROLL KING	Thomas Browne Henry
BOYG	Henry Kleinbach
TROLL BRAT	David Brady
COTTON	John Waldron
BALLON	Wallace Dow
EBERKOPF	*Lee J. Cobb*
TRUMPETERSTRAALE	William Osborne Booth
ANITRA	Mary Hutchinson
HUHU	*Abner M. Kramer*
FELLAH	*Gordon Patterson*
HUSSEIN	Howard Chamberlin
SHERIFF	*John Waldron*
BUTTON-MOLDER	*Henry Kleinbach*
LEAN ONE	Charles Levinson

McMillan Theater (New York, N.Y.), March 13, 1937

PRODUCERS: Tatterman Marionettes and William Duncan-Edward Mabley, Inc. of Cleveland. DIRECTOR: Edward Mabley. MARIONETTE CONSTRUCTION: Roy Patton, Harry Patton, Carl Saleske. SETTINGS AND COSTUMES: Terence von Duren. MUSIC: Edvard Grieg. PUPPETEERS: George Brengel, Frank Dodge, Charles Horine, Kathryn Horine, Ellen Mahar, Wayne McMeekan [David Wayne], Elden Smith.

Kirby Memorial Theater (Amherst, Mass.), Acts I, II, III, January 11, 1940; Acts IV, V, April 11, 1940.

PRODUCER: Amherst College Department of Dramatics. DIRECTOR: Curtis Canfield. SETTINGS AND COSTUMES: Charles Rogers. PUPPETS: Alice Cleland. MUSIC: Edvard Grieg. CHOREOGRAPHY: Virginia Haglin.

PEER GYNT	John H. Reber
AASE	Margaret Marsh
ASLAK	George Hunter
MADS MOEN	Robert Byrne
HIS FATHER	Robert M. Smith
HIS MOTHER	Irene Salmon
NEWCOMER	David Smiley
HIS WIFE	Dorothy Wellington
SOLVEIG	Shirley Haller
HELGA	Genevieve Nichols
HEGSTAD FARMER	William Leslie
INGRID	Margery Phleger
HERD GIRLS	Janet Morgan, Elizabeth K. Merrick, Kathleen Callahan
WOMAN IN GREEN	Katherine Canfield
TROLL KING	Philip Orth
BOYG	*William Leslie*
KARI	Frances White
TROLL BRAT	Eric Hamp
COTTON	*David Smiley*
BALLON	William Holdsworth
EBERKOPF	Nelson Warner
TRUMPETERSTRAALE	Warren Lux
ANITRA	Virginia Haglin
SEA CAPTAIN	Carl Andrews
COOK	Henry S. Kingman
STRANGE PASSENGER	Wallace Alexander
PASTOR	Clinton Blake
BUTTON-MOLDER	Robert M. Smith
LEAN ONE	*William Leslie*

Union Theater (Madison, Wis.), May 2, 1950

PRODUCER: University of Wisconsin Department of Speech. DIRECTOR: Ronald Mitchell. SETTINGS AND MASKS: Joan Hurst. COSTUMES: Jean Jacobsen. LIGHTING: David Weiss. MUSIC: Harald Saeverud. CHOREOGRAPHY: Joan Jones.

PEER GYNT	Erik Bye
AASE	Talie Handler
ASLAK	Robert Petersen
MASTER OF CEREMONIES	John Shabaz
MADS MOEN	Paul Bird
HIS FATHER	Allen Blomquist
HIS MOTHER	Kathleen Rockwell
NEWCOMER	Charles Webster
HIS WIFE	Sari Schneider
SOLVEIG	Colette Slightam
HEGSTAD FARMER	Joseph Capello
INGRID	Irmie Wolff
HERD GIRLS	Ellen Moore, Doris Senasac, Phyllis Silverman
WOMAN IN GREEN	Diane Foster
TROLL KING	Elwin Reynolds
COURTIER TROLL	Richard Zingsheim
BOYG	*Erik Bye*
KARI	Betty Bevis
TROLL BRAT	Tommy Wills
COTTON	*Elwin Reynolds*
BALLON	Eugene De Caprio
EBERKOPF	*Allen Blomquist*
TRUMPETERSTRAALE	*Joseph Capello*
THIEF	Ralph Zauner
FENCE	William Johnson
ANITRA	Leah Mandelker
BEGRIFFENFELDT	Warren Enters

FELLAH	*Paul Bird*
HUSSEIN	*William Johnson*
SEA CAPTAIN	Milton Ferry
STRANGE PASSENGER	*John Shabaz*
COOK	Donald Newell
BUTTON-MOLDER	Jerry McNeely

ANTA Playhouse (New York, N.Y.), January 28, 1951

PRODUCERS: Cheryl Crawford and Roger L. Stevens. DIRECTOR: Lee Strasberg. SETTINGS: Donald Oenslager. COSTUMES: Rose Bogdanoff. MUSIC: Lan Adomian, and Hillel and Aviva. CHOREOGRAPHY: Valerie Bettis.

PEER GYNT	John Garfield
AASE	Mildred Dunnock
ASLAK	John Randolph
MASTER OF CEREMONIES	Ray Gordon
MADS MOEN	Mahlon Naill
HIS FATHER	Edward Binns
HIS MOTHER	Lisa Baker
NEWCOMER	Joseph Anthony
HIS WIFE	Anne Hegira
SOLVEIG	Pearl Lang
HEGSTAD FARMER	Nehemia Persoff
INGRID	Rebecca Darke
HERD GIRLS	Lucile Patton, Barbara Gaye,
	Beverlee Bozeman
WOMAN IN GREEN	Sherry Britton
TROLL KING	*Nehemia Persoff*
BOYG	*John Randolph*
KARI	*Lisa Baker*
TROLL BRAT	Ed Horner
COTTON	Richard Purdy
BALLON	*Joseph Anthony*
EBERKOPF	*Edward Binns*

TRUMPETERSTRAALE	*John Randolph*
THIEF	*Ray Gordon*
FENCE	*Ed Horner*
ANITRA	Sono Osato
BEGRIFFENFELDT	*Joseph Anthony*
HUSSEIN	*Richard Purdy*
BUTTON-MOLDER	Karl Malden

Phoenix Theater (New York, N.Y.), January 12, 1960

PRODUCERS: T. Edward Hambleton and Norris Houghton. DIRECTOR: Stuart Vaughan. SETTINGS AND COSTUMES: Will Steven Armstrong. LIGHTING: Tharon Musser. MUSIC: David Amram. CHOREOGRAPHY: John Waller.

PEER GYNT	Fritz Weaver
AASE	Joanna Roos
ASLAK	Rex Everhart
MADS MOEN	Nicholas Kepros
HIS FATHER	Elliott Sullivan
HIS MOTHER	Joanne Ellsperman
NEWCOMER	John Heffernan
SOLVEIG	Inga Swenson
HELGA	Jan Jarrett
HEGSTAD FARMER	Patrick Hines
INGRID	Alice Drummond
HERD GIRLS	Jenifer Heyward,
	Juliet Randall, Marcie Hubert
WOMAN IN GREEN	Patricia Falkenhain
TROLL KING	Eric Berry
COURTIER TROLL	Albert Quinton
BOYG	*Albert Quinton*
KARI	Patricia Ripley
TROLL BRAT	*Nicholas Kepros*
COTTON	*Patrick Hines*

BALLON	*Eric Berry*
EBERKOPF	*Rex Everhart*
THIEF	*Nicholas Kepros*
FENCE	*Elliott Sullivan*
ANITRA	Gerry Jedd
BEGRIFFENFELDT	*Patrick Hines*
FELLAH	*Albert Quinton*
HUSSEIN	Edwin Sherin
SEA CAPTAIN	*Elliott Sullivan*
STRANGE PASSENGER	J. D. Cannon
BUTTON-MOLDER	*J. D. Cannon*

Adams Memorial Theater (Williamstown, Mass.), June 30, 1967

PRODUCER: The Williamstown Theater. DIRECTOR: Nikos Psacharopoulos. SETTINGS, COSTUMES, AND PROJECTIONS: John Conklin. LIGHTING: Peter Hunt. MUSIC: Arthur Rubenstein.

PEER GYNT	Robert Symonds
AASE	Margaret Barker
ASLAK	David Ackroyd
MADS MOEN	Ladislau Brown
HIS FATHER	Donald Ecklebarger
HIS MOTHER	Batya Hilsen
NEWCOMER	Robert Ingham
HIS WIFE	Karlene Counsman
SOLVEIG	Barbette Tweed
HELGA	Betsy Peck
INGRID	Christine Reilly
WOMAN IN GREEN	Priscilla Pointer
TROLL KING	Tony Capodilupo
COURTIER TROLL	Tom Sawyer
TROLL BRAT	Bill Donovan
COTTON	*Robert Ingham*

BALLON	*Tom Sawyer*
EBERKOPF	*Tony Capodilupo*
ANITRA	Portia Patterson
BEGRIFFENFELDT	William Swetland
HUHU	Alan Holzman
FELLAH	*David Ackroyd*
HUSSEIN	Ronald Silver
PASTOR	*David Ackroyd*
BUTTON-MOLDER	William Hansen
LEAN ONE	*Tom Sawyer*

Delacorte Theater (New York, N.Y.), July 8, 1969

PRODUCER: New York Shakespeare Festival. DIRECTOR: Gerald Freedman. SETTING: Ming Cho Lee. COSTUMES: Theoni V. Aldredge. LIGHTING: Martin Aronstein. MUSIC: John Morris. CHOREOGRAPHY: Joyce Trisler.

PEER GYNT	Stacy Keach
AASE	Estelle Parsons
ASLAK	Michael Baseleon
MADS MOEN	Robert Stattel
HIS FATHER	Albert Stratton
HIS MOTHER	Mary Nall
NEWCOMER	John Heffernan
HIS WIFE	Paulita Sedgwick
SOLVEIG	Judy Collins
HELGA	Lisa Griffin
HEGSTAD FARMER	James Cahill
INGRID	Olympia Dukakis
HERD GIRLS	Marilyn Meyers, Esther Koslow, Maria Di Dia
WOMAN IN GREEN	*Olympia Dukakis*
TROLL KING	*James Cahill*
COURTIER TROLL	*Albert Stratton*

BOYG	*Stacy Keach*
KARI	Janet Dowd
TROLL BRAT	Frances Patrelle
ADMIRAL	*Michael Baseleon*
GENERAL	*Robert Stattel*
INDUSTRIALIST	*Albert Stratton*
DIPLOMAT	*James Cahill*
ANITRA	*Olympia Dukakis*
BEGRIFFENFELDT	*Michael Baseleon*
HUSSEIN	*Robert Stattel*
STRANGE PASSENGER	*Albert Stratton*
PASTOR	*John Heffernan*
BUTTON-MOLDER	*John Heffernan*
LEAN ONE	*Robert Stattel*

George Washington University Center Theater (Washington, D.C.), May 2, 1970

PRODUCERS: John F. Kennedy Center for the Performing Arts, The Smithsonian Institution, American College Theater Festival, and Hanover College Theater. DIRECTOR AND DE-SIGNER: Tom G. Evans. COSTUMES: Jenny Parker. LIGHT-ING: Joel McCarty. MUSIC: Howard Blanning.

PEER GYNT	Roger Bulington
AASE	Rene Handren
SOLVEIG	Trish Doherty
ENSEMBLE	Howard Blanning, Vicky Calvert, John Duvall, Chip Egan, Jeri Elmont, Kris Harper, Lon Huber, Kathy King, John Martin, Marty Patterson, Hunt Prothro, Tom Statton, Sara Stites, David Terry, Diane Watt, Bob Weaver

University Theater (Athens, Ga.), November 18, 1970

PRODUCER: University of Georgia Department of Drama and Theater. DIRECTOR: Anne Gullestad. SETTING AND LIGHTING: Jonne Thornton. COSTUMES: Jackson Kesler. MUSIC: Arne Nordheim. CHOREOGRAPHY: Leslie Carter.

PEER GYNT	Wayland Winstead
AASE	Roberta Illg
ASLAK	Charles Orck
MASTER OF CEREMONIES	Terrence Jones
MADS MOEN	Joseph Caruana
HIS FATHER	Rick Hammond
HIS MOTHER	Leara Rhodes
NEWCOMER	Bob Weir
HIS WIFE	Jane Holder
SOLVEIG	Meade Hindman
HELGA	Linda Duck
HEGSTAD FARMER	Richard LeVene
INGRID	Vicki Baskin
HERD GIRLS	Caren Schrier, Dierdre Pierce, Evelyn Moricle
WOMAN IN GREEN	Marilyn Hickey
TROLL KING	Marshall Rosenblum
COURTIER TROLL	John Arey
KARI	LaFaye Baxter
TROLL BRAT	Christine Cotter
COTTON	Eddie Terry
BALLON	Eui-Hyum Paik
EBERKOPF	*Rick Hammond*
TRUMPETERSTRAALE	Allen W. Lyndrup
THIEF	Hugh Cobb
FENCE	*Bob Weir*
ANITRA	Anne Joseph
BEGRIFFENFELDT	James Hindman
HUSSEIN	*Richard LeVene*

SEA CAPTAIN	*Rick Hammond*
STRANGE PASSENGER	Charles Hadley
COOK	Frank New
SHERIFF	Steve DeArmoun
BUTTON-MOLDER	George Black
LEAN ONE	Larry Stoller

University Playhouse (Kansas City, Mo.), August 8, 1974

PRODUCER: Missouri Repertory Theater. DIRECTOR: Adrian Hall. SETTINGS: John Ezell. COSTUMES: Douglas A. Russell. LIGHTING: Marc Schlackman. MUSIC: Richard Cumming. SOUND: Bruce Richardson.

YOUNG PEER GYNT	Robert Elliott
OLD PEER GYNT	Vincent Dowling
AASE	Frances Peter
ASLAK	Howard Renensland, Jr.
MADS MOEN	Michael LaGue
HIS FATHER	George C. Berry
HIS MOTHER	Caroline Campbell
NEWCOMER	Walter W. Atamaniuk
HIS WIFE	Harriet Levitt
SOLVEIG	Carol Pfander
HELGA	Gabrielle Weeks
HEGSTAD FARMER	Art Ellison
INGRID	Loren Beth Brown
WOMAN IN GREEN	Susan Borneman
TROLL KING	Martin Marinaro
KARI	Alison Bowyer
COTTON	Al Christy
BALLON	Steven Ryan
EBERKOPF	*Walter W. Atamaniuk*
TRUMPETERSTRAALE	Robert Scogin
THIEF	Henry Stram

FENCE	Cary Groner
ANITRA	Michele Garrison
BEGRIFFENFELDT	John Q. Bruce, Jr.
HUHU	Stuart Brooks
FELLAH	Frederic-Winslow Oram
HUSSEIN	Paul Casey
SEA CAPTAIN	Roger Atwell
STRANGE PASSENGER	Ken Graham
COOK	Steve Scearcy
PASTOR	*Walter W. Atamaniuk*
SHERIFF	Donald J. Quinn
BUTTON-MOLDER	John Maddison
LEAN ONE	David Peter Lauria

Geary Theater (San Francisco, Calif.), March 9, 1976

PRODUCER: American Conservatory Theater. DIRECTOR: Allen Fletcher. SETTINGS: Ralph Funicello. COSTUMES: Robert Blackman. LIGHTING: Dirk Epperson. MUSIC: Larry Delinger. SOUND: Bartholomeo Rago. CHOREOGRAPHY: John Pasqualetti.

STORY TELLERS	Ronald Blossom, Charles Coffey, Linda Connor, Gina Franz, Janice Garcia, Nathan Haas, Michael-Keys Hall, Willys I. Peck, Jr., Stephen Schnetzer, Peter Schuck, Sandra Shotwell, Anne Deavere Smith
PEER GYNT	Daniel Davis
AASE	Joy Carlin
ASLAK	Charles Hallahan
MASTER OF CEREMONIES	Daniel Kern
MADS MOEN	Rick Hamilton

HIS FATHER	Raye Birk
HIS MOTHER	Candace Barrett
NEWCOMER	Charles H. Hyman
HIS WIFE	Marrian Walters
SOLVEIG	Francine Tacker
HELGA	Shoshana Colman
HEGSTAD FARMER	Joseph Bird
INGRID	Hope Alexander-Willis
HERD GIRLS	Barbara Dirickson,
	Deborah May,
	Franchelle Stewart Dorn
WOMAN IN GREEN	*Hope Alexander-Willis*
TROLL KING	*Joseph Bird*
COURTIER TROLL	*Daniel Kern*
BOYG	Sydney Walker
KARI	Anne Lawder
TROLL BRAT	Al White
RICH MERCHANT	*Al White*
CHIEF MONKEY	*Joseph Bird*
THIEVES	*Daniel Kern*, Lawrence Hecht
ANITRA	*Hope Alexander-Willis*
BEGRIFFENFELDT	James R. Winker
BOATSWAIN	*Al White*
STRANGE PASSENGER	Earl Boen
PASTOR	William Paterson
SHERIFF	*Charles H. Hyman*
BUTTON-MOLDER	*Sydney Walker*
LEAN ONE	*James R. Winker*

SELECTED
BIBLIOGRAPHY

SELECTED BIBLIOGRAPHY

THE MAN AND THE LIFE

Heiberg, Hans. *Ibsen, a Portrait of the Artist.* Trans. Joan Tate. Coral Gables, Florida: University of Miami Press, 1969.

Ibsen, Bergliot. *The Three Ibsens, Memories of Henrik Ibsen, Suzannah Ibsen and Sigurd Ibsen.* Trans. Gerik Schjelderup. New York: American-Scandinavian Foundation, 1952.

Koht, Halvdan. *Life of Ibsen.* New ed. Trans. and ed. Einar Haugen and A. E. Santiello. New York: Benjamin Blom, Inc., 1971.

Meyer, Michael. *Ibsen, a Biography.* Garden City, N.Y.: Doubleday, 1971.

Sprinchorn, Evert, ed. *Ibsen, Letters and Speeches.* New York: Hill and Wang, 1964.

Zucker, Adolf E. *Ibsen the Master Builder.* New York: Octagon Books, 1973 [1929].

THE PLAYWRIGHT AND THE PLAY

Anderssen, Odd-Stein. "Before the Centenary of *Peer Gynt.*" *World Theater*, XII, 4 (Winter, 1963-64), 281-300.

Arestad, Sverre. "*Peer Gynt* and the Idea of Self." *Modern Drama*, III, 2 (Sept. 1960), 103-22.

Auden, W. H. *The Dyer's Hand and Other Essays.* New York: Random House, 1962. "Genius & Apostle," 433-55.

Bradbrook, M. C. *Ibsen the Norwegian, a Revaluation.* New ed. London: Chatto and Windus, 1966.

Brandes, Georg. *Henrik Ibsen, a Critical Study.* New York: Benjamin Blom, Inc., 1964 [1899].

Burke, Kenneth. *A Grammar of Motives.* Los Angeles: University of California Press, 1969, 433-39.

Clurman, Harold. *Ibsen.* New York: The Macmillan Company, 1977.

Davies, Trevor H. *Spiritual Voices in Modern Literature.* New York: George H. Doran Company, 1919. "Ibsen: 'Peer Gynt,' The Ignominy of Half-Heartedness," 41-69.

Downs, Brian W. *Ibsen, the Intellectual Background.* New York: Cambridge University Press, 1948.

————. *A Study of Six Plays by Ibsen.* New York: Cambridge University Press, 1950.

Egan, Michael, ed. *Ibsen, the Critical Heritage.* Boston: Routledge & Kegan Paul, 1972.

Eikeland, P. J. *Ibsen Studies.* New York: Haskell House Publishers, Ltd., 1970 [1931].

Fjelde, Rolf. "*Peer Gynt*, Naturalism and the Dissolving Self." *The Drama Review*, XIII, 2 (Winter 1968), 28-43.

Gaskell, Ronald. "Symbol and Reality in *Peer Gynt.*" *Drama Survey*, IV, 1 (Spring 1965), 57-64.

Glicksberg, Charles I. *The Self in Modern Literature.* University Park, Pa.: Pennsylvania State University Press, 1963. "The Ibsenite Self," 12-26.

Groddeck, Georg. "Peer Gynt," in *Ibsen: A Collection of Critical Essays.* Ed. Rolf Fjelde. Englewood Cliffs, N.J.: Prentice-Hall, 1965, 63-79.

Guthrie, Tyrone. "Some Afterthoughts on *Peer Gynt.*" *The Norseman*, V, 3 (May & June 1947), 204-5.

Haugen, Einar. *Ibsen's Drama: Author to Audience.* Minneapolis: University of Minnesota Press, 1979.

Huneker, James. *Iconoclasts, a Book of Dramatists.* New York: Charles Scribner's Sons, 1905. "Henrik Ibsen," 1-138.

Hurt, James R. "Fantastic Scenes in *Peer Gynt.*" *Modern Drama*, V, 1 (May 1962), 37-41.

Jeffreys, Harold. "Ibsen's *Peer Gynt*: a psychoanalytic study." *Psychoanalytic Review*, XI (Oct. 1924), 361-402.

Johnston, Brian. *To the Third Empire: Ibsen's Early Drama.* Minneapolis: University of Minnesota Press, 1980.

Jorgenson, Theodore. *Henrik Ibsen, a Study in Art and Personality.* Northfield, Minn.: St. Olaf Press, 1945.

Knight, G. Wilson. *Henrik Ibsen.* New York: Grove Press, 1963.

Lavrin, Janko. *Ibsen, an Approach.* London: Methuen & Co. Ltd., 1950.

Logeman, Henri. *A Commentary on Henrik Ibsen's Peer Gynt: Its Language, Literary Associations and Folklore.* The Hague: Martinus Nijhoff, 1917.

Lucus, F. W. *The Drama of Ibsen and Strindberg.* New York: The Macmillan Company, 1962.

Lund, Mary Graham. "The Existentialism of Ibsen." *The Personalist*, XLI, 3 (Summer 1960), 310-17.

MacFarlane, James W. ed. *The Oxford Ibsen*, III, *Brand, Peer Gynt.* New York, Oxford University Press, 1972. "Scenario and Draft Manuscripts," 454-82.

MacFarlane, James W. and Graham Orton, ed. *The Oxford Ibsen*, I, *Early Plays*. New York: Oxford University Press, 1970. "On the Heroic Ballad and Its Significance for Literature," 672-84.

Rorrison, Hugh. "Berlin's Democratic Theatre and Its 'Peer Gynt.' " *Theatre Quarterly*, IV, 13 (February-April 1974), 15-35.

Schiff, Timothy. "Providence and Dispensation in Henrik Ibsen's *Peer Gynt*." *Scandinavian Studies*, LI, 4 (Autumn 1979), 375-91.

Shaw, George Bernard. *Our Theater in the Nineties*. II. London: Constable and Company, Ltd., 1954 [1932]. "Peer Gynt in Paris" [21 November 1896] , 248-56.

_____. *The Quintessence of Ibsenism*. New York: Hill & Wang, 1957 [1913].

Smith, Denzell. "The Relationship of Setting and Idea in *Peer Gynt*." *Modern Drama*, XIII, 2 (Sept. 1970), 169-73.

Thune, Enraf. "The Paradox of the Boyg: A Study in Peer Gynt's Humanization." *Modern Drama*, XVIV (March 1976), 88-99.

Valency, Maurice. *The Flower and the Castle, an Introduction to the Modern Drama: Ibsen and Strindberg*. New York: The Macmillan Company, 1963.

Wicksteed, Philip H. *Four Lectures on Henrik Ibsen: Dealing Chiefly with His Metrical Works*. Port Washington, N.Y.: Kennikat Press, 1969 [1892].

Williams, Raymond. "Ibsen's Non-Theatrical Plays 'Brand' and 'Peer Gynt.' " *Ibsenårbok 1960-62*. Skien, Norway: Oluf Rasmussens Boktrykkeri, 1962, 186-92.

Zentner, Jules. "Figures of Estrangement — Peer Gynt's Other Selves." *Edda*, LXXIII, 2 (1973), 73-78.

_____. *"Peer Gynt* — The Quest for Shine and the Giving Way of a Loop." *Scandinavica*, IX, 2 (Nov. 1970), 116-26.

Zucker, A. E. "Goethe and Ibsen's Button-Moulder." *Publications of the Modern Language Association of America*, LVII, 4 (Dec. 1942), 1101-7.

HENRIK IBSEN, generally acknowledged as the master builder of modern drama, was born on March 20, 1828, in Skien, Norway. He began his writing career as a poet, soon turning to a series of verse and prose plays, mainly on Norwegian historical themes. At thirty-eight, exhausted by his efforts to create a national theater, he left his native land for twenty-seven years of voluntary exile in the south of Europe. *Brand, Peer Gynt,* and *Emperor and Galilean,* works of his middle period, expressed his philosophy of the individual self and of the course of civilization. In 1877, with *Pillars of Society,* he embarked on that cycle of twelve probing, evocative, ostensibly realistic plays which confirmed his international standing as the foremost dramatist of his age. Ibsen died of a stroke in Oslo on May 23, 1906.

ROLF FJELDE, born in New York City of Scandinavian ancestry, was educated at Yale University, including the Yale School of Drama, and at Columbia University. His poetry and criticism has appeared in many leading periodicals, as well as in two collections of verse; and his original plays and Ibsen translations have been staged in England, Norway, Canada, and throughout the United States. He has edited *Ibsen: A Collection of Critical Essays* in the Twentieth Century Views Series and translated the final twelve-play realistic cycle in the volume *Ibsen: The Complete Major Prose Plays.* Mr. Fjelde is founding president of the Ibsen Society of America. He currently teaches drama and film at Pratt Institute and dramatic literature at the Juilliard School.